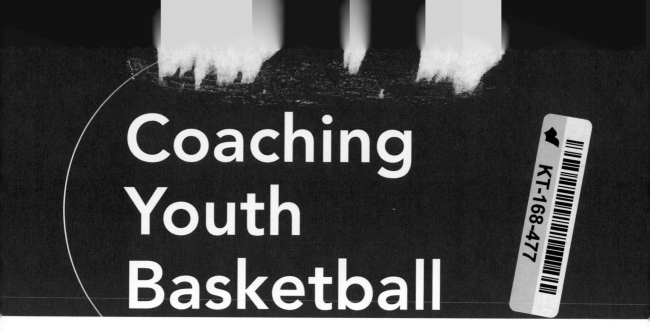

Coaching Youth Basketball

FIFTH EDITION

American Sport Education Program with Don Showalter

USA Basketball Head Coach
Men's Developmental National Team

Human Kinetics

Library of Congress Cataloging-in-Publication Data

Coaching youth basketball / American Sport Education Program
with Don Showalter. -- 5th ed.
    p. cm.
 ISBN-13: 978-1-4504-1972-7 (soft cover)
 ISBN-10: 1-4504-1972-0 (soft cover)
 1. Basketball for children--Coaching. 2. Basketball--Coaching.
I. Showalter, Don. II. American Sport Education Program.
 GV885.3.C63 2012
 796.323083--dc23

                        2012007721

ISBN-10: 1-4504-1972-0 (print)
ISBN-13: 978-1-4504-1972-7 (print)

The web addresses cited in this text were current as of March 2012, unless otherwise noted.

Acquisitions Editor: Justin Klug; **Developmental Editor:** Laura E. Podeschi; **Assistant Editor:** Tyler Wolpert; **Copyeditor:** Patrick Connolly; **Permissions Manager:** Martha Gullo; **Graphic Designer:** Nancy Rasmus; **Graphic Artist:** Tara Welsch; **Cover Designer:** Keith Blomberg; **Photographer (cover):** Dale Garvey; **Photographer (interior):** Neil Bernstein; **Visual Production Assistant:** Joyce Brumfield; **Photo Production Manager:** Jason Allen; **Art Manager:** Kelly Hendren; **Associate Art Manager:** Alan L. Wilborn; **Illustrations:** © Human Kinetics, unless otherwise noted; **Printer:** Versa Press

We thank Next Generation School in Champaign, Illinois, for assistance in providing the location for the photo shoot for this book.

Copies of this book are available at special discounts for bulk purchase for sales promotions, premiums, fund-raising, or educational use. Special editions or book excerpts can also be created to specifications. For details, contact the Special Sales Manager at Human Kinetics.

Printed in the United States of America   10 9 8 7 6 5 4 3 2 1

The paper in this book is certified under a sustainable forestry program.

Human Kinetics
Website: www.HumanKinetics.com

United States: Human Kinetics
P.O. Box 5076
Champaign, IL 61825-5076
800-747-4457
e-mail: humank@hkusa.com

Canada: Human Kinetics
475 Devonshire Road Unit 100
Windsor, ON N8Y 2L5
800-465-7301 (in Canada only)
e-mail: info@hkcanada.com

Europe: Human Kinetics
107 Bradford Road
Stanningley
Leeds LS28 6AT, United Kingdom
+44 (0) 113 255 5665
e-mail: hk@hkeurope.com

Australia: Human Kinetics
57A Price Avenue
Lower Mitcham, South Australia 5062
08 8372 0999
e-mail: info@hkaustralia.com

New Zealand: Human Kinetics
P.O. Box 80
Torrens Park, South Australia 5062
0800 222 062
e-mail: info@hknewzealand.com

E5585

Coaching Youth Basketball

FIFTH EDITION

Contents

Foreword

When you watch a college, WNBA, or NBA basketball game, it looks so simple. Two teams take the court looking to accomplish the same goal—win. The athletes make the game look simple, but many viewers don't have a clue about just how much hard work and practice the players had to put in to make the game seem so basic. When players are recruited for college basketball, you hear all about what they were able to accomplish in high school. But where do you think they first learned how to play? For a very select few, high school was the first time they'd ever played organized basketball. But the majority began learning the game and the skills at the youth level.

From local YMCA to community recreational leagues, youth basketball remains one of the most popular sports for young kids. It's a way to teach kids about the game as well as the importance of living a healthy, active lifestyle and other critical life lessons such as teamwork, respect, and dedication. But aside from those key lessons, kids learn how to have fun!

Throughout my coaching career I have had the honor and privilege of coaching young men who share my passion for this great game. But all that is seen on television, read in the papers, or discussed by media is the outcome of games. You never hear about how they are able to use the sport to develop into productive citizens, respectful people, and future leaders. That is truly a shame, because the game is so much more—and it all begins at the youth level. In *Coaching Youth Basketball*, USA Basketball's Don Showalter teams with the American Sport Education Program to show you the proper way to develop skills, communicate with young players, and help kids get everything possible out of the game. This resource will give you everything you need from the first practice through the final game, and it will do so by teaching you how to keep kids engaged and excited to play and learn the game.

I've been fortunate to coach almost every level of the game over the years, and it becomes more and more rewarding every single day. Working with young kids is both a challenge and a joy. Remember that although you might not coach the next LeBron James or Derrick Rose, you have the ability to affect a child's life both on and off the court. I encourage you to treat every moment as if it could be your very last time interacting with your young players. Always remember that whether you are in a paid position or working as a volunteer coach, you're still a coach, and the young kids look up to you. Most important, have fun—it's the only way to ensure that the kids will, too!

Best wishes.

Roy Williams
Head men's basketball coach, University of North Carolina

Welcome to the fifth edition of *Coaching Youth Basketball*. Being a coach is truly one of the most important professions—whether it is a volunteer or compensated position—that a person can undertake. The rewards of coaching young people are great, and you make an impact on each of the players you coach. We have included a great deal of information related to managing, teaching, and practicing at the youth level.

The information provided in the following pages will help guide you as you coach your team. I have used much of this information to coach the USA Basketball Developmental Teams (U16 and U17) to gold medals in international competition. I have also used this information to coach players at the elementary and junior high levels. I hope this source helps you as you begin your own coaching endeavor. Have fun!

Don Showalter

Head coach of the USA Basketball Men's Developmental National Team

Varsity boys' basketball coach—City High School, Iowa City, Iowa

Acknowledgments

Many people had much to do with editing this edition. The USA Basketball staff are unbelievable and have provided me with tremendous opportunities most high school coaches only dream about in their career; Jim Tooley, Sean Ford, and BJ Johnson are great people. Thanks to Annie Byrne for her help in writing the Considerations When Coaching Females sidebars in this edition. Laura Podeschi from Human Kinetics was outstanding to work with and provided great guidance throughout the project. My longtime assistant coaches—Chris Kern, Kelby Bender, and Bud Bender—also deserve recognition because they have been a huge part of my success and have done much during our summer development so I could work with USA Basketball. Coaches who have had a great impact on my coaching career are John Wooden, Coach K (Mike Krzyzewski), Roy Williams, and Tates Locke, to name just a few. Finally, the support of a family is crucial in a coach's success, and my wife of 39 years, Vicky Showalter, has been a rock.

Don Showalter

Drill Finder

Key to Diagrams

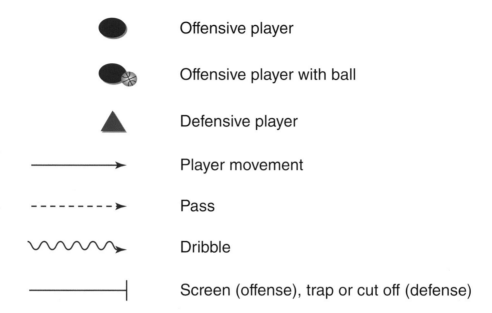

Offensive player

Offensive player with ball

Defensive player

Player movement

Pass

Dribble

Screen (offense), trap or cut off (defense)

Part I

Managing

Have you purchased the traditional coaching tools such as a whistle, coaching attire, sport shoes, and a clipboard? They'll help you in the act of coaching, but to be successful, you'll need five other tools that cannot be bought. These tools are available only through self-examination and hard work; they're easy to remember with the acronym COACH:

C	Comprehension
O	Outlook
A	Affection
C	Character
H	Humor

Comprehension

Comprehension of the rules and skills of basketball is required. You must understand the elements of the sport. To improve your comprehension of basketball, take the following steps:

- Read about the rules of basketball beginning on page 27 in chapter 2 of this book.
- Read about the fundamental skills of basketball in chapters 4 and 7.
- Read additional basketball coaching books, including those available from the American Sport Education Program (ASEP).
- Contact youth basketball organizations.
- Attend basketball coaching clinics.
- Talk with more experienced coaches.
- Observe local college, high school, and youth basketball games.
- Watch basketball games on television.

In addition to having basketball knowledge, you must implement proper training and safety methods so that your players can participate with little risk of injury. Even then, injuries may occur. And more often than not, you'll be the first person responding to your players' injuries, so be sure you understand the basic emergency care procedures described in chapter 2. Also, read in that chapter how to handle more serious sport injury situations.

Outlook

This coaching tool refers to your perspective and goals—what you seek as a coach. The most common coaching objectives are to (a) have fun; (b) help players develop their physical, mental, and social skills; and (c) strive to win. Thus, your outlook involves your priorities, your planning, and your vision for the future. See the Assessing Your Priorities sidebar (page 4) to learn more about the priorities you set for yourself as a coach.

ASEP has a motto that will help you keep your outlook in line with the best interests of the kids on your team. It summarizes in four words all you need to remember when establishing your coaching priorities:

Athletes First, Winning Second

This motto recognizes that striving to win is an important, even vital, part of sports. Instilling a competitive nature in your players is very important because they will need this competitive mind-set in the job world as well. But the motto emphatically states that no efforts in striving to win should be made at the expense of the players' well-being, development, and enjoyment. Take the following actions to better define your outlook:

- With the members of your coaching staff, determine your priorities for the season.
- Prepare for situations that may challenge your priorities.
- Set goals for yourself and your players that are consistent with your priorities.
- Plan how you and your players can best attain your goals.
- Review your goals frequently to be sure that you are staying on track.

Affection

Another vital tool you will want to have in your coaching kit is a genuine concern for the young people you coach. This requires having a passion for kids, a desire to share with them your enjoyment and knowledge of basketball, and the patience and understanding that allow all your players to grow from their involvement in sport. You can demonstrate your affection and patience in many ways, including the following:

- Make an effort to get to know each player on your team.
- Treat each player as an individual.
- Empathize with players trying to learn new and difficult skills.
- Treat players as you would like to be treated under similar circumstances.
- Control your emotions.
- Show your enthusiasm for being involved with your team.
- Keep an upbeat tempo and positive tone in all of your communications.
- Strive to get to know your players off the court, and plan ways for them to get to know each other and the coaches in a noncompetitive environment (e.g., pizza parties, bowling, watching college games together, or movie nights).

Assessing Your Priorities

Even though all coaches focus on competition, we want you to focus on *positive* competition—keeping the pursuit of victory in perspective by making decisions that, first, are in the best interest of the players, and second, will help to win the game.

So, how do you know if your outlook and priorities are in order? Here's a little test:

1. Which situation would you be most proud of?
    a. *knowing that each participant enjoyed playing basketball*
    b. *seeing that all players improved their basketball skills*
    c. *winning the league championship*

2. Which statement best reflects your thoughts about sport?
    a. *If it isn't fun, don't do it.*
    b. *Everyone should learn something every day.*
    c. *Sport isn't fun if you don't win.*

3. How would you like your players to remember you?
    a. *as a coach who was fun to play for*
    b. *as a coach who provided a good base of fundamental skills*
    c. *as a coach who had a winning record*

4. Which would you most like to hear a parent of a player on your team say?
    a. *Mike really had a good time playing basketball this year.*
    b. *Nicole learned some important lessons playing basketball this year.*
    c. *Willie played on the first-place basketball team this year.*

5. Which of the following would be the most rewarding moment of your season?
    a. *having your team want to continue playing, even after practice is over*
    b. *seeing one of your players finally master the skill of dribbling*
    c. *winning the league championship*

Look over your answers. If you most often selected *a* responses, then having fun is most important to you. A majority of *b* answers suggests that skill development is what attracts you to coaching. And if *c* was your most frequent response, winning is tops on your list of coaching priorities. If your priorities are in order, your players' well-being will take precedence over your team's win–loss record every time.

Character

The fact that you have decided to coach young basketball players probably means that you think participation in sport is important. But whether that participation develops character in your players depends as much on you as it does on the sport itself. How can you help your players build character?

Having good character means modeling appropriate behaviors for sport and life. That means more than just saying the right things. What you say and what you do must match. There is no place in coaching for the "Do as I say, not as I do" philosophy. Challenge, support, encourage, and reward every youngster, and your players will be more likely to accept—even celebrate—their differences. Be in control before, during, and after all practices and games. And don't be afraid to admit that you were wrong. No one is perfect!

Each member of your coaching staff should consider the following steps to becoming a good role model:

- Take stock of your strengths and weaknesses.
- Build on your strengths.
- Set goals for yourself to improve on areas that are not as strong.
- If you slip up, apologize to your team and to yourself. You'll do better next time.

Humor

Humor is an often-overlooked coaching tool. It means having the ability to laugh at yourself and with your players during practices and games. Nothing helps balance the seriousness of a skill session like a chuckle or two. And a sense of humor puts in perspective the many mistakes your players will make. So don't get upset over each miscue or respond negatively to erring players. Allow yourself and your players to enjoy the ups, and don't dwell on the downs.

Here are some tips for injecting humor and fun into your practices:

- Make practices fun by including a variety of activities.
- Keep all players involved in games and skill practices.
- Consider laughter by your players to be a sign of enjoyment, not of waning discipline.
- Do not use sarcasm aimed at any player as a means of humor.
- Be able to laugh at yourself first.
- Smile!

1

Responsibilities

Coaching at all levels involves much more than designing offensive plays or drawing up defenses. Coaching involves accepting the tremendous responsibility you face when parents put their children into your care. As a basketball coach, you'll be called on to do the following:

1. **Provide a safe physical environment.** Playing basketball holds inherent risks, but as a coach you're responsible for regularly inspecting the courts and equipment used for practice and competition (see the Facilities and Equipment Checklist in the appendix on page 247).

2. **Communicate in a positive way.** As you can already see, you have a lot to communicate. You'll communicate not only with your players and their parents but also with the coaching staff, officials, administrators, and others. Communicate in a way that is positive and that demonstrates that you have the best interests of the players at heart.

COACHING TIP Set a goal for yourself to make at least two positive comments to each player during each practice.

3. **Teach the fundamental skills of basketball.** When teaching the fundamental skills of basketball, keep in mind that basketball is a game, and therefore, you want to be sure that your players have fun while they are learning the skills. We ask that you help all players be the best they can be by creating a fun, yet productive, practice environment in which players learn and practice the needed skills in a manner that they enjoy (see part II for more information). Additionally, to help your players improve their skills, you need to have a sound understanding of offensive and defensive skills. We'll provide information to assist you in gaining that understanding (see chapters 4 and 7).

4. **Teach the rules of basketball.** You need to introduce the rules of basketball and incorporate them into individual instruction (see page 27 in chapter 2 for more information). Many rules can be taught in practice, including offensive rules (such as double dribble, traveling, the three-second rule, over-and-back violations, and free-throw violations) as well as defensive rules (such as fouling and the five-second rule on closely guarding an opponent). You should also plan to go over the rules with your players any time an opportunity naturally arises in practices.

5. **Direct players in competition.** Your responsibilities include determining starting lineups and a substitution plan, relating appropriately to officials and to opposing coaches and players, and making sound tactical decisions during games (see chapter 3 for more information on coaching during games). Remember that the focus is not on winning at all costs, but on coaching your kids to compete well, do their best, improve their basketball skills, and strive to win within the rules.

6. **Help your players become fit and value fitness for a lifetime.** We want you to help your players be fit so they can play basketball safely and successfully. We also want your players to learn to become fit on their own, understand the value of fitness, and enjoy training. Thus, we ask you not to make them do push-ups or run laps for punishment. Make it fun to get fit for basketball, and make it fun to play basketball so that they'll stay fit for a lifetime.

7. **Help young people develop character.** Character development includes learning, caring, being honest and respectful, taking responsibility, and demonstrating good sporting behavior during practices and games. Teaching these intangible qualities to your players is no less important than teaching them the skill of shooting the basketball. We ask you to teach these values to players by demonstrating and encouraging behaviors that express these values at all times. For example, in teaching good team defense, stress to young players the importance of learning their assignments, helping their teammates, playing within the rules, showing respect for their opponents, and understanding that they are responsible for winning the individual battle on every play—even though they may not always be recognized individually for their efforts.

These are your responsibilities as a coach. Remember that every player is an individual. You must provide a wholesome environment in which every player has the opportunity to learn how to play the game without fear while having fun and enjoying the overall basketball experience.

Safety

One of your players appears to break free downcourt, dribbling the ball toward the basket for an apparent layup. Out of nowhere races a defender who catches up with and accidentally undercuts your player. You see that your player is not getting up and seems to be in pain. What do you do?

No coach wants to see players get hurt. But injury remains a reality of sport participation; consequently, you must be prepared to provide first aid when injuries occur and to protect yourself against unjustified lawsuits. Fortunately, coaches can institute many preventive measures to reduce the risk. In this section, we describe steps you can take to prevent injuries, chapter 2 covers first aid and emergency responses for when injuries occur, and your legal responsibilities as a coach.

You can't prevent all injuries from happening, but you can take preventive measures that give your players the best possible chance for injury-free participation. To help you create the safest possible environment for your players, we'll explore what you can do in these areas:

- Preseason physical examination
- Physical conditioning
- Player matchups and inherent risks
- Proper supervision and record keeping
- Environmental conditions

Preseason Physical Examination

We recommend that your players have a physical examination before participating in basketball. The exam should address the most likely areas of medical concern and identify youngsters at high risk. We also suggest that you have players' parents or guardians sign a participation agreement form (this will be discussed in more detail later in this chapter) and an informed consent form to allow their children to be treated in case of an emergency. For a sample form, please see the Informed Consent Form on page 248 of the appendix.

Physical Conditioning

Players need to be in shape (or get in shape) to play the game at the level expected. They must have adequate cardiorespiratory fitness and muscular fitness.

Cardiorespiratory fitness involves the body's ability to use oxygen and fuels efficiently to power muscle contractions. As players get in better shape, their bodies are able to more efficiently deliver oxygen to fuel muscles and carry off carbon dioxides and other wastes. Basketball requires lots of running and exertion; most players will be moving nearly continuously and making short bursts throughout a game. Youngsters who aren't as fit as their peers often overextend in trying to keep up, which can result in light-headedness, nausea, fatigue, and potential injury.

Try to remember that the players' goals are to participate, to learn, and to have fun. Therefore, you must keep the players active, attentive, and involved with every phase of practice. If you do, the players will attain higher levels of cardiorespiratory fitness as the season progresses simply by taking part in practice. However, you should watch closely for signs of low cardiorespiratory fitness; don't let your players do much until they're fit. You might privately counsel youngsters who appear overly winded, suggesting that they train outside of practice (under proper supervision) to increase their fitness.

Muscular fitness encompasses strength, muscular endurance, power, speed, and flexibility. This type of fitness is affected by physical maturity, as well as strength training and other types of training. Your players will likely exhibit a relatively wide range of muscular fitness. Those who have greater muscular fitness will be able to run faster and jump higher. They will also sustain fewer muscular injuries, and any injuries that do occur will tend to be minor. And in case of injury, recovery is faster for those with higher levels of muscular fitness.

Two other components of fitness and injury prevention are the warm-up and the cool-down. Although young bodies are generally very limber, they can become tight through inactivity. The warm-up should address each muscle group and elevate the heart rate in preparation for strenuous activity. Players should warm up for 5 to 10 minutes using a combination of light running, jumping, and stretching. As practice winds down, slow players' heart rates with an easy jog or walk. Then have the players stretch for 5 minutes to help prevent tight muscles before the next practice or game.

Player Matchups and Inherent Risks

We recommend that you group teams in 2-year age increments if possible. You'll encounter fewer mismatches in physical maturation with narrow age ranges. Even so, two 12-year-old boys might differ by 90 pounds in weight, a foot in height, and 3 or 4 years in emotional and intellectual maturity. This presents dangers for the less mature. Whenever possible, you should match players against opponents of similar size and physical maturity. Such an approach gives smaller, less mature youngsters a better chance to succeed and avoid injury while providing more mature players with a greater challenge. Closely supervise games so that the more mature do not put the less mature at undue risk.

COACHING TIP If your players vary largely in size, you should consider installing a rule that does not allow players to double-team or steal the ball from a dribbler during practices. This may help prevent bigger players from overpowering smaller players and stealing the ball at every opportunity.

Although proper matching helps protect you from certain liability concerns, you must also warn players of the inherent risks involved in playing basketball, because "failure to warn" is one of the most successful arguments in lawsuits against coaches. So, thoroughly explain the inherent risks of basketball, and make sure each player knows, understands, and appreciates those risks. You can learn more about these risks by talking with your league administrators.

The preseason parent-orientation meeting is a good opportunity to explain the risks of the sport to both parents and players. It is also a good time to have both the players and their parents sign a participation agreement form or waiver releasing you from liability should an injury occur. You should work with your league when creating these forms or waivers, and the forms should be reviewed by legal counsel before presentation. These forms or waivers do not relieve you of responsibility for your players' well-being, but they are recommended by lawyers and may help you in the event of a lawsuit.

Proper Supervision and Record Keeping

To ensure players' safety, you must provide both general supervision and specific supervision. *General supervision* means that you are in the area of activity so that you can see and hear what is happening. You should be

- on the court and in position to supervise the players even before the formal practice or game begins,
- immediately accessible to the activity and able to oversee the entire activity,
- alert to conditions that may be dangerous to players and ready to take action to protect players,
- able to react immediately and appropriately to emergencies, and
- present on the court until the last player has been picked up after the practice or game.

Specific supervision is the direct supervision of an activity at practice. For example, you should provide specific supervision when you teach new skills and should continue it until your players understand the requirements of the activity, the risks involved, and their own ability to perform in light of these risks. You must also provide specific supervision when you notice players breaking rules or a change in the condition of your players. As a general rule, the more dangerous the activity, the more specific the supervision required. This suggests that more specific supervision is required with younger and less experienced players.

COACHING TIP Supervision is very important to ensure that the basketball skills you teach are performed in a consistent manner. The more adults that can help supervise the skills, the better the players can learn and perform those skills.

As part of your supervisory duties, you are expected to foresee potentially dangerous situations and to be positioned to help prevent them. This requires that you know basketball well, especially the rules that are intended to provide for safety. Prohibit dangerous horseplay, and hold training sessions only under safe weather conditions (as discussed in Environmental Conditions). These specific supervisory activities, applied consistently, will make the play environment safer for your players and will help protect you from liability if a mishap occurs.

For further protection, keep records of your season plans, practice plans, and players' injuries. Season and practice plans come in handy when you need evidence that players have been taught certain skills, whereas accurate, detailed injury report forms offer protection against unfounded lawsuits. Ask for these forms from your sponsoring organization (see page 249 in the appendix for the Injury Report Form), and hold onto these records for several years so that an "old basketball injury" of a former player doesn't come back to haunt you.

Environmental Conditions

Even though basketball is a game that is typically played indoors, the versatility of the game allows it to be played outside as well. Many players will practice on their own at outside courts, and many camps and youth practices are held outside because gym space is often not available. Most health problems caused by environmental factors are related to excessive heat or cold, although you should also consider other environmental factors such as severe weather and air pollution. A little thought about the potential problems and a little effort to ensure adequate protection for your players will prevent most serious emergencies related to environmental conditions.

COACHING TIP Encourage players to drink plenty of water before, during, and after training. Water makes up 45 to 65 percent of a youngster's body weight, and losing even a small amount of water can cause severe consequences in the body's systems. It doesn't have to be hot and humid for players to become dehydrated, nor is thirst an accurate indicator. In fact, by the time players are aware of their thirst, they are long overdue for a drink.

Heat

On hot and humid days, the body has difficulty cooling itself. Because the air is already saturated with water vapor (humidity), sweat doesn't evaporate as easily. Therefore, body sweat is a less effective cooling agent, and the body retains extra heat. Hot, humid environments put players at risk of heat exhaustion and heatstroke (see more on these in chapter 2 on page 26). And if *you* think it's hot or humid, it's worse for the kids, not only because they're more active, but also because kids under the age of 12 have more difficulty regulating their body temperature than adults do. To provide for players' safety in hot or humid conditions, take the following preventive measures:

- Monitor weather conditions and adjust training sessions accordingly. Table 1.1 lists some warm-weather precautions for various temperatures.
- Acclimatize players to exercising in high heat and humidity. Athletes can adjust to high heat and humidity in 7 to 10 days. During this period, hold practices at low to moderate activity levels and give the players fluid breaks every 20 minutes or less.
- Switch to light clothing. Players should wear shorts and white T-shirts.

TABLE 1.1 Warm-Weather Precautions

Temperature (°F)	Humidity	Precautions
80-90	<70%	Monitoring of athletes prone to heat illness
	≥70%	5 min rest after 30 min of practice
90-100	<70%	5 min rest after 30 min of practice
	≥70%	Short practices in evening or early morning

- Identify and monitor players who are prone to heat illness. This would include players who are overweight, heavily muscled, or out of shape and players who work excessively hard or have suffered previous heat illness. Closely monitor these players and give them fluid breaks every 15 to 20 minutes.

- Make sure players replace fluids lost through sweat. Encourage players to drink 17 to 20 ounces of fluid 2 to 3 hours before each practice or game, to drink 7 to 10 ounces every 20 minutes during and after each practice and game, and to drink 16 to 24 ounces of fluid for every pound lost. Fluids such as water and sports drinks are preferable during games and practices (suggested intakes are based on NATA [National Athletic Trainers' Association] recommendations). The amount of fluid is generally the same for each age group; however, prepubescent players should drink more water than sports drinks.

- Encourage players to replenish electrolytes, such as sodium (salt) and potassium, that are lost through sweat. The best way to replace these nutrients—as well as others such as carbohydrates (energy) and protein (muscle building)—is by eating a balanced diet. Experts say that additional salt intake may be helpful during the most intense training periods in the heat.

Cold

When a person is exposed to cold weather, the body temperature starts to drop below normal. To counteract this, the body shivers to create heat and reduces blood flow to the extremities to conserve heat in the core of the body. But no matter how effective the body's natural heating mechanism is, the body will better withstand cold temperatures if it is prepared to handle them. To reduce the risk of cold-related illnesses, make sure players wear appropriate protective clothing, and keep the players active to maintain body heat. Also monitor the windchill factor because it can drastically affect the severity of players' responses to the weather. The windchill factor index is shown in figure 1.1.

Temperature (°F)

Wind speed (mph)	0	5	10	15	20	25	30	35	40
Flesh may freeze within one minute									
40	-29	-22	-15	-8	-1	6	13	20	27
35	-27	-21	-14	-7	0	7	14	21	28
30	-26	-19	-12	-5	1	8	15	22	28
25	-24	-17	-11	-4	3	9	16	23	29
20	-22	-15	-9	-2	4	11	17	24	30
15	-19	-13	-7	0	6	13	19	25	32
10	-16	-10	-4	3	9	15	21	27	34
5	-11	-5	1	7	13	19	25	31	36

Windchill temperature (°F)

FIGURE 1.1 Windchill factor index.

Adapted from National Weather Service, 2009, NWS windchill chart. [Online]. Available: www.nws.noaa.gov/om/windchill/index.shtml [February 3, 2012].

Severe Weather

Severe weather refers to a host of potential dangers, including lightning storms, tornadoes, hail storms, and heavy rains. When people are playing basketball outside, lightning is of special concern because it can come up quickly and can cause great harm or even kill. For each 5-second count from the flash of lightning to the bang of thunder, lightning is one mile away. A flash–bang of 10 seconds means lightning is two miles away; a flash–bang of 15 seconds indicates that lightning is three miles away. A practice or competition should be stopped for the day if lightning is six miles away or closer (30 seconds or fewer from flash to bang). In addition to these suggestions, your school, league, or state association may also have rules that you will want to consider in severe weather.

Safe places to take cover when lightning strikes include fully enclosed metal vehicles with the windows up, enclosed buildings, and low ground (under cover of bushes, if possible). It's not safe to be near metal objects such as flag poles, fences, light poles, and metal bleachers. Also avoid trees, water, and open fields.

You should cancel practice when under either a tornado watch or warning. If you are practicing or competing when a tornado is nearby, you should get inside a building if possible. If you cannot get into a building, lie in a ditch or other low-lying area or crouch near a strong building, using your arms to protect your head and neck.

The keys to handling severe weather are caution and prudence. Don't try to get that last 10 minutes of practice in if lightning is on the horizon. Don't continue to play in heavy rain. Many storms can strike both quickly and ferociously. Respect the weather and play it safe.

Air Pollution

Poor air quality and smog can present real dangers to your players. Both short- and long-term lung damage are possible from breathing polluted air. Although it's true that participating in clean air is not possible in many areas, restricting activity is recommended when the air quality ratings are lower than moderate or when there is a smog alert in your area. Your local health department or air quality control board can inform you of the air quality ratings for your area and when restricting activities is recommended.

Teaching

In coaching, teaching involves teaching skills to players. When teaching a basketball skill, you should demonstrate the skill in a simple form so the players can understand the hows and whys of the skill (see part II for more details). This may vary depending on the age and development of your players. In addition to teaching basketball skills, you should teach your players how to demonstrate good sporting behavior on and off the court and how to develop friendships with teammates, opponents, officials, and coaches. The goal is for players to learn life skills that will have benefits long after the basketball season is done.

Organization

Organization should be a top priority for every coach. As you continue to coach young players, you should keep a good record of what you have done, identifying what worked well and what can be improved on for next season.

Here are some ideas that will help you to be more organized:

- Keep a daily journal of what worked well in practice and what did not work well.
- Organize your notes into a notebook for easy reference during future seasons.
- Keep all your practice plans from one year to the next in a binder. This will be a great reference when you are planning practices in upcoming seasons.
- Keep all the player information in a file or on your computer. You may have the same players from one year to the next, so this will be handy for your reference.
- Keep a log of your games. Write a short scouting report on the teams you played. These scouting reports will be helpful when you play the team in the next season, especially if the team has the same coach.
- Keep a record of your meetings with parents, players, and other people associated with your program. This will be of value in future seasons; if necessary, you can refer back to this record to see what has been discussed previously.

Fun

Regardless of where you are in your season, you must create an environment that welcomes learning and promotes teamwork while still allowing players to have fun. Following are seven tips that will help you and your coaching staff get the most out of your practices:

1. Stick to the practice times agreed on as a staff.
2. Start and end each practice as a team.
3. Keep the practice routine as consistent as possible so that the players can feel comfortable.
4. Be organized in your approach by moving quickly from one drill to another and from one period to another.
5. Tell your players what the practice will include before the practice starts.
6. Allow the players to take water breaks whenever possible.
7. Focus on providing positive feedback.

You may also want to consider using games to make practices more fun. In chapters 6 and 9, you will find 47 gamelike drills. During your season, it may be fun to use the games toward the end of the week to add variety to your practices.

Preparations

2

You've learned about the tools you need for coaching—comprehension, outlook, affection, character, and humor—as well as your responsibilities as a coach, some ways to provide safety for your players, techniques for teaching, and how to make basketball fun. These are essentials for effective coaching; without them, you'd have a difficult time managing your team. But you must also be sure to take the appropriate steps to prepare for your season. This chapter examines how to develop a season plan and practice plans. In addition, the chapter provides you with the knowledge you'll need as a coach, including information on how the game is played, descriptions of the rules of basketball, and details on how to handle injuries.

Season Planning

Your season plan acts as a snapshot of the entire season. Before the first practice with your players, you must sit down as a coaching staff and develop a season plan. To do this, simply write down each practice and game date on a calendar, and then go back and number your practices. These practice numbers will become the foundation of your season plan. Now you can work through the season plan, moving from practice to practice, to create a quick overview of what you hope to cover in each practice. You should note the purpose of the practice, the skills you will cover, and the activities you will use for that particular practice.

Parent Preseason Meeting

A player's parents need to be assured that their son or daughter is under the direction of a coach who is both knowledgeable about the sport and concerned about the youngster's well-being. You can put their worries to rest by holding a preseason parent-orientation meeting in which you describe your background and your approach to coaching.

Preseason Meeting Outline

1. Outline the paperwork that is needed:
   - Copy of the player's birth certificate
   - Completed player's application and payment record
   - Report card from the previous year
   - Informed consent form (see page 248 of the appendix)
2. Go over the inherent risks of basketball and other safety issues.
3. Inform parents of the date and time that uniforms and equipment will be handed out.
4. Review the season practice schedule, including the date, location, and time of each practice.
5. Go over the proper gear and attire that should be worn at each practice session.
6. Discuss nutrition, hydration, and rest for players.
7. Explain the goals for the team.
8. Cover methods of communication: e-mail list, emergency phone numbers, interactive website, and so on.
9. Discuss ways that parents can help with the team.
10. Discuss standards of conduct for coaches, players, and parents.
11. Provide time for questions and answers.

If parents contact you with comments or concerns during the season, you should listen to them closely and try to offer positive responses or solutions. If you need to communicate with parents, the best plan is to catch them after a practice, give them a phone call, or send a note through e-mail or the U.S. mail. Messages sent to parents through young players are too often lost, misinterpreted, or forgotten. Remember, it is better to communicate with parents too much rather than too little.

Following is more detailed information about season plans for each particular age group—ages 5 and 6, 7 and 8, 9 and 10, 11 and 12, and 13 and 14.

> **COACHING TIP** While developing your season plan, keep in mind that you will want to incorporate gamelike activities into your practices. These activities focus on replicating the game environment. Using gamelike activities better develops the players both physically and mentally to the demands of the game.

Season Plan for Ages 5 and 6

The players in this age group will be new to playing basketball, and you will be required to thoroughly explain and demonstrate basketball terms to your players. The recommended ball-to-player ratio is 1:1, so you should plan for individual activities in your practices. You must also plan to take time to review skills learned in previous practices. For the 5- and 6-year age group, the following concepts and skills should be covered during the season:

- **Psychology.** Sharing, fair play, parental involvement, "how to play," emotional management
- **Fitness.** Balance, running, jumping, warm-up (introduce the idea of how to warm up), movement education
- **Technical skills.** Moving with and without the ball, footwork, dribbling, shooting, passing
- **Tactical skills.** Which basket to shoot at

Season Plan for Ages 7 and 8

Most of the players in this age group have had exposure to basketball, but some may still be newer to the sport. The season plan for this age group builds on the season plan for ages 5 and 6 as players refine fundamental skills. The recommended ball-to-player ratio is 1:5, so you can plan for individual, pairs, and both small- and larger-group activities. For the 7- and 8-year age group, the following concepts and skills should be covered during the season:

- **Psychology.** Teamwork, confidence, desire, mental rehearsal, intrinsic motivation, handling distress, how to learn from each game, good sporting behavior, parental involvement, emotional management
- **Fitness.** Speed, strength, aerobic exercise
- **Technical skills.** Passing (chest, bounce, overhead, and one-handed push passes), dribbling (speed, control, crossover, and backup dribbles), shooting (layups, set and jump shots, and free throws), offensive and defensive footwork (slides, pivots, jump stops, and cuts)

- **Tactical skills.** Playing on and off the ball, passing around defensive players, fast break (two-on-one, three-on-two, and four-on-three drills; filling lanes; and outletting the ball), communication, halftime analysis, offensive sets and specific plays, defensive principles including man-to-man and zone defense

Season Plan for Ages 9 and 10

The season plan for this age group is similar to the season plan for ages 7 and 8 as players continue to refine fundamental skills. The recommended ball-to-player ratio is again 1:5, so you can plan for individual, pair, and both small- and larger-group activities. For the 9- and 10-year age group, the same concepts and skills covered with ages 7 and 8 above should be covered during the season.

Season Plan for Ages 11 and 12

At this stage, players are refining the skills they have learned from past years. This season plan builds on the plans for previous age groups and adds a few new skills. Many of the skills are the same as those presented in younger age groups, but in the 11- and 12-year age group, emphasis will be placed on different aspects of the game. For the 11- and 12-year age group, the following concepts and skills should be covered during the season:

- **Psychology.** Teamwork, confidence, desire, mental rehearsal, intrinsic motivation, handling distress, how to learn from each game, good sporting behavior, parental involvement, emotional management
- **Fitness.** Speed, strength, aerobic exercise
- **Technical skills.** Passing (overhead passes and passing off the dribble), shooting (set shots, power shots, and jump shots off the pass and dribble), post moves, defensive slides
- **Tactical skills.** Set plays for man-to-man and zone offenses, full-court defense for man-to-man and zone, fast break (lanes and secondary break), full-court press break on offense, inbounds plays, passing around the defense, jump ball situations

Season Plan for Ages 13 and 14

As in the previous age group, at this stage, players are refining the skills they have learned from past years. The skills are the same as those presented in younger age groups, but like the 11- and 12-year age group, emphasis in the 13- and 14-year age group will be placed on different aspects of the game. For the 13- and 14-year age group, the same concepts and skills covered with ages 11 and 12 above should be covered during the season.

Practice Planning

Coaches rarely believe they have enough time to practice everything they want to cover. To help organize your thoughts and help you stay on track toward your practice objectives, you should create practice plans. These plans help you better visualize and prepare so that you can run your practices effectively.

First and foremost, your practice plans should be age appropriate for the age group you are coaching. The plans should incorporate all of the skills and concepts presented in the particular age group's season plan and should include activities that move from simple to more complex.

The practice plans for ages 5 and 6 should focus mostly on individual skill development. Games (such as those where players play 2v2 and 3v3) should be incorporated to help develop these skills.

The practice plans for the 7- and 8-year age group will be much the same as in the 5- and 6-year age group. Practice plans will still focus mostly on individual skill development, though more advanced skills relating to team offense and defense will be introduced throughout the season.

The practice plans for ages 9 and 10 will be more advanced while still focusing on individual skill development. The advanced skills introduced at this level will focus on the basics of team offense and defense, as well as on team skills such as fast break transition and coordinated screens and cuts on offense.

The practice plans for ages 11 and 12 will begin to shift focus from individual skill development to further developing team offenses and defenses. Most drills will involve working on multiple skills at one time. The advanced skills introduced at this level will focus on additional aspects of team offense and defense, the fast break, and out-of-bounds plays.

The practice plans for the 13- and 14-year age group will continue to focus on the development of team offenses and defenses. In addition to working on advanced skills related to team offense and defense, the fast break, and out-of-bounds plays, this age group should focus on the skills that the players will need for their positions, such as post and perimeter play.

For sample practice plans for each age group, refer to part III.

Facilities and Equipment

Be sure to regularly examine the court on which your players practice and play. Remove hazards, report conditions you cannot remedy, and request maintenance as necessary. If unsafe conditions exist, you should either make adaptations to prevent risk to your players' safety or stop the practice or game until safe conditions have been restored. You can also prevent injuries by checking the quality and fit of uniforms, practice attire, and any protective equipment used by your players. Refer to the Facilities and Equipment Checklist in the appendix (page 247) to help guide you in verifying that facilities and equipment are safe.

First Response

No matter how good your prevention program and planning are, injuries most likely will occur. When injury does strike, chances are you will be the one in charge. The severity and nature of the injury will determine how actively involved you'll be in treating it. But regardless of how seriously a player is hurt, it is your responsibility to know what steps to take. Therefore, you must be prepared to take appropriate action and provide basic emergency care when an injury occurs.

Being Prepared

Being prepared to provide basic emergency care involves many things, including being trained in cardiopulmonary resuscitation (CPR) and first aid, having a first aid kit on hand, and having an emergency plan.

CPR and First Aid Training

We recommend that all coaches receive CPR and first aid training from a nationally recognized organization such as the National Safety Council, the American Heart Association, the American Red Cross, or the American Sport Education Program (ASEP). You should be certified based on a practical test and a written test of knowledge. Training in CPR should include obstructed airway procedures and basic life support for both children and adults.

Emergency Plan

An emergency plan is the final tool in being prepared to take appropriate action for severe or serious injuries. The plan calls for three steps:

1. **Evaluate the injured player.** Use your CPR and first aid training to guide you. Be sure to keep these certifications up to date. Practice your skills frequently to keep them fresh and ready to use if and when you need them.

2. **Call the appropriate medical personnel.** If possible, delegate the responsibility of seeking medical help to another calm and responsible adult who attends all practices and games. Write out a list of emergency phone numbers and keep it with you at practices and games. Include the following phone numbers:

- Rescue unit
- Hospital
- Physician
- Police
- Fire department

Take each player's emergency information to every practice and game (see the Emergency Information Card in the appendix on page 250). This information includes the person to contact in case of an emergency, what types of medications the player is using, what types of drugs the player is allergic to, and so on.

Give an emergency response card (see the Emergency Response Card in the appendix on page 251) to the contact person calling for emergency assistance. Having

First Aid Kit

A well-stocked first aid kit should include the following:

- Antibacterial soap or wipes
- Arm sling
- Athletic tape (one and a half inches wide)
- Bandage scissors
- Bandage strips (assorted sizes)
- Blood spill kit
- Cell phone
- Contact lens case
- Cotton swabs
- Elastic wraps (three inches, four inches, and six inches)
- Emergency blanket
- Examination gloves (latex free)
- Eye patch
- Foam rubber (one-eighth inch, one-fourth inch, and one-half inch)
- Insect sting kit
- List of emergency phone numbers
- Mirror
- Moleskin
- Nail clippers
- Oral thermometer (to determine if a player has a fever caused by illness)
- Penlight
- Petroleum jelly
- Plastic bags for crushed ice
- Prewrap (underwrap for tape)
- Rescue breathing or CPR face mask
- Safety glasses (for assistance in first aid)
- Safety pins
- Saline solution for eyes
- Sterile gauze pads (three-inch and four-inch squares; preferably nonstick)
- Sterile gauze rolls
- Sunscreen (sun protection factor, or SPF, of 30 or greater)
- Tape adherent and tape remover
- Tongue depressors
- Tooth saver kit
- Triangular bandages
- Tweezers

Adapted, by permission, from M. Flegel, 2008, *Sport first aid*, 4th ed. (Champaign, IL: Human Kinetics), 20.

this information ready should help the contact person remain calm. You must also complete an injury report form (see page 249 in the appendix) and keep it on file for any injury that occurs.

3. **Provide first aid.** If medical personnel are not on hand at the time of the injury, you should provide first aid care to the extent of your qualifications. Again, although your CPR and first aid training will guide you, you must remember the following:

- Do not move the injured player if the injury is to the head, neck, or back; if a large joint (ankle, knee, elbow, or shoulder) is dislocated; or if the pelvis, a rib, or an arm or leg is fractured.

- Calm the injured player and keep others away from her as much as possible.
- Evaluate whether the player's breathing has stopped or is irregular, and if necessary, clear the airway with your fingers.
- Administer CPR as directed in the CPR certification course recommended by your school, league, or state association.
- Remain with the player until medical personnel arrive.

Emergency Steps

You must have a clear, well-rehearsed emergency action plan. You want to be sure you are prepared in case of an emergency because every second counts. Your emergency plan should follow this sequence:

1. Check the player's level of consciousness.
2. Send a contact person to call the appropriate medical personnel and to call the player's parents.
3. Send someone to wait for the rescue team and direct them to the injured player.
4. Assess the injury.
5. Administer first aid.
6. Assist emergency medical personnel in preparing the player for transportation to a medical facility.
7. Appoint someone to go with the player if the parents are not available. This person should be responsible, calm, and familiar with the player. Assistant coaches or parents are best for this job.
8. Complete an injury report form while the incident is fresh in your mind (see page 249 in the appendix).

Taking Appropriate Action

Proper CPR and first aid training, a well-stocked first aid kit, and an emergency plan help prepare you to take appropriate action when an injury occurs. In the previous section, we mentioned the importance of providing first aid to the extent of your qualifications. Don't "play doctor" with injuries; sort out minor injuries that you can treat from those that need medical attention. Now let's look at taking the appropriate action for minor injuries and more serious injuries.

Minor Injuries

Although no injury seems minor to the person experiencing it, most injuries are neither life threatening nor severe enough to restrict participation. When these injuries occur, you can take an active role in their initial treatment.

Scrapes and Cuts   When one of your players has an open wound, the first thing you should do is put on a pair of disposable latex-free examination gloves or some other effective blood barrier. Then follow these four steps:

1. Stop the bleeding by applying direct pressure with a clean dressing to the wound and elevating the injured area if possible. The player may be able to apply this pressure while you put on your gloves. Do not remove the dressing if it becomes soaked with blood. Instead, place an additional dressing on top of the one already in place. If bleeding continues, keep elevating the injured area above the heart and maintain pressure.

2. Cleanse the wound thoroughly once the bleeding is controlled. A good rinsing with a forceful stream of water, and perhaps light scrubbing with soap, will help prevent infection.

3. Protect the wound with sterile gauze or a bandage strip. If the player continues to participate, apply protective padding over the injured area.

4. Remove and dispose of gloves carefully to prevent you or anyone else from coming into contact with blood.

For bloody noses not associated with serious facial injury, have the player sit and lean slightly forward. Then pinch the player's nostrils shut. If the bleeding continues after several minutes, or if the player has a history of nosebleeds, seek medical assistance.

COACHING TIP   You shouldn't let a fear of acquired immune deficiency syndrome (AIDS) and other communicable diseases stop you from helping a player. You are only at risk if you allow contaminated blood to come in contact with an open wound on your body, so the examination gloves that you wear will protect you from AIDS if one of your players carries this disease. Check with your sport director, your league, or the Centers for Disease Control and Prevention (CDC) for more information about protecting yourself and your participants from AIDS.

Strains and Sprains   The physical demands of playing basketball often result in injury to the muscles or tendons (strains) or to the ligaments (sprains). When your players suffer minor strains or sprains, you should immediately apply the PRICE method of injury care:

P	Protect the player and the injured body part from further danger or trauma.
R	Rest the injured area to avoid further damage and foster healing.
I	Ice the area to reduce swelling and pain.
C	Compress the area by securing an ice bag in place with an elastic wrap.
E	Elevate the injury above heart level to keep blood from pooling in the area.

Bumps and Bruises   Inevitably, basketball players make contact with each other and with the ground. If the force applied to a body part at impact is great enough, a bump or bruise will result. Many players continue playing with such sore spots, but if the bump or bruise is large and painful, you should take appropriate action. Again, use the PRICE method for injury care and monitor the injury. If swelling, discoloration, and pain have lessened, the player may resume participation with protective padding; if not, the player should be examined by a physician.

Serious Injuries

Head, neck, and back injuries; fractures; and injuries that cause a player to lose consciousness are among a class of injuries that you cannot and should not try to treat yourself. In these cases, you should follow the emergency plan outlined on pages 20 to 22.

 If you suspect that a player has received a blow to the head, no matter how mild the symptoms, you should view it as a serious injury. If the player has only mild symptoms, such as a headache, call the parents and have them take the player to a doctor immediately. You should alert emergency medical services (EMS) immediately if the player has lost consciousness or has impaired memory, dizziness, ringing in the ears, blood or fluid draining from the nose or ears, or blurry vision. For more information, see the Heads Up: Concussion in Youth Sports fact sheet that follows (this fact sheet is provided by the Centers for Disease Control and Prevention; www.cdc.gov). If you suspect that a player has a spine injury, joint dislocation, or bone fracture, do not remove any of the player's equipment unless you have to do so to provide lifesaving CPR.

Heads Up: Concussion in Youth Sports

What Is a Concussion?

A concussion is a brain injury. Concussions are caused by a bump or blow to the head. Even a "ding," "getting your bell rung," or what seems to be a mild bump or blow to the head can be serious.

 You can't see a concussion. Signs and symptoms of concussion can show up right after the injury or may not appear or be noticed until days or weeks after the injury. If a player reports any symptoms of concussion, or if you notice the symptoms yourself, seek medical attention right away.

What Are the Signs and Symptoms of a Concussion?

SIGNS OBSERVED BY COACHES, PARENTS, OR GUARDIANS

If a player has experienced a bump or blow to the head during a game or practice, look for any of the following signs and symptoms of a concussion:

- Appears dazed or stunned
- Is confused about assignment or position
- Forgets an instruction
- Is unsure of game, score, or opponent
- Moves clumsily

- Answers questions slowly
- Loses consciousness (even briefly)
- Shows behavior or personality changes
- Can't recall events before hit or fall
- Can't recall events after hit or fall

SYMPTOMS REPORTED BY ATHLETE

- Headache or "pressure" in head
- Nausea or vomiting
- Balance problems or dizziness
- Double or blurry vision
- Sensitivity to light
- Sensitivity to noise
- Feeling sluggish, hazy, foggy, or groggy
- Concentration or memory problems
- Confusion
- Does not "feel right"

How Can You Help Players Prevent a Concussion?

Every sport is different, but all coaches can take steps to help protect their players from concussion.

- Ensure that the players follow their coach's rules for safety and the rules of the sport.
- Encourage players to practice good sporting behavior at all times.
- Make sure the players wear the right protective equipment for their activity. Protective equipment should fit properly, be well maintained, and be worn consistently and correctly.
- Learn the signs and symptoms of a concussion.

What Should You Do if You Think a Player Has a Concussion?

1. **Seek medical attention right away.** A health care professional will be able to decide how serious the concussion is and when it is safe for the player to return to sports.

2. **Keep the player out of play.** Concussions take time to heal. Don't let the player return to play until a health care professional says it's OK. Athletes who return to play too soon—while the brain is still healing—risk a greater chance of having a second concussion. Repeat concussions can be very serious. They can cause permanent brain damage, affecting the person for a lifetime.

3. **Tell other coaches about any recent concussion.** All coaches should know if a player has had a recent concussion in *any* sport. Other coaches might not know about a concussion that the player suffered in another sport or activity unless you tell them.

Adapted from Centers for Disease Control and Prevention, 2007, Heads up: Concussion in youth sports: A fact sheet for parents. [Online]. Available: www.cdc.gov/concussion/pdf/parents_Eng.pdf [February 3, 2012].

In the following sections, we examine more closely your role in preventing heat cramps, heat exhaustion, and heatstroke. Additionally, please refer to table 2.1 for an illustrative example of the signs and symptoms associated with heat exhaustion and heatstroke.

Heat Cramps Tough practices combined with heat stress and substantial fluid loss from sweating can provoke muscle cramps commonly known as heat cramps. Cramping is most common during the early part of the season when the weather is the hottest and the players may be the least adapted to heat. The cramp, a severe tightening of the muscle, can drop players and prevent continued play. Dehydration, electrolyte loss, and fatigue are the contributing factors. The immediate treatment is to have the player cool off and slowly stretch the contracted muscle. The player may return to play later that same day or the next day provided the cramp doesn't cause a muscle strain.

Heat Exhaustion Heat exhaustion is a shocklike condition caused by dehydration and electrolyte depletion. Symptoms include headache, nausea, dizziness, chills, fatigue, and extreme thirst. Profuse sweating is a key sign of heat exhaustion. Other signs include pale, cool, and clammy skin; rapid, weak pulse; loss of coordination; and dilated pupils.

A player suffering from heat exhaustion should rest in a cool, shaded area; drink cool fluids, particularly those containing electrolytes; and apply ice to the neck, back, or abdomen to help cool the body. If you believe a player has heat exhaustion, seek medical attention. Under no conditions should the player return to activity that day or before he regains all the weight lost through sweat. If the player has to see a physician, the player shouldn't return to the team until he has a written release from the physician.

Heatstroke Heatstroke is a life-threatening condition in which the body stops sweating and body temperature rises dangerously high. It occurs when dehydration causes a malfunction in the body's temperature control center in the brain. Symptoms include the feeling of being extremely hot, nausea, confusion, irritability, and fatigue. Signs include hot, dry, and flushed or red skin (this is a key sign); lack of sweat; rapid pulse; rapid breathing; constricted pupils; vomiting; diarrhea; and possibly seizures, unconsciousness, or respiratory or cardiac arrest.

TABLE 2.1 Signs and Symptoms of Heat Exhaustion and Heatstroke

Heat exhaustion	Heatstroke
Dizziness	Dizziness
Headache	Headache
Fatigue	Disoriented, combative, or unconscious
Dehydration	Dehydration
Profuse sweating	Hot and wet or dry skin
Mildly increased body temperature	Markedly increased body temperature
Nausea or vomiting	Nausea or vomiting
Diarrhea	Diarrhea
Rapid, weak pulse	
Muscle cramps	

If you suspect that a player is suffering from heatstroke, send for emergency medical assistance immediately and cool the player as quickly as possible. Remove excess clothing and equipment from the player, and lower her body temperature by using cool, wet towels; by pouring cool water over her; or by placing her in a cold bath. Apply ice packs to the armpits, neck, back, abdomen, and between the legs. If the player is conscious, give her cool fluids to drink. If the player is unconscious, place the player on her side to allow fluids and vomit to drain from the mouth. A player who has suffered heatstroke may not return to the team until she has a written release from a physician.

Knowledge of Rules

The game is governed by a thick rule book. This introduction to the basic rules of basketball won't cover every rule of the game but instead will give you what you need to work with players who are 5 to 14 years old. Here, we cover specifics about some of the basics of the game, such as the number of players, ball and court size, and game length, depending on your team's age group. We also describe specifics such as equipment, player positions, scoring, fouls, and how to start and restart games.

How the Game Is Played

Basketball is a fast-paced game where the objective is to put the ball into the basket. Although the concept is simple, specific offensive and defensive aspects of the game are executed differently based on the level of play and the game situation. Additionally, the court that the game is played on may vary depending on the age level of your players and the facility where the game is played. Figure 2.1 shows the court markings for a standard basketball court.

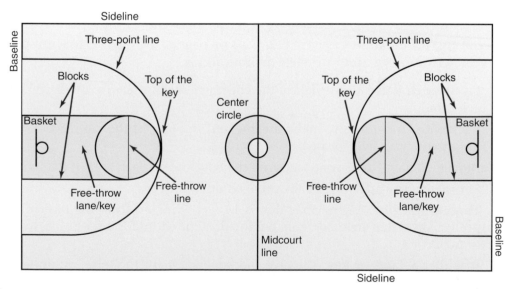

FIGURE 2.1 Standard basketball court markings.

Age Modifications for Basketball

Before we begin, let's consider some of the modifications that can be made to accommodate different age groups. Things such as the size of the court, the size of the ball, the number of players on the court, and the duration of the game can be adjusted for the various age groups to help accommodate players' development and skill levels. Suggested adjustments are as follows:

	5 and 6 years	7 and 8 years	9 and 10 years	11 and 12 years	13 and 14 years
Players on team	5	5	5	5	5
Players on court	5v5	5v5	5v5	5v5	5v5
Ball size	Junior (#5)	Women's (#6)	Women's (#6)	Regulation (#7, or #6 in some states)	Regulation (#7, or #6 in some states)
Court size	Short court	Short court	Short court	Full court	Full court
Free-throw distance	9 ft	9 ft	9 ft	12 to 15 ft	12 to 15 ft
Game length	24 min	24 min	24 min	32 min	32 min
Time-outs	4	4	4	4	4
Basket height	7 ft	8 ft	8 ft	9 to 10 ft	9 to 10 ft

Several areas of the court shown in figure 2.1 on page 27 are referred to with special basketball terminology. Here are a few definitions:

- **Frontcourt.** Refers to the half of the court where your team's offensive basket is located.
- **Backcourt.** Includes the midcourt line and the half of the court where your opponent's basket is located.
- **Blocks.** Square markings 6 feet from the baseline on each side of the lane.
- **Perimeter.** The area outside the three-second lane area.
- **Three-point line.** A semicircle that is 19 feet, 9 inches from the basket at all points. Shots that are made from behind this line count for three points instead of two.
- **Free-throw lane or key.** The area that extends from the baseline under the basket to the free-throw line; it's also called the *three-second lane.*
- **Top of the key.** The semicircle that extends beyond the free-throw line.

Player Equipment

Basketball requires very little player equipment. Players should wear basketball shoes so they have proper traction on the court. They should wear clothing such as athletic shorts and tank tops or loose-fitting shirts so they have the freedom of movement needed to run, jump, and shoot. Players may choose to wear safety glasses or goggles to protect their eyes from injury. Also, players who have conditions affecting the knees or elbows may want to wear soft pads to protect them. Players may not wear jewelry during games.

You must examine the condition of each item you distribute to players. Also make sure that the pieces of equipment they furnish themselves meet acceptable standards.

COACHING TIP You should ensure that each player on your team is outfitted properly and correctly. Early in the season, before games begin, take time out of practice to demonstrate how uniforms and equipment should be handled and worn.

Player Positions

Young players should be given a chance to play a variety of positions, on both offense and defense. By playing different positions, they'll have a better all-around playing experience and may stay more interested in the sport. Furthermore, they'll gain a better understanding of the many technical and tactical skills used in the game. This will also help them appreciate the efforts of their teammates who play positions they find difficult.

COACHING TIP For younger players, especially those who are 5 to 8 years old, you may want to avoid labeling your players by positions. These players should be allowed to experiment with all positions.

Player positions in basketball are typically given a number (1 through 5) for each player on the court. Following are descriptions of these positions.

• **Guards.** A basketball team usually has two guards in the game at all times. The guards play farthest from the basket, on the perimeter. The point guard (the 1 position) is played by the team's best dribbler and passer. The off-guard (the 2 position) is often played by the best long-range shooter and second-best dribbler. Guards are usually the best ball handlers and outside shooters on the team. They tend to be shorter and quicker than the other players and have good dribbling and passing skills.

• **Forwards.** A team usually plays with two forwards in its lineup. Forwards are typically taller than guards, and they play closer to the basket. The smaller forward (the 3 position) is also referred to as the wing, and this position is often filled by the most versatile and athletic member of the team. This forward must be able to play in the lane and on the perimeter on offense, and on defense, he must be able to guard small and quick or big and strong opponents. The other forward position (the 4 position) is filled by a bigger player; this forward should be able to shoot the ball accurately from within 12 feet of the basket and rebound the ball when shots are missed. This is a good spot to assign to one of your bigger players and better rebounders—one who can also shoot the ball from anywhere in the lane area.

- **Center.** Most basketball teams designate one player on the court as their center. The center (the 5 position, which is also called the post position) is frequently the tallest or biggest player on the team. That extra size is helpful in maneuvering for shots or rebounds around the basket. A tall center can also make it difficult for opposing teams to shoot near the basket. A center should have "soft" hands to catch the passes thrown into the lane area by guards and forwards.

Rules of Play

Basketball rules are designed to make the game run smoothly and safely and to prevent either team from gaining an unfair advantage. Throw out the rules and a basketball game can quickly turn chaotic. Following is an overview of some of the basic rules in basketball.

Starts and Restarts

In regulation play, a jump ball at center court is used to start games and overtime periods, which are played when teams are tied at the end of regulation time. During jump balls, the official tosses up the ball between two players, usually each team's center or best leaper. Each player attempts to tip the ball to a teammate (who must be outside of the center circle) to gain possession of the ball. Another jump ball situation is simultaneous possession of the ball by players from opposing teams. In this case, teams alternate possession; the team that did not win the first jump ball takes the ball out of bounds in the next jump ball situation.

Play stops during intermissions and time-outs, but also when the ball goes out of bounds and when an official calls a violation or a foul (as discussed later in this chapter). The clock restarts when the ball is touched following an inbounds pass or a missed free throw.

Scoring

In regulation play, teams are awarded two points for every shot made from inside the three-point line, and they are given three points for shots made from beyond the three-point stripe. A successful free throw is worth one point. (Players may not enter the lane until the free throw has hit the rim. If the free throw doesn't hit the rim, the ball is awarded to the opposing team out of bounds.) The team that scores the most points over the course of the game is the winner.

Fouls

Basketball is a contact sport, with players in close proximity and in constant motion. The rules of the game discourage rough play or tactics that allow a team to gain an advantage through brute force. Therefore, fouls are called when officials see illegal physical contact between two or more players based on these principles:

- The first player to establish position (to become stationary or set) on the court has priority rights to that position.
- A body part cannot be extended into the path of an opponent.

- The player who moves into the path of an opponent—especially an airborne opponent—when contact occurs is responsible for the contact.
- All players have the right to the space extending straight up from their feet on the floor. This is called the principle of verticality.

A team that fouls too much pays for it, because fouls carry with them increasingly severe penalties. A player who has five fouls must sit out for the remainder of the game. In regulation play, a team that has more than a specified number of fouls in a quarter or half gives the opposing team a bonus situation: The member of the team who was fouled is allowed to shoot free throws. If the foul is a nonshooting—or personal—foul, the player shoots one free throw and, if she makes it, shoots a second one (this is called one-and-one). Table 2.2 lists the most common personal fouls and their penalties.

If the foul is a shooting foul—in other words, a foul in which a defender makes contact with a player who is shooting the basketball—the player shoots two free throws.

TABLE 2.2 Personal Fouls and Penalties

Type of foul	Description of foul	Penalty
Blocking	Physically impeding the progress of another player who is still moving.	Foul
Charging	Running into or pushing a defender who is stationary.	Foul
Hand-checking	Using the hands to check the progress of an offensive player when that player is in front of the defender who is using the hands.	Foul
Holding	Restricting the movement of an opponent.	Foul
Illegal screen	A form of blocking in which the player setting the screen is still moving when the defender makes contact.	Don't call except for the older age groups (11 and 12, 13 and 14)
Over-the-back	Infringing on the vertical plane of, and making contact with, a player who is in position and attempting to rebound.	Don't call except for the older age groups (11 and 12, 13 and 14)
Pushing	Impeding the progress or otherwise moving a player by pushing or shoving.	Foul
Reaching in	Extending an arm and making contact with a ball handler in an attempt to steal the ball.	Foul
Tripping	Extending a leg or foot and causing an opponent to lose balance or fall.	Foul

Emphasize to your players the importance of keeping their hands off the shooter, establishing position, using the feet to maintain position (rather than reaching in with the hands), and not attempting to rebound over an opponent who has established position.

Other types of fouls exist, such as a technical foul; this is a foul that does not involve contact with the opponent while the ball is alive (e.g., use of profanity, delay of game, unsporting conduct). Intentional and flagrant fouls relate to extreme behaviors and should not (we hope) come up with your players. If they do, players who are guilty of unsporting conduct during a game are usually ejected and assessed a technical foul, and they should be counseled by the coach. In such a case, the opposing team is awarded two free throws and possession of the ball.

Violations

Violations are mistakes made by the offensive team that will result in the ball being given to the defensive team. Turnovers—the loss of the ball to the defense—caused by violations will be one of your continuing frustrations as a basketball coach. Violations are categorized as either ballhandling or clock violations. Table 2.3 shows our recommendations for modifying the rules for these violations based on the age group of your team.

TABLE 2.3   Rule Modifications for Violations

		Age group				
Violation	Description	5 and 6 years	7 and 8 years	9 and 10 years	11 and 12 years	13 and 14 years
Ballhandling violations						
Double dribble	Resuming dribbling after having stopped (when no defender interrupts the player's possession of the ball) or dribbling with both hands at the same time.	Allow one violation per player possession; gradually tighten up this allowance.	Allow one violation per player possession; gradually tighten up this allowance.	Allow one violation per player possession; gradually tighten up this allowance.	Call.	Call.

Violation	Description	Age group				
		5 and 6 years	7 and 8 years	9 and 10 years	11 and 12 years	13 and 14 years
Ballhandling violations *(continued)*						
Over-and-back	The return of the ball to the backcourt when last touched by an offensive player in the frontcourt.	Don't call.	Don't call.	Don't call.	Don't call.	Don't call.
Traveling	Taking more than one step without dribbling; also called carrying the ball or palming the ball when a player turns the ball a complete rotation in the hand between dribbles.	Give an extra step for starting and stopping; gradually tighten up this allowance.	Give an extra step for starting and stopping; gradually tighten up this allowance.	Give an extra step for starting and stopping; gradually tighten up this allowance.	Call.	Call.
Clock violations						
Inbounds	On any inbounds play, the player throwing the ball in has 5 seconds to release the ball.	Don't call.	Don't call.	Give warnings early in the season; call after midseason.	Call.	Call.
Lane	An offensive player cannot be in the lane (in the key) for more than 3 seconds at a time.	Don't call.	Don't call.	Give warnings early in the season; call after midseason.	Call.	Call.

(continued)

TABLE 2.3   Rule Modifications for Violations *(continued)*

Violation	Description	Age group				
		5 and 6 years	7 and 8 years	9 and 10 years	11 and 12 years	13 and 14 years
Clock violations (continued)						
Backcourt	A team must advance the ball into its frontcourt within 10 seconds after gaining possession in the backcourt.	Don't call.	Don't call.	Give warnings early in the season; call after midseason.	Call.	Call.
Shot clock	The ball must leave an offensive player's hands before the shot clock expires. The ball must subsequently hit the rim on that shot or it will be a violation.	Don't use.	Don't use.	Don't use.	Don't use.	Don't use.

Substitutions

A substitution is when a player who is out of the game takes the place of a player who is on the playing floor. Players coming into the game must go to the scorer's table and give the scorekeeper their number and the number of the player they are replacing so that this information can be recorded. The substitute must then wait at the scorer's table until the referee motions for him to enter the game. Any number of players (ranging from one to five players) can be substituted at a time; substitutions are allowed at any time during stopped-clock situations.

Time-Outs

When a time-out is called, play stops so that the coaches can visit with their team off the playing floor. A time-out may be called by a player or a coach by giving the proper signal to the official during any dead-ball situation or if your team has possession of the ball. A time-out is designated as a 30-second time-out or a 1-minute time-out by the coach of the team that called it. Each team is allowed five time-outs (three 1-minute time-outs and two 30-second time-outs) per game; an extra 1-minute time-out is allowed for each overtime.

Officiating

Basketball rules are enforced by officials. In youth basketball, there are typically two officials overseeing the game. Officials have many responsibilities during a game, including effectively communicating their calls to other members of the staff (such as the scorers and timers) and to the players, coaches, and spectators. Figure 2.2, *a* through *u*, shows some common officiating signals.

If you have a concern about how a game is being officiated, you should address the officials respectfully. Do so immediately if at any time you think that the officiating jeopardizes the safety of your players.

(continued)

FIGURE 2.2 Officiating signals: *(a)* starting the clock, *(b)* stopping the clock for a jump ball, *(c)* beckoning a sub in on a dead ball, *(d)* stopping the clock for a foul, *(e)* scoring one point (two fingers for scoring two points), and *(f)* scoring three points.

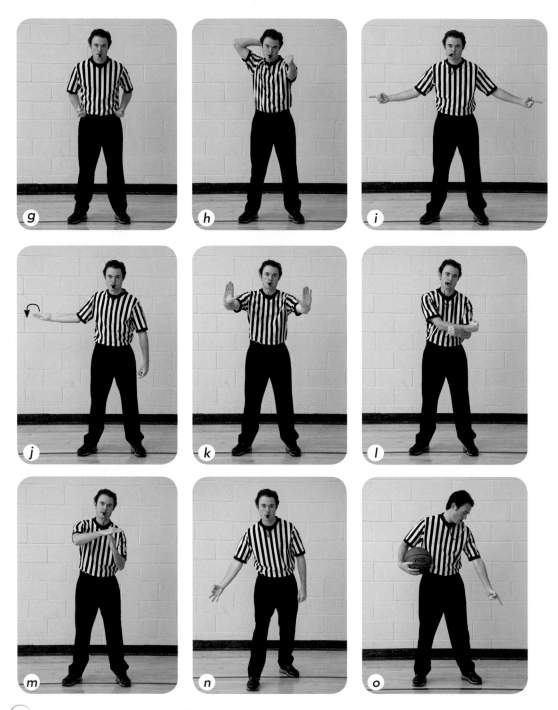

FIGURE 2.2 (continued) Officiating signals: (g) blocking, (h) charging, (i) bonus situation, (j) over-and-back or carrying the ball, (k) pushing, (l) illegal use of hands, (m) technical foul, (n) three-second violation, and (o) designating out-of-bounds spot.

FIGURE 2.2 (continued)   Officiating signals: (p) traveling, (q) holding, (r) kicking, (s) no score, (t) illegal dribble, and (u) hand check.

3

Game Days

Games provide the opportunity for your players to show what they've learned in practice. Just as your players' focus shifts on game days from learning and practicing to competing, your focus shifts from teaching skills to coaching players as they perform those skills in games. Of course, the game is a teaching opportunity as well, but the focus is on performing what has been learned, participating, and having fun.

In the previous chapter, you learned how to prepare for your season and practices. In this chapter, you will learn how to coach your players on game day. We provide important coaching principles that will guide you before, during, and after the game.

Game Strategy

Some coaches burn the midnight oil as they devise a complex plan of attack. Team tactics at this level, however, don't need to be complex—especially for the younger age groups. The focus should be on consistent execution, moving the ball on offense, and playing good team defense. You should emphasize the importance of teamwork, of every player fulfilling her role on offense and defense, and of every player knowing her assignments. This should be done during each practice so the players know their roles during the game well before the game starts. As you become more familiar with your team's tendencies and abilities, you can help them focus on specific tactics that will help them play better.

Creating a Game Plan

Just as you need a practice plan for what you will cover at each practice, you also need a game plan for game day. As a coach for youth basketball, your game plan will vary depending on the age group you are working with. As you begin planning and mapping out how your game days will progress, you should keep the following age-related points in mind.

Ages 5 and 6	<ul><li>Encourage players to try their best.</li><li>Focus on helping players develop their individual skills for team competition.</li><li>Although the use of games is important, do not spend too much time just playing games without time for proper skill instruction.</li></ul>
Ages 7 and 8	<ul><li>Focus on helping players develop their individual skills as well as more general team concepts, both offensive and defensive.</li><li>Encourage players to evaluate their skills and to work on these skills on their own time.</li></ul>
Ages 9 and 10	<ul><li>The strengths and weaknesses of the opposition are of little concern at this age; the focus should be on helping your team execute the skills they have learned.</li><li>Use simple team offenses that make it easy for your players to execute the techniques and skills learned in practice.</li><li>Remind players of one offensive and one defensive aspect that they have learned, and have them focus on these aspects for the game.</li><li>Give players a starting lineup before the first game.</li></ul>
Ages 11 and 12	<ul><li>Begin to use team drills that emphasize several skills at the same time.</li><li>Start to use full-court drills that include passing and shooting so the players use these skills in full-court work.</li><li>Begin to implement some team strategy related to defenses and offenses that can be played in games.</li></ul>
Ages 13 and 14	<ul><li>Players should begin to focus on one or two of the opponent's strengths and weaknesses, and they should be able to take advantage of this while the game is being played.</li><li>Teams will sometimes adjust their play based on the opponent, but the main focus is still the proper execution of the techniques and skills learned in practice.</li><li>Use more complex team offenses and defenses that will take advantage of the opponent's weaknesses.</li></ul>

COACHING TIP When developing your game plan, keep in mind that your players need to understand what you expect of them both offensively and defensively during the game. Be clear about this in the days leading up to a game. Take time at the beginning or end of each practice to discuss these expectations.

During the week before a game, you should inform players of the tactics that you think will work and that you plan to use in the game. Pick out several offensive sets and plays and the main defense that you want to use in the game. Try to practice these at every practice, and make certain that every player understands the plays and that the team can run them without error. Limiting the number of plays allows you to repeat them during practice and instill in your players the confidence that they can execute the plays that will be called during the game.

Depending on the age level, experience, and knowledge of your players, you may want to let them help you determine the first offensive play or set and the defense that you will call in the game. It is the coach's role to help youngsters grow through the sport experience. Allowing player input helps your players learn the game and involves them at a planning level often reserved solely for the coach. It also gives them a feeling of ownership. Rather than just carrying out orders for the coach, they're executing the plan of attack that they helped create. Youngsters who have a say in how they approach a task often respond with more enthusiasm and motivation. This technique also builds trust between the players and coach.

Pregame Warm-Ups

Players need to both physically and mentally prepare for a game once they arrive, and physical preparation involves warming up. We suggest that players arrive 30 to 45 minutes before the game to warm up. You should arrive at the game site 45 to 60 minutes before the game so you can check the facility (see the Facilities and Equipment Checklist in the appendix on page 247), check in with the site coordinator and officials, and greet your players as they arrive to warm up. You will want to conduct the pregame warm-up similar to practice warm-ups. Before game day, you should walk the players through the steps for how they will enter and where they will line up on the court for the warm-up. The warm-up should consist of a few brief games or drills that focus on skill practice, stretching, and exercises or activities that involve a range of motion, such as passing drills that get the players running while catching the ball.

You should refrain from delivering a long-winded pep talk (2 to 3 minutes is fine, but do not go over 5 minutes), but you can help players mentally prepare for the game by reminding them of the skills they've been working on in recent practices and by focusing their attention on their strengths and what they've been doing well. Also take time to remind players that they should work as a team, play hard and smart, and have fun!

You should have a preset plan or routine that is used before every game. This can help alleviate nerves and build confidence in your players, especially those in younger age groups. A pregame routine will also help players forget outside concerns and get into the frame of mind to focus on the game.

Game Time

Although you won't need to create a complex game strategy, as mentioned before, you will need to make tactical decisions in several areas throughout a game. You'll make decisions about who starts the game and when to enter substitutes, about making slight adjustments to your team's tactics, and about dealing with players' performance errors.

Lineup and Substitutions

When considering playing time, make sure that everyone on the team gets to play at least half of each game. This should be your guiding principle as you consider starting and substitution patterns. It is also nice if each player has a chance to start one game during your season. Realize that some players may play better in a starting role than when coming off the bench. We suggest you consider two options in substituting players:

1. **Substituting individually.** Replace one player with another. This offers you a lot of latitude in deciding who goes in when, and it gives you the greatest combination of players throughout the game. Keeping track of playing time can be difficult, but this task could be made easier by assigning it to an assistant or a parent.

You may want to try substituting players by time left in the quarter, especially when working with younger age groups. For example, you can let a substitute know that she will play the last four minutes of each quarter, or that she will replace a player at the six-minute mark of the quarter. This will let the player know when she can expect to get into the game and will help the player be more prepared for her playing time.

In addition, if a player plays so hard that she asks to be taken out of a game, you should allow her to go back in when she is ready. This will let your players know that they can play hard without worrying that another individual will sub in for them and they will not get back in the game.

2. **Substituting by quarters.** The advantage of substituting players after each quarter is that you can easily track playing time, and players know how long they will be in before they might be replaced. When substituting by quarters, you should still keep track of the actual number of minutes that each player is on the court.

Time-Outs and Intermissions

At the younger age levels (5 and 6, 7 and 8, or 9 and 10), you probably won't adjust your team tactics, or plays, too significantly during a game. Rather, you'll focus on the basic tactics, and during breaks in the game, you'll emphasize the specific tactics your team needs to work on. However, coaches of 11- to 14-year-olds might have reason to make tactical adjustments to improve their team's chances of performing well and winning. As games progress, assess your opponents' style of play and tactics, and make adjustments that are appropriate—that is, those that your players are prepared for. You may want to consider the following examples when adjusting team tactics:

- How does your opponent usually initiate their attack? Do they aim to get around, over, or through your defense? This can help you make defensive adjustments.
- Who are the strongest players on the opposing team? The weakest players? As you identify strong players, you'll want to assign more skilled players to defend them.
- Are the opponent's forwards fast and powerful? Do they come to the ball, or do they try to run behind the defense and receive passes? Their mode of attack should influence how you instruct your players to defend them.
- On defense, does your opponent play a high-pressure game, or do they retreat once you've gained possession of the ball? Either type of defense could call for a different strategy from you.
- Ask your players, "What does the player you are guarding do well?" Then ask, "Do you think you can stop the player from doing that?" This will help players adjust their game to what the opponent does best.

Knowing the answers to such questions can help you formulate an effective game plan and make proper adjustments during a game. However, don't stress tactics too much during a game. Doing so can take the fun out of the game for the players. If you don't trust your memory, carry a pen and pad to note which team tactics and individual skills need attention at the next practice. This is also a good job for your assistant.

Interaction With Opposing Coaches and Officials

You must respect the opponents and officials you encounter in your competitions. Without them, there wouldn't be a competition. Opponents provide opportunities for your team to test itself, improve, and excel. Officials help provide a fair and safe experience for players and, as appropriate, help them learn the rules of the game.

You and your team should show respect for opponents and officials by giving your best efforts and being civil. Don't allow your players to "trash talk" or taunt an opponent or an official. Such behavior is disrespectful to the spirit of the competition, and you should immediately remove a player from a game if that player disobeys your team rules in this area.

Remember, too, that officials at this level are quite often teenagers—in many cases not much older than the players themselves—and the level of officiating should be

Communicating With Parents

The groundwork for your communication with parents will have been laid in the parent preseason meeting (page 16), where the parents learned the best ways to support their kids'—and the whole team's—efforts on the court. You should encourage parents to judge success based not just on the outcome of the game, but also on how the kids are improving their performances.

If parents yell at the kids for mistakes made during the game, make disparaging remarks about the officials or opponents, or shout instructions on which tactics to use, you should ask them to refrain and to instead support team members through their comments and actions. These standards of conduct should all be covered in the parent preseason meeting.

When time permits, as parents gather before a game (and before the team has entered), you can let them know in a general sense what the team has been focusing on during the past week and what your goals are for the game. However, your players must come first during this time, so focus on your players during the pregame warm-up.

After a game, quickly come together as a coaching staff and decide what to say to the team. Then, if the opportunity arises, you can informally assess with parents how the team did based not on the outcome, but on meeting performance goals and playing to the best of their abilities. Help parents see the game as a process, not solely as a test that is pass or fail, or win or lose. Encourage parents to reinforce that concept at home. Always remove yourself from parents who have a complaint directly after a game. Give yourself and the parents 24 hours before you address any issue.

commensurate to the level of play. In other words, don't expect perfection from officials any more than you do from your own players. Especially at younger levels, the officials won't make every call, because to do so would stop the game too frequently. You may find that officials at younger levels only call the most flagrant violations—those directly affecting the outcome of the game. As long as the calls are being made consistently on both sides and the violations are being addressed, most of your officiating concerns will be alleviated.

If you yell at or disagree with the officials constantly, you are giving your team an excuse for not playing well or losing the game. Don't give your players an excuse for losing or playing poorly by blaming the officials.

Postgame Conduct

When the game is over, join your team in congratulating the coaches and players of the opposing team, then be sure to thank the officials. Remember to check on any injuries players sustained during the game, and instruct players on how to care for them at home. Be prepared to speak with the officials about any problems that occurred during the game. Then, hold a brief postgame meeting to ensure that your players are on an even keel, whether they won or lost.

Your first concern after a game should be your players' attitudes and mental well-being. You don't want them to be too high after a win or too low after a loss. This is the time you can be most influential in keeping the outcome in perspective and keeping the players on an even keel.

COACHING TIP To keep your players on an even keel after a game, you may want to bring up the next opponent. This works extremely well after a big win; the players are left thinking about the next game as opposed to only the game they just played.

When celebrating a victory, make sure your team does so in a way that doesn't show disrespect for the opponents. It's okay and appropriate to be happy and celebrate a win, but don't allow your players to taunt the opponents or boast about their victory. If your team was defeated, your players will naturally be disappointed. But, if your team has made a winning effort, let them know this. After a loss, help the players keep their chins up and maintain a positive attitude that will carry over into the next practice and game. Winning and losing are a part of life, not just a part of sport. If players can handle both equally well, they'll be successful in whatever they do.

After the game, gather your team in a designated area for a short postgame meeting. Before this meeting, decide as a coaching staff what you will say and who will say it. Be sure that the staff speaks with one voice following the game.

If your players have performed well in a game, you should be sure to compliment and congratulate them. Tell them specifically what they did well, whether they won or lost. This will reinforce their desire to repeat their good performances. Don't use this time after a game to criticize individual players for poor performances in front of teammates or attempt to go over tactical problems and adjustments. You should help players improve their skills, but do so at the next practice. Immediately after a game, players won't absorb much tactical information.

Finally, make sure your players have transportation home. Be the last one to leave in order to ensure full supervision of your players.

Keeping a Proper Perspective

Winning games is the short-term goal of your basketball program. The long-term goal is helping your players learn the techniques and tactics and rules of basketball, how to become fit, and how to be good sports in basketball and in life. Your young players are "winning" when they are becoming better human beings through their participation in basketball. Keep that perspective in mind when you coach. You have the privilege of setting the tone for how your team approaches the game. Keep winning and all aspects of the competition in proper perspective, and your young players will likely follow suit.

Part II

Teaching

Coaching basketball is about teaching kids how to play the game by

teaching them skills, fitness, and values. It's also about "coaching" players before, during, and after games. Teaching and coaching are closely related, but there are important differences. In the following sections, we focus on principles of teaching, especially on teaching technical and tactical skills. These principles apply to teaching values and fitness concepts as well. Armed with these principles, you will be able to design effective and efficient practices. Then you will be able to teach the skills and plays necessary to be successful in basketball (which are outlined in chapters 4, 5, 7, and 8).

Teaching Basketball Skills

Many people believe that the only qualification needed for teaching a skill is to have performed it. Although it's helpful to have performed it, teaching it successfully requires much more than that. And even if you haven't performed the skill before, you can still learn to teach successfully with the useful acronym IDEA:

I	Introduce the skill.
D	Demonstrate the skill.
E	Explain the skill.
A	Attend to players practicing the skill.

Introduce the Skill

Players, especially those who are young and inexperienced, need to know what skill they are learning and why they are learning it. You should therefore follow these three steps every time you introduce a skill to your players:

1. Get your players' attention.
2. Name the skill.
3. Explain the importance of the skill.

Get Your Players' Attention

Because youngsters are easily distracted, you should do something to get their attention. Some coaches use interesting news items or stories. Others use jokes. And still others simply project enthusiasm to get their players to listen. Whatever method you use, speak slightly above your normal volume and look your players in the eye when you speak.

Also, position players so they can see and hear you. Arrange the players in two or three evenly spaced rows, facing you. (Make sure they aren't looking into the sun or at a distracting activity.) Then ask whether all of them can see you before you begin to speak.

Name the Skill

More than one common name may exist for the skill you are introducing, but you should decide as a staff before the start of the season which one you'll use (and then stick with it). This will help prevent confusion and enhance communication among your players. When you introduce the new skill, call it by name several times so that the players automatically correlate the name with the skill in later discussions.

Explain the Importance of the Skill

As Rainer Martens, the founder of the American Sport Education Program (ASEP), has said, "The most difficult aspect of coaching is this: Coaches must learn to let athletes learn. Sport skills should be taught so they have meaning to the child, not just meaning to the coach." Although the importance of a skill may be apparent to you, your players may be less able to see how the skill will help them become better basketball players. Offer them a reason for learning the skill, and describe how the skill relates to more advanced skills.

Demonstrate the Skill

The demonstration step is the most important part of teaching sport skills to players who may never have done anything closely resembling the skill. They need a picture, not just words. They need to see how the skill is performed. If you are unable to perform the skill correctly, ask an assistant coach, one of your players, or someone more skilled to perform the demonstration.

COACHING TIP You may want to write out in detail each skill you will teach. This can clarify what you will say and how you will demonstrate and teach each skill to your players.

These tips will help make your demonstrations more effective:

- Use correct form.
- Demonstrate the skill several times.
- Slow the action, if possible, during one or two performances so players can see every movement involved in the skill.
- Perform the skill at different angles so your players can get a full perspective of it.
- Demonstrate the skill with both the right and left arms and legs.

Explain the Skill

Players learn more effectively when they're given a brief explanation of the skill along with the demonstration. You should use simple terms and, if possible, relate the skill to previously learned skills. Ask your players whether they understand your description. A good technique is to ask the team to repeat your explanation. Ask questions such as "What are you going to do first?" and "Then what?" If players look confused or uncertain, you should repeat your explanation and demonstration. If possible, use different words so your players get a chance to try to understand the skill from a different perspective.

Complex skills are often better understood when they are explained in more manageable parts. For instance, if you want to teach your players how to perform the crossover dribble, you might take the following steps:

1. Show them a correct performance of the entire skill, and explain its function in basketball.
2. Break down the skill and point out its component parts (such as controlling the dribble at knee level, dribbling with the head up to see the rim, and protecting the ball with the body and the nondribbling hand) to your players.
3. Have players perform each of the component parts you have already taught them.
4. After players have demonstrated their ability to perform the separate parts of the skill in sequence, reexplain the entire skill.
5. Have players practice the skill in gamelike conditions.

Young players have short attention spans, and a long demonstration or explanation of a skill may cause them to lose focus. Therefore, you should spend no more than a few minutes altogether on the introduction, demonstration, and explanation phases. Then involve the players in drills or games that call on them to perform the skill.

Attend to Players Practicing the Skill

If the skill you selected was within your players' capabilities and you have done an effective job of introducing, demonstrating, and explaining it, your players should be

How to Properly Run Your Drills

Before running a drill that teaches technique, you should do the following:

- Name the drill.
- Explain the skill or skills to be practiced.
- Position the players correctly.
- Explain what the drill will accomplish.
- State the command that will start the drill.
- Identify the signal that will end the drill, such as a whistle.

Once the drill has been introduced and repeated a few times in this manner, you will find that merely calling out the name of the drill is sufficient; your players will automatically line up in the proper position to run the drill and practice the skill.

ready to attempt the skill. Some players, especially those in younger age groups, may need to be physically guided through the movements during their first few attempts. Walking unsure players through the skill in this way will help them gain confidence to perform the skill on their own.

You should look at the entire skill and then break it down into components. For example, when teaching the skill of shooting the basketball, you can use the acronym "BEEF" to break down the skill into components that will help your players learn the proper technique for shooting the ball:

B	Balance (position the shooting foot slightly ahead of the other foot for balance)
E	Elbow (the elbow should be in a straight line with the shooting foot and knee)
E	Eyes (the eyes should be focused on the rim and never watch the ball in flight)
F	Follow-through (after the release, the thumb of the shooting hand should be pointed down)

Your teaching duties, though, don't end when all your players have demonstrated that they understand how to perform a skill. In fact, your teaching role is just beginning as you help your players improve their skills. A significant part of your teaching consists of closely observing the hit-and-miss trial performances of your players. You will shape players' skills by detecting errors and correcting them using positive feedback. Keep in mind that your positive feedback will have a great influence on your players' motivation to practice and improve their performances.

Remember, too, that some players may need individual instruction. So set aside a time before, during, or after practice to give individual help.

Helping Players Improve Skills

After you have successfully taught your players the fundamentals of a skill, your focus will be on helping them improve the skill. Players learn skills and improve on them at different rates, so don't get frustrated if progress seems slow. Instead, help them improve by shaping their skills and detecting and correcting errors.

Shaping Players' Skills

One of your principal teaching duties is to reward positive effort or behavior—in terms of successful skill execution—when you see it. A player makes a good pass in practice, and you immediately say, "That's the way to extend! Good follow-through!" This, plus a smile and a thumbs-up gesture, go a long way toward reinforcing that technique in that player. However, sometimes you may have a long dry spell before you see correct techniques to reinforce. It's difficult to reward players when they don't execute skills correctly. How can you shape their skills if this is the case?

Shaping skills takes practice on your players' part and patience on yours. Expect your players to make errors. Telling the player who made the great pass that she did a good job doesn't ensure that she'll have the same success next time. Seeing inconsistency in your players' technique can be frustrating. It's even more challenging to stay positive when your players repeatedly perform a skill incorrectly or have a lack of enthusiasm for learning. It can certainly be frustrating to see players who seemingly don't heed your advice and continue to make the same mistakes.

Although it is normal to get frustrated sometimes when teaching skills, part of successful coaching is controlling this frustration. Instead of getting upset, use these six guidelines for shaping skills:

1. **Think small initially.** Reward the first signs of behavior that approximate what you want. Then reward closer and closer approximations of the desired behavior. In short, use your reward power to shape the behavior you seek.

2. **Break skills into small steps.** For instance, in learning to dribble, one of your players does well in keeping the ball close to his body, but he's bouncing the ball too high and doesn't effectively shield it from defenders. Reinforce the correct technique of keeping the ball close, and teach him how to dribble at knee level. Once he masters this, you can focus on getting him to shield the ball from defenders.

3. **Develop one component of a skill at a time.** Don't try to shape two components of a skill at once. For example, in rebounding, players must first block their opponents out, then go for the ball. Players should focus first on one aspect (blocking out by putting their back against their opponent's chest and creating a wide base), then on the other (putting their hands up and going for the ball). Players who have problems mastering a skill often do so because they're trying to improve two or more components at once. You should help these players to isolate a single component.

4. **Use reinforcement only occasionally, for the best examples.** By focusing only on the best examples, you will help players continue to improve once they've mastered the basics. When the coach uses occasional reinforcement during practice, this allows players to have more contact time with the ball rather than having to constantly stop and listen to the coach. Basketball skills are best learned through a lot of repetition, such as drills, and the coach needs to make the best use of team practice time by allowing the players as much time with the ball as possible.

COACHING TIP For older age groups or players with advanced skills, coaches can ask players to "self-coach." With the proper guidance and a positive team environment, young players can think about how they perform a skill and how they might be able to perform it better. Self-coaching is best done at practice, where a player can experiment with learning new skills.

5. **Relax your standards.** As players focus on mastering a new skill or attempt to integrate it with other skills, their old, well-learned skills may temporarily degenerate, and you may need to relax your expectations. For example, a player has learned how to shoot the ball and is now learning how to combine that skill with the dribble.

While learning to combine the two skills and getting the timing down, the player's shooting may be poor. A similar degeneration of ball skills may occur during growth spurts while the coordination of muscles, tendons, and ligaments catches up to the growth of bones.

6. **Go back to the basics.** If, however, a well-learned skill degenerates for long, you may need to restore it by going back to the basics. For example, you may need to go back to the "BEEF" method of shooting technique to help restore the player's skill.

Detecting and Correcting Errors

Good coaches recognize that players make two types of errors: learning errors and performance errors. Learning errors are ones that occur because players don't know how to perform a skill; that is, they have not yet developed the correct motor pattern in the brain to perform a particular skill. Performance errors are made not because players don't know how to execute the skill, but because they have made a mistake in executing what they do know. There is no easy way to know whether a player is making learning or performance errors; part of the art of coaching is being able to sort out which type of error each mistake is.

The process of helping your players correct errors begins with you observing and evaluating their performances to determine if the mistakes are learning or performance errors. You should carefully watch your players to see if they routinely make the errors in both practice and game settings, or if the errors tend to occur only in game settings. If the latter is the case, then your players are making performance errors. For performance errors, you need to look for the reasons your players are not performing as well as they know how; perhaps they are nervous, or maybe they get distracted by the game setting. If the mistakes are learning errors, then you need to help them learn the skill, which is the focus of this section.

When correcting learning errors, there is no substitute for knowledge of the skills. The better you understand a skill—not only how it is performed correctly but also what causes learning errors—the more helpful you will be in correcting your players' mistakes.

> **COACHING TIP** Correcting errors is part of what coaching is all about, but don't get caught up in correcting errors all the time. Give positive feedback when a player makes small steps toward progress, but give players some freedom to figure it out on their own.

One of the most common coaching mistakes is to provide inaccurate feedback and advice on how to correct errors. Don't rush into error correction; wrong feedback or poor advice will hurt the learning process more than no feedback or advice at all. If you are uncertain about the cause of the problem or how to correct it, you should continue to observe and analyze until you are more sure. As a rule, you should see the error repeated several times before attempting to correct it.

Correct One Error at a Time

Suppose Jill, one of your forwards, is having trouble with her shooting. She's doing some things well, but you notice that she's extending her arm on too flat a trajectory, resulting in too low an arc, and she's not squaring up to face the basket on all of her shots. What do you do?

First, decide which error to correct first, because players learn more effectively when they attempt to correct one error at a time. Determine whether one error is causing the other; if so, have the player correct that error first, because it may eliminate the other error. In Jill's case, however, neither error is causing the other. In such cases, players should correct the error that is easiest to correct and will bring the greatest improvement when remedied. For Jill, this probably means squaring up to the basket. Correcting this error will likely motivate her to correct the other error.

Use Positive Feedback to Correct Errors

The positive approach to correcting errors includes emphasizing what to do instead of what not to do. Use compliments, praise, rewards, and encouragement to correct errors. Acknowledge correct performance as well as efforts to improve. By using positive feedback, you can help your players feel good about themselves and promote a strong desire to achieve.

When you're working with one player at a time, the positive approach to correcting errors includes four steps:

1. **Praise effort and correct performance.** Praise the player for trying to perform a skill correctly and for performing any parts of it correctly. Praise the player immediately after he performs the skill, if possible. Keep the praise simple: "Good try," "Way to hustle," "Good extension," or "That's the way to follow through." You can also use nonverbal feedback, such as smiling, clapping your hands, or any facial or body expression that shows approval.

Make sure you're sincere with your praise. Don't indicate that a player's effort was good when it wasn't. Usually a player knows when he has made a sincere effort to perform the skill correctly and perceives undeserved praise for what it is—untruthful feedback to make him feel good. Likewise, don't indicate that a player's performance was correct when it wasn't.

> **COACHING TIP**   Set a goal for yourself to make at least two positive comments to each player during each practice.

2. **Give simple and precise feedback to correct errors.** Don't burden a player with a long or detailed explanation of how to correct an error. Give just enough feedback so that the player can correct one error at a time. Before giving feedback, recognize that some players readily accept it immediately after the error; others will respond better if you slightly delay the correction.

For errors that are complicated to explain and difficult to correct, you should try the following:

- Explain and demonstrate what the player should have done. Do not demonstrate what the player did wrong.

- Explain the causes of the error (if the causes aren't already obvious).

- Explain why you are recommending the correction you have selected (if it's not obvious).

3. **Make sure the player understands your feedback.** If the player doesn't understand your feedback, she won't be able to correct the error. Ask the player to repeat the feedback and to explain and demonstrate how it will be used. If the player can't do this, you should be patient and present your feedback again. Then have the player repeat the feedback after you're finished.

4. **Provide an environment that motivates the player to improve.** Your players won't always be able to correct their errors immediately, even if they do understand your feedback. Encourage them to "hang tough" and stick with it when corrections are difficult or when players seem discouraged. For more difficult corrections, you should remind players that it will take time, and that the improvement will happen only if they work at it. Encourage those players with little self-confidence. Saying something like, "You were dribbling at a much better speed today; with practice, you'll be able to keep the ball closer to you and shield it from defenders," can motivate a player to continue to refine his dribbling skills.

Other players may be very self-motivated and need little help from you in this area; with them you can practically ignore step 4 when correcting an error. Although motivation comes from within, you should try to provide an environment of positive instruction and encouragement to help your players improve.

A final note on correcting errors: Team sports such as basketball provide unique challenges in this endeavor. How do you provide individual feedback in a group setting using a positive approach? Instead of yelling across the court to correct an error (and embarrassing the player), you can pull the player aside to make the correction. This type of feedback has several advantages:

- The player will be more receptive to the one-on-one feedback.
- The other players are still active and still practicing skills, and they are unable to hear your discussion.
- Because the rest of the team is still playing, you'll feel compelled to make your comments simple and concise—which is more helpful to the player.

This doesn't mean you can't use the team setting to give specific, positive feedback. You can do so to emphasize correct group and individual performances. Use this team feedback approach only for positive statements, though. Keep any negative feedback for individual discussions.

4

Offensive Skills

This chapter focuses on the offensive techniques that players need to learn in order to perform effectively in youth basketball games. Remember to use the IDEA approach to teaching skills: introduce, demonstrate, and explain the skill, and attend to players as they practice the skill. This chapter also ties directly into the practice plans in chapters 10 to 14, describing the technical skills that you'll teach at the practices outlined there. If you aren't familiar with basketball skills, you may find it helpful to watch a video so you can see the skills performed correctly. Also, the Coaching Youth Basketball Online Course offered by the American Sport Education Program (ASEP) can help you further understand these skills (you can take this course by going to www.ASEP.com).

The information in this book is limited to basketball basics. As your players advance in their skills, you will need to advance your knowledge as a coach. You can do this by learning from your experiences, watching and talking with more experienced coaches, and studying resources on advanced skills.

The offensive technical skills you will teach your players include positioning and footwork, dribbling, passing and catching, shooting, and rebounding. Mastering these skills will allow your players to better execute your offensive tactics—or plays—during the game (see chapter 5). These basic technical skills serve as the foundation for playing basketball well at all levels. Basketball players practice these techniques at every practice, from youth basketball to the pros.

Offensive Positioning

When on the offensive side of play, the player must always try to maintain a good offensive position. This position is often called the ready position; when the player has the ball, the position can be referred to as the triple-threat position.

Ready Position

The ready position—sometimes called *basketball position*—is the position from which all offensive moves should be made. From this ready position, the offensive player can perform any offensive skill—shooting, running, passing, dribbling, screening, pivoting, or jumping—in a very efficient manner because the player is ready to move quickly in any direction. In the ready position, the feet are shoulder-width apart or wider, and the knees are bent and out from the body (see figure 4.1). The hands and arms are above the waist to make the player seem as big as possible.

The coach should emphasize the ready position in all drills so that it becomes a habit for the players when performing all skills.

FIGURE 4.1   Ready position.

Triple-Threat Position

Whenever a player receives the ball, she should assume the triple-threat position. The triple-threat position is a version of the ready position in which the player squares up to the basket. This position allows the offensive player to see the entire court. It also puts the player in a position where she can make one of three choices—to shoot, pass, or dribble—without letting the defense know which option she is going to use.

When assuming the triple-threat position, the player should be square to the basket with her body facing the basket and the defender so that she is in a good position to shoot, pass, or drive to the right or left. The player should hold the ball to the side toward the hip, with elbows out; the player's hands should always remain in shooting position, with one hand behind the ball and the other hand on the side, allowing her to shoot the ball quickly and in rhythm, if necessary. The shooting foot, which is the foot

FIGURE 4.2   Triple-threat position.

on the same side as the shooting hand, should be positioned slightly ahead of the other foot so that the player is in balance to take a shot if she chooses to do so (see figure 4.2). To keep a defender off guard, a player in the triple-threat position should move the ball, keeping the ball close to the chest and never lower than the waist.

Offensive Footwork

Good footwork is important for both offense and defense, but offensive players have an advantage over defenders because they know what moves they are going to make and when. Offensive players use footwork to fake defenders off balance, to move off screens, to cut to the basket, to avoid charging into a defender, and to elude a blockout when going for a rebound. We'll explore four types of basic footwork—cuts, jump stops, pivots, and jab steps.

When executing basic footwork correctly, a team's offense will continue to improve; therefore, the coach should take special note of footwork and make corrections when necessary.

Cuts

Offensive players use cuts to change direction quickly (while staying in balance) and "lose" their opponents in order to get open for passes or shots. Defenders will find it difficult to keep up if they are unable to respond correctly to the cut.

A player executes a cut by planting one foot on the court at the end of a slightly shortened stride, then pushing off that foot to shift his momentum in another direction. For example, if a player wants to cut to the right, he will first plant the left foot (see figure 4.3a) and then push off of it. Then, he will turn the unplanted foot in the direction he wants to go and will lead with that leg as he bursts in the new direction (see figure 4.3b). When cutting, a player should bend the knees to lower his center of gravity and provide explosiveness from the legs. After cutting, he should always strive to get his lead hand up as a target for a pass. If a player is off balance when making a cut, it is usually because of two things: The player is not low enough, and the player's head is not over his feet.

Three types of cuts that offensive players use to get open are V-cuts, L-cuts, and backdoor cuts.

FIGURE 4.3 Proper body positioning for a cut to the right.

V-Cut

A V-cut is used by an offensive player to get open at the wing when the defensive player has a foot and hand in the passing lane and is trying to deny a pass to the offensive player. The ideal place for the offensive player to receive the ball is at the wing position, which is even with the free-throw line halfway between the free-throw lane and the sideline. The V-cut should be the offensive player's first option in getting to this position because it is the easiest cut to use and the quickest method to get open. To execute a V-cut, the offensive player moves from the wing position and takes her defender to the basket. She then plants the foot closest to the basket and pushes off toward the wing

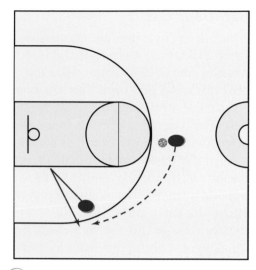

FIGURE 4.4   V-cut.

position to receive the ball (see figure 4.4). The offensive player should come out on a different line than the one she used when making her cut to the basket (hence the V-cut).

COACHING TIP   Younger players commonly take an arced path when cutting, or they slow down, taking short steps before the cut. You should teach your players that cuts must be hard, sharp, and explosive in order to be most effective and to keep the defense on edge.

L-Cut

An L-cut is also used by an offensive player to get open at the wing when a defender has a foot and hand in the passing lane, trying to deny the pass. Again, the ideal place for the offensive player to receive the ball is at the wing position. The L-cut is used when the V-cut will not get the offensive player open to catch the ball. To execute an L-cut, the offensive player should first be in the ready position. He moves to a spot just outside the free-throw lane (about even with the middle of the lane) and then takes the defensive player slowly to the elbow of the free-throw line. He plants his inside foot and crosses over with the outside foot to move straight out to the wing to receive the ball (see figure 4.5).

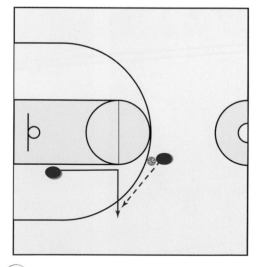

FIGURE 4.5   L-cut.

Backdoor Cut

A backdoor cut is used by an offensive player when a defender has a foot and hand in the passing lane to deny a pass from the outside into the wing position. This cut is used to reduce the pressure at the wing. Because the defender is denying the pass to the wing, the offensive player must execute a backdoor cut toward the basket to get open. To execute a backdoor cut, the player should move to the outside by taking her defensive player a step above the three-point line. She then plants the foot closest to the half-court line and quickly cuts behind her defender and toward the basket (see figure 4.6).

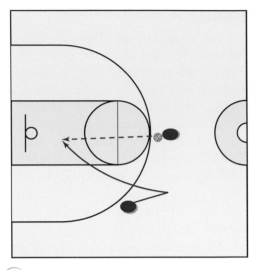

FIGURE 4.6   Backdoor cut.

Jump Stops

A jump stop is used to stop quickly when on the run, with or without the ball. It is a necessary maneuver almost any time a pass is received at any position on the floor. The jump stop is particularly advantageous when a player receives a pass while facing away from the basket in the low-post area, which is anywhere within eight feet of the basket, because it will allow the player to use either foot as her pivot foot; this gives the offensive player an advantage.

To jump stop, a player on the run (see figure 4.7a) quickly stops her body under control by allowing both feet to hit the floor at the same time and assuming the ready position, with the feet about shoulder-width apart, the knees flexed, and her weight shifted slightly forward to the balls of the feet (see figure 4.7b). The player's arms should be in a position above the waist, ready to receive the ball, and the head should be up and positioned over the

FIGURE 4.7   Jump stop.

waist. If a player tends to lose her balance when making the jump stop, you should teach her to shift her weight to the back of the feet, with the head back and in line with the body (loss of balance is commonly a result of the player's head being positioned too far forward in front of the feet).

After completing the jump stop, the player can then choose either foot as a pivot foot, but she may not change that pivot foot while in possession of the ball (see Pivots for more information).

Pivots

A pivot takes place when one foot is lifted off the floor while the other foot is used to turn the body. When players receive the ball, they can use either a front or back pivot to protect the ball from the defense, to pass to a teammate, or to make a move to the basket. A pivot can be made while on the run with or without the ball, for example, when performing a crossover dribble or a V-cut. A pivot can also be made when a player is stationary, such as when a player uses it to gain an advantage.

Front Pivot

A front pivot is when the turn of the pivot moves forward. Players should use a front pivot in situations where they are facing the basket. When a player is facing the basket, a front pivot will allow him to keep his eyes on the basket and not turn his back to his teammates. To execute a front pivot, the player must assume a ready position—with the feet about shoulder-width apart and the knees bent (see figure 4.8a)—and maintain this position throughout the pivot. The player then turns his body by lifting one foot and moving his body forward (see figure 4.8b). The player should keep his weight on the ball of the pivot foot; that is, the foot that remains on the court.

FIGURE 4.8 Front pivot.

Back Pivot

A back pivot is when the turn of the pivot moves backward. Players use a back pivot when a defender is guarding them very closely and they cannot make the front pivot without committing a violation or foul. Players will often use the back pivot in an effort to avoid contact with the defensive player. To execute a back pivot, the player must assume a ready position—with the feet about shoulder-width apart and the knees bent (see figure 4.9*a*)—and maintain this position throughout the pivot. The player takes a drop step, also called a *reverse turn*, by allowing his back to lead the way and lifting one foot and then dropping it back (see figure 4.9*b*). The player should keep his weight on the ball of the pivot foot (the foot that remains on the court).

Once a pivot foot is chosen, the player cannot lift or slide that foot, because doing so would become a violation called *traveling*. However, when attempting a pass or shot, the player may lift the designated pivot foot—providing the player releases the ball before the pivot foot again hits the floor.

FIGURE 4.9   Back pivot.

Jab Steps

A jab step—also called a *drive step*—is a short, 8- to 10-inch (20 to 25 cm) step made straight toward the defender with the nonpivot foot. A player will use a jab step to create space between herself and the defensive player.

To execute a jab step, the player catches the ball from a teammate and immediately assumes the triple-threat position and squares up to the basket (see figure 4.10*a*). The player's weight should be on the pivot foot, and the player takes a short step directly at the defensive player with the other foot (see figure 4.10*b*).

FIGURE 4.10   Jab step.

Dribbling

Simply stated, dribbling is used to maintain possession of the ball while moving by bouncing the ball on the floor. At the start of the dribble, the ball must leave the hand before the player lifts her pivot foot from the floor (as discussed in Pivots on page 59), and the player may not touch the ball simultaneously with both hands while dribbling or allow it to come to a rest in her hand.

Dribbling is an integral part of the sport of basketball and is vital to individual and team play; however, it is also the most misused fundamental skill in the game. Excessive dribbling with no purpose can quickly destroy teamwork and the morale of your team. For example, if a player dribbles too much, teammates will tend not to move or react, making the defense's job much easier. When learning the skill of dribbling, young players must first understand that all dribbling must have a purpose, such as to advance the ball up the court or to the basket, or to make the passing angle better to get a pass to an open teammate. Players must also keep their dribble in motion until a shot or pass is available; picking up—or "killing"—the dribble in a poor position without an option of a pass or a shot often results in a turnover.

COACHING TIP   When dribbling, players should strive to stay in the middle of the court and stay away from the sidelines and corners. It is much more difficult for the defense to trap or double-team a dribbler in the middle of the floor. Players should visualize the sideline as another defender and should continually work to stay away from it.

When dribbling, your players should first maintain the ready position, keeping the knees bent and the rear down, and establish a feel for the ball with the pads of the

fingers. Players should work to keep the dribble under control by always bouncing the ball below waist height and even lower when being guarded closely by a defender. The ball should be kept close to the body, and the player should protect the dribble from the defender with the nondribbling hand and arm. The head should always be up so that the player can "see the rim" and be aware of what is happening on the rest of the court, such as the location of defenders and teammates (see figure 4.11).

FIGURE 4.11   Proper body positioning for a dribble.

Dribbling Don'ts

Dribbling can be a very effective weapon to use in many situations, but as we have learned, it is often an overused offensive skill. Following are a few key "don'ts" to teach your players:

- Don't dribble with the head down. When players dribble with their head down, they are not able to see teammates who are open for a pass.
- Don't always use the same hand when dribbling. Players should be able to dribble with either hand.
- Don't dribble the ball out from the body in traffic because this will make it much more difficult to protect the ball from defensive players.
- Don't automatically start dribbling after receiving a pass. After receiving the pass, players should first square up to the basket in a triple-threat position and look to see what shooting or passing options are available to them.
- Don't pick up or stop the dribble until a clear shot or pass option becomes available.
- Don't dribble into a crowd—the ball is more likely to be stolen.
- Don't try to get fancy when good fundamental dribbling will do the job.
- Don't hesitate. Players should be assertive and confident when dribbling the ball.

Coaches should help players learn at a young age how to dribble with both hands. The ability to dribble with the weak hand as well as the strong hand is one key in advancing a player's skill level. When a player can move effectively in either direction with a dribble, this forces the defender to play in a more squared up position to the dribbler and allows the offensive player more freedom to go in either direction. Young players should also work on their ability to change speed and direction while dribbling, because this makes it more difficult for the defender to anticipate the offensive player's next move.

Players can use many types of dribbles; however, we're going to take a look at two of the most common dribbles that are used in youth basketball—the power dribble and the crossover dribble. We also discuss dribbling techniques that players should use when driving to the basket.

Power Dribble

A power dribble is a hard dribble that allows the player to make a move in a close space and free himself from tight defense. The power dribble is most often used on a drive to the basket, but it can also be used to get out of a congested area, such as when a player secures a rebound but is surrounded by defenders with no open teammate to pass to.

The power dribble calls on many of the same fundamentals as described previously for dribbling, but it combines them with an explosive first step toward the basket or in the direction the player is moving. The ball is put down hard on the floor, almost as if it is being thrown (see figure 4.12), as the offensive player takes several quick steps with the dribble, typically to the left or right of the defensive player.

FIGURE 4.12   Power dribble.

As with all dribbles, players should be taught to keep the head up and "see the rim" so that they are aware of what is happening on the court. Additionally, the player should dribble off the finger pads with fingertip control, flexing the wrist and fingers to impart force to the ball without pumping the arm.

Crossover Dribble

The crossover dribble is a type of dribble where the dribbler actually crosses the ball in front of the defensive player in order to make a change in direction (left or right), typically from the strong hand to the weak hand. A player should use a crossover dribble when overplayed by the defender, meaning that the defender is trying to restrict the direction that the offensive player may go. The crossover dribble is used in the open court on a fast break or to create space between the dribbler and the defender for a drive to the basket or for a better shot or pass.

To execute the crossover dribble, the player should first plant the foot on the side of the body that he is dribbling on (see figure 4.13a). The player then crosses the ball in front, switching the dribble from one hand to the other on the bounce (see figure 4.13b), while crossing the leg over in front of the defender in the direction that he wants to go (see figure 4.13c). After changing direction, the player should remember to get his nondribbling hand up for protection.

FIGURE 4.13   Crossover dribble.

Driving to the Basket

When the ball handler finds an opening, he will make a drive to the basket. To execute this drive properly, the player should take a longer step—called a *drive step*—in a straight line to the basket, close to his defender, while keeping his weight on the pivot foot (see figure 4.14a). The drive step should move past the defender's lead foot, cutting off the defender's retreat by closing the gap between the offensive player and the defender's retreat step. The offensive player then takes a long dribble with the outside hand (the hand farthest away from the defender) and makes the drive while keeping the head up and the eyes on the basket (see figure 4.14b). After driving by the defender, the player should be alert for defensive help and should finish by going in strong for a layup or passing to an open teammate who can score.

FIGURE 4.14 Drive step.

Passing

Effective passing is the key to moving the ball into position to take high-percentage shots. Players pass the ball to maintain possession and to create scoring opportunities. Passes should usually be short and crisp, and they should arrive above the waist and within easy reach of the receiver. Long or slow passes are likely to be stolen, and players should avoid throwing too hard or using passes that are difficult to control. Additionally, if possible, passes should be thrown to the receiver's side that is farthest from the defender.

We'll take a closer look at three types of passes: chest pass, bounce pass, and overhead pass.

COACHING TIP Teach your players that a pass travels much faster than a dribble, so before dribbling, a player should always first look for an opportunity to pass to an open teammate.

Chest Pass

The chest pass is made when the ball is thrown with two hands from the passer's chest area to the receiver's chest area. Chest passes are used often because they can be made quickly and accurately from most positions on the floor.

To execute the chest pass, the player should begin in the ready position and step toward the target, extending a leg, the back, and the arms, to initiate the pass (see figure 4.15a on page 66). The pass should be started with the elbows in, and then the wrists and fingers should be forced through the ball, releasing it off the first and second fingers of both hands to give the ball backspin and direction. To get good backspin on the ball, the player should follow through with the fingers pointed at the target, palms facing out, and with the thumb of both hands pointed down (see figure 4.15b on page 66).

FIGURE 4.15   Chest pass.

> **COACHING TIP**   Although all passers need to see their targets, more advanced players should practice seeing their targets without looking at them, by looking or faking away before passing. This will help the passer better conceal where she intends to pass the ball.

Bounce Pass

It is sometimes easier for a passer to get the ball to a teammate by bouncing the ball once on the court before it reaches the receiver. For example, if a defender is guarding a player with both hands overhead, this may prevent a pass from being made through the air to a teammate. Players should use bounce passes when they are closely guarded and do not have the space to extend their arms for a chest pass.

To execute the bounce pass, the player should first assume the triple-threat position, with the head up and with the ball held in both hands toward one hip to protect the ball from the defender. The player should step toward the target (see figure 4.16a) and snap the thumbs down and together on the release (as shown in figure 4.16b) to impart backspin on the ball, which will slow the pass down a little as it hits the floor. The player should make the pass at waist level and aim to bounce the ball on the court about two-thirds of the way between herself and the receiver so that the receiver is able to catch it at waist level.

FIGURE 4.16   Bounce pass.

COACHING TIP   Often, a player's strong hand tends to dominate on a pass, forcing the ball in one direction or another versus straight ahead. Players should focus on forcing the weak hand through the ball in order to place an equal distribution of force on the ball and keep it moving straight ahead on the pass.

Overhead Pass

An overhead pass is used when a player is closely guarded and forced to pass over a defender—for example, when making an outlet pass to start a fast break or a lob pass to a player cutting backdoor to the basket. The overhead pass is also an option for feeding the low post.

To execute the overhead pass, the player should start in the triple-threat position, holding the ball above the forehead with the elbows in and flexed at about 90 degrees (see figure 4.17a). The player should be careful not to bring the ball back behind the head, because from this position, it takes longer to make the pass, and it is easier for a defender to come in from behind and make a steal. The player then steps in the direction of the target and extends the legs and back, quickly passing the ball by extending the arms, flexing the wrists and fingers, and releasing the ball off the first and second fingers of both hands. The player follows through with the fingers pointing at the target and the palms facing down (see figure 4.17b).

FIGURE 4.17   Overhead pass.

Catching

Even the best passes are of little value if they aren't caught, and sloppy receiving technique is often the cause of turnovers and missed scoring opportunities.

To receive a pass properly, the player should first show a target to the passer by putting an arm up or out to the side and should call for the ball (see figure 4.18*a*). She should then move to meet the pass—ideally stepping toward the ball, not away—and watch the ball into her hands (see figure 4.18*b*). The player's hands should be relaxed—with palms facing the passer and thumbs together in a *W* position—and should "give" with the ball as it is caught.

When possible, players should come to a jump stop after receiving a pass; their feet should be positioned shoulder-width apart in triple-threat position. From this position, players should pivot to face the basket, looking for an open teammate, a shot, or a lane to dribble the ball to the basket.

FIGURE 4.18 Catching a pass.

Shooting

Most players love the chance to put the basketball through the hoop and will be highly motivated to learn proper shooting technique. However, many players spend hours shooting the basketball but never become very good shooters because they practice shots that they never take in game competition. After your players learn the fundamentals of the shot, you should make sure that they practice shooting under game conditions.

Players should first learn how to select high-percentage shots only—in other words, shots that are likely to go in. Obviously, the closer the player is to the basket when the shot is attempted, the better the chance that the shot will go in. Other factors that determine a high-percentage shot include the defensive pressure, the position of the shooter, the team offense, and the time and score of the game. High-percentage opportunities for a shot also vary depending on the player's shooting skill and the position that the player plays on the team.

When shooting, players should also learn to focus on a specific target, usually the rim or backboard. The middle of the rim should be the target for most shots, but when players are at a 30- to 60-degree angle from the hoop, they should sight the corner of the square on the backboard for a bank shot. If the angle is correct, using the backboard will help the ball go into the basket.

Players can shoot the ball in a variety of ways, including set and jump shots, free throws, layups, and shooting off a dribble.

Achieving Arc on the Shot

Many players tend to shoot "line drives" at the hoop, rather than achieving a proper arc on the ball when taking a shot. This arc can improve the chances of making a shot because a proper arc allows the ball to be somewhat off the mark and still go in the basket.

Arc is determined by the placement of the arm and hand during and after the shot. To achieve arc on the shot, players should shoot the ball up, then out, toward the basket. The player's shoulders should be relaxed and in a forward position. The player should move the hands closer together if they are too far apart; she should raise her shooting arm higher to provide more arc. A good way to check for proper arc is to examine the positioning of the shooting-arm elbow. The elbow should end up above eye level on the follow-through for the shot.

Set Shots

Set shots are shots taken without a jump during the shot, such as the type of shot used for free throws. A jump shot, as the name implies, is a shot taken using a jump during the shot (see page 72). Although the most common shot at higher levels of play is the jump shot, young players who lack the leg strength and coordination to spring from the floor while shooting will more often shoot set shots.

COACHING TIP   Teach younger players the mechanics of the set shot first, and they will be able to advance to the jump shot as they increase their strength and improve their coordination.

When executing the set shot, players should first square up to the basket, with the foot on the shooting-hand side positioned up to 6 inches (15 cm) in front of the other foot, creating a comfortable, balanced base of support. The ball should lie on the finger pads of each hand, with the shooting hand behind and slightly underneath the ball and with the nonshooting hand balancing the ball from the side (see figure 4.19a). The player then bends the knees to get momentum for the shot—using the legs, not the arms, for power; at the same time, the player bends the shooting-arm elbow to approximately a 90-degree angle, keeping the forearm perpendicular to the floor and in front of the cocked wrist as the ball is brought up to the shooting position above the forehead (see figure 4.19b). As the legs extend, the player releases the ball by extending the elbow, bringing the wrist forward, and moving the fingers of the shooting hand up and through the ball. The player should follow through after the release by extending the shooting arm, dropping the wrist, and pointing the index finger of the shooting hand directly at the basket; the thumb on the shooting hand ends in the down position after the shot (see figure 4.19c).

FIGURE 4.19   Set shot.

For a set shot, players should understand that the nonshooting arm and hand should maintain their supportive position on the side of the ball until after the release—the nonshooting hand should not be used to help push the ball to the basket. To verify proper positioning of the nonshooting hand, ensure that the thumb of the nonshooting hand is pointed back to the ear and not at the basket.

Jump Shots

A jump shot is similar to the set shot except that the player aligns the ball higher at the point of release and shoots after jumping, rather than shooting with the simultaneous extension of the legs while on the floor. Also, because the player jumps first and then shoots, the upper body, arm, wrist, and fingers must generate more force.

When a player is executing a jump shot, the movement above the waist is similar to that of the set shot. The shooting hand should be positioned behind the ball, with the elbow in line with the basket, and the nonshooting hand should be positioned to the side of the ball (see figure 4.20a). For the jump shot, however, the player should jump straight up off both feet—fully extending the ankles, knees, back, and shoulders—and should take the shot just before reaching the peak of the jump (see figure 4.20b). For a jump shot, the ball must be put into motion as the player is jumping in order to impart that power onto the ball. If a player releases the ball too late, the shot will most likely be short. The player should follow through on the jump shot with the shooting arm extended and the nonshooting hand in position with the thumb pointing back toward the ear (see figure 4.20c).

FIGURE 4.20 Jump shot.

The height of the player's jump depends on the range of the shot. On shots close to the basket when the player is closely guarded, she will have to jump higher than her defenders. On longer-range jump shots, she will usually have more time and defenders are not quite as close; therefore, the player won't have to jump as high for these shots. When using a jump shot, however, more force from the legs should be used for shooting the ball rather than for jumping high. Balance and control are more important than gaining maximum height on a jump.

Free Throws

Although the mechanics of a free throw are similar to a set shot (see figure 4.19 on page 71), free-throw shooting requires a great deal of concentration because the shooter is by himself at the free-throw line. Success in free-throw shooting largely depends on the player's ability to be relaxed and confident in order to concentrate fully on the shots being taken.

Establishing a consistent rhythm and a set routine will help players achieve this relaxation and confidence. A routine, for example, can include dribbling a set number of times; checking mechanics; breathing deeply and exhaling fully; consciously relaxing the shoulders, arms, hands, and fingers; letting them drop and loosen; and so forth. Players may also use visualization techniques to mentally practice shooting the free throw and to focus on positive thoughts, such as *I'm a good shooter* and "seeing" the ball going through the basket.

Layups

The highest-percentage shot—and therefore the most desirable—is a layup. A layup is a one-handed shot taken within three feet of the basket. A layup is typically shot using the hand farthest from the basket in an effort to protect the ball from defenders. Teach players to use their left hand when shooting layups from the left side of the basket and their right hand when shooting from the right side of the basket.

When executing a layup, the player begins by striding from a 45- to 60-degree angle to the hoop and then planting the foot opposite the shooting hand (see figure 4.21a on page 74). The player explodes off the planted foot straight up into the air (see figure 4.21b). At the top of the jump, the player releases the ball by bringing the shooting hand, which is underneath the ball and near the shoulder, straight up toward

COACHING TIP Right-handed players are likely to find left-handed layups troublesome, and vice versa. The strength and coordination of younger players are not yet advanced enough to perform the layup easily from both sides of the basket. You can help your players learn to use the left hand on the left side of the basket, for example, by teaching them to visualize the left knee and left elbow attached with a string. As the left elbow goes up to release the ball, the left knee also comes up, and the player jumps off the right foot.

FIGURE 4.21   Layup.

the basket (see figure 4.21c). As in the set shot, the index finger of the shooting hand should be pointed directly at the basket or the appropriate spot on the backboard.

When shooting a layup, the player should aim to shoot high off the backboard so that the ball drops in the basket. This way, even if the player is fouled on the shot, the ball will have a chance to go in.

Shooting Off the Dribble

Shooting off the dribble is simply taking a shot after using a dribble to get into a better shooting position. The dribble also helps the shooter get more power into the shot than when a shot is taken directly from a pass.

When shooting off a dribble, the player should first achieve a balanced stance with the knees bent. She should pick up the ball while facing the basket in position to shoot. The player shouldn't reach for the ball but should instead pick it up in front of the shooting knee (the knee on the same side of the body as the shooting hand) as the ball bounces up. When a player is dribbling to the strong-hand side (see figure 4.22a), she should jump behind her last dribble (see figure 4.22b) and pick the ball up in front of her shooting knee using the strong-side hand; the nonshooting hand will be positioned on the side of the ball for the shot (see figure 4.22c). When a player is dribbling to his weak-hand side (see figure 4.23a), he will pick the ball up off the last dribble (see figure 4.23b) with the weak-side hand and bring the ball to the shooting hand for the shot (see figure 4.23c).

FIGURE 4.22   Shooting the ball from the strong-side dribble.

FIGURE 4.23   Shooting the ball from the weak-side dribble.

Offensive Rebounding

An offensive rebound is a rebound secured by the offensive team when one of its own players misses a shot. Successful offensive rebounding by your players adds greatly to your team's chances to score. Possession of the ball comes more often from missed shots than any other way, and a team that can control the backboard usually controls the game. More than any other basic basketball skill, the success of offensive rebounding relies largely on players' desire and courage. Good rebounders must be able to anticipate missed shots and determine how hard or how soft, and to what side of the rim, the ball will rebound. They must also know where their opponents are at all times.

When preparing to rebound a ball, the offensive player should be in the ready position with the hands above the shoulders (see figure 4.24a) so that she can achieve maximum height on her jump to go after the ball. The hands and arms need to be fully extended so the player gets the ball at the peak of her jump instead of allowing the ball to come down to the player. A player should catch the rebound firmly with both hands (see figure 4.24b), and after controlling a rebound, the player should keep the ball at chin level with the elbows out (see figure 4.24c). The player must protect the ball while maintaining the ready position with the ball at the chin and the elbows out, but at the same time the player must avoid swinging the elbows to draw a foul.

FIGURE 4.24 Securing the rebound.

Rebounding Shots From the Side

For a shot taken from the side, offensive players should be aware that the ball is likely to rebound to the opposite side of the basket. Players should not watch the ball in flight; instead, they should look for an opening on the opposite side so that they can position themselves for the rebound. The offensive player can get into offensive rebound position by taking a V-cut (discussed previously on page 57) toward the baseline in order to get inside position on the defender. The player can also use a pivot (discussed previously on page 59) to make a spin move around the defender.

Rebounding Shots From the Front

Offensive rebounding for shots taken from the front is similar to rebounding the shots from the side, except that shots taken from the front will usually rebound straight out from the rim. The offensive player can use the same tactics to get into offensive rebound position in front of the rim—taking a V-cut to get inside position on the defender or using a pivot to make a spin move around defenders.

COACHING TIP A player should avoid reaching over an opponent when getting "boxed out" by the defense (see Defensive Rebounding in chapter 7) or else it is likely that a foul will be called. Emphasize the importance of jumping straight up for the rebound. By jumping vertically, not only will a player achieve great height, but she'll also avoid needless fouls.

Rebounding Free Throws

When rebounding free throws, the offensive player should line up as far up the lane as possible (in his box). When the ball hits the rim, the player should immediately step down the lane hard and quick to try to beat the inside defender for the rebound. This will make it more difficult for the defensive rebounder to make contact and block out the offensive player.

5

Offensive Tactics

Once your players understand and can properly execute the individual offensive technical skills, they can begin putting them together into offensive tactics. As you probably already know, the primary offensive objective in basketball is to move the ball effectively so that you can score. A secondary goal, then, is to maintain ball possession so that the opposing team cannot score. The following tactics will help your team accomplish these goals.

Coordinating an Offensive Attack

When coordinating your offensive attack, above all else, you must strive to maintain court balance and spacing to provide opportunities for players to be in a position to score. The execution of these objectives differs depending on whether your team is up against a man-to-man or zone defense.

Jump Balls

The jump ball occurs when both teams have equal control of the ball, as in the start of the game or overtime periods. How players are positioned for a jump ball depends on whether your team has the better chance of controlling the tip—that is, winning the jump ball. If the player jumping for you has the advantage, your team should align in an offensive formation and attempt to score off the play. If, however, it appears that the opposing team will gain possession, a defensive setup is appropriate. The jumper should tip the ball to an open spot where two teammates are next to each other without an opponent in between.

Against Man-to-Man Defense

Against man-to-man defense, the most important thing for your players to learn is proper spacing so that the defenders cannot easily double-team the offensive player with the ball (see Creating Passing Lanes on page 80 for more information). For youth players, an offensive set that works well against man-to-man defense is one where the point guard (1) leads the attack with the wings (2 and 3) stationed at the free-throw line extended—approximately 17 feet from the basket—and the two post players (4 and 5) positioned on the free-throw line blocks (see figure 5.1). When the ball is passed to a wing, the point guard screens away for the other

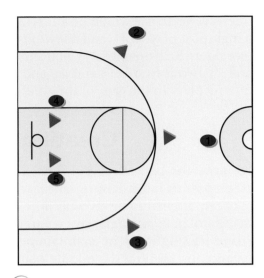

FIGURE 5.1 Offensive set against a man-to-man defense.

wing, and a post player screens away for the opposite post player. At times, the point guard may cut to the basket instead of setting the screen; when this happens, to regain court balance, the opposite wing will fill the front spot. The post players may also step out to the wing positions to set a ball screen and create a two-man pick-and-roll.

Against Zone Defense

Against a zone defense, your players need to move quickly and strive to find positions in gaps of the defense. If players dribble the basketball between the gaps in a zone defense, this will often make two defenders cover the dribbler and leave a player open for a shot. When your team faces a 2-3 zone defense (see figure 5.2a), a good

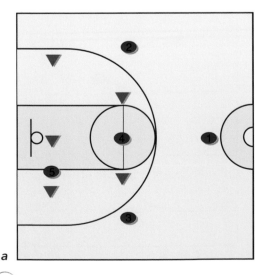

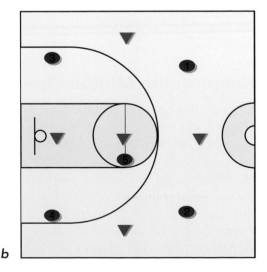

a   b

FIGURE 5.2 Offensive sets against a zone defense.

offensive set to use would be a 1-3-1 set with a point guard (1), two wings (2 and 3), a high-post player (4), and a low-post player (5). When facing a 1-3-1 zone defense (see figure 5.2*b* on page 79), you should use a 2-1-2 offensive set with two guards (1 and 2), two forwards (3 and 4), and a post player (5) in the middle. In a 2-1-2, the offense plays in the gaps of the zone defense.

Creating Passing Lanes

To move the ball effectively, your team needs to move well without the ball and create passing lanes. Passing lanes are spaces or open areas where passes can be made

between offensive players with little risk of being stolen by the defensive team. Players create passing lanes by maintaining court balance, by keeping the middle open, and by quickly moving to a vacated spot. Passing lanes can also be created by screens, which will be covered in Setting and Using Screens on the following page.

Maintaining Court Balance

Court balance is necessary to allow the offense to make passes and cuts. Offensive players should start in an open formation about 12 to 15 feet apart. This spacing will make it more difficult for the defenders to double-team and will allow better opportunities for screens and cuts. Offensive players should be spaced high at the top, wide on the wings, and at the midpoints between the basket and corners on the baseline (see figure 5.3).

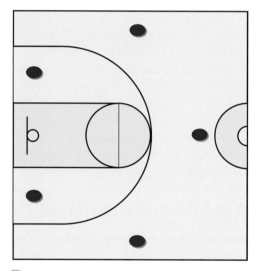

FIGURE 5.3 Open spacing formation.

Keeping the Middle Open

Keeping the middle, or lane area, open is a very good offensive maneuver because it enables cutters to cut through the lane to receive the ball without much traffic. When a player cuts to the basket and doesn't receive a pass, the player should continue through and fill an open spot on the side of the court with fewer players, which is usually the opposite side from where the player came. This will keep the middle open and the floor balanced (see figure 5.4).

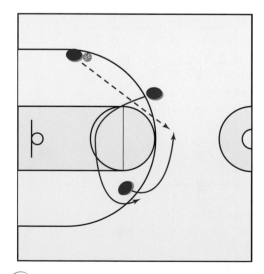

FIGURE 5.4 Filling an open spot on a cut.

Additionally, players must be aware that they shouldn't stay in the post area (high, mid, or low post) for more than three counts. A violation will occur after three seconds in the lane, and the middle area will get congested if the player continues to go into the post areas.

Moving to a Vacated Spot

When a player cuts, the player who is the next player away from the cutting player should move quickly to the vacated spot. This is especially important when the player has to cut from the top position (the position at the top of the key that the point guard typically covers), because floor balance is needed so that players are in the proper position for the rebound and to stop the fast break. This top position is where the offense usually starts, depending on the offensive set being used. But as players move to various spots on the court in response to defensive movement, this point position needs to be covered by different players so that good court balance is maintained. When replacing the player at the

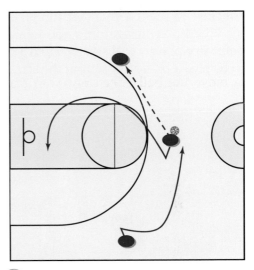

FIGURE 5.5 Moving to a vacated spot when a cut is taken from the point.

point, the new player should swing wide above the three-point line, creating a better passing angle from the wing (see figure 5.5). The new player needs to get open for a pass at the top of the key, and if the player receives a pass, this is a good opportunity to reverse the ball to the other side of the court and make a cut to the basket.

Setting and Using Screens

Screens can be set for a player with or without the ball. They are used to help players get open for passes and shots. In figure 5.6, the low player sets a screen—also called a *pick*—by positioning as a stationary barrier on one side of his teammate's defender, thus blocking that defender's path as the teammate cuts around the screen to get open for a pass. A player will typically set a screen perpendicular to the path of the defender and will "screen away" from the ball—that is, set the screen for a player without the ball who is located on the opposite side of the court from the ball (the weak side). This way, the player for whom the screen is set will be moving toward the passer after coming off the screen.

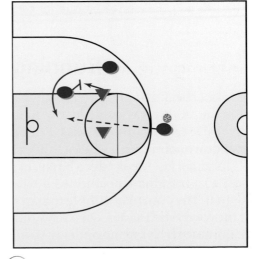

FIGURE 5.6 Setting a screen.

When setting a screen, the player should use a wide two-footed jump stop (see page 58 of chapter 4) to avoid an illegal moving screen. The player should stand erect with the feet planted shoulder-width apart and the arms down in front or crossed at the chest (see figure 5.7a). The screener should keep the arms and knees in as the defender fights through. The cutter—the player for whom the screen is set—should cut close to the screener (see figure 5.7b) and actually brush the screener on the way by. When playing against a good defensive team, the cutter may be covered because defensive players will switch when a screen is set. But the screener may often be open to receive a pass after setting the screen.

FIGURE 5.7   Proper technique for setting and using a screen.

Running a Fast Break

The fast break usually develops after a rebound, a steal, or possibly after a basket, and it is the fastest way to make the transition from defense to offense. As soon as the defensive team gains possession, it becomes the offensive team and tries to push the ball downcourt quickly before the other team can get back on defense.

To start a fast break after a basket or steal, players use a quick pass, known as an *outlet pass,* to a teammate positioned downcourt from the player in possession of the basketball. They can also dribble to start the break, but passing is the first option because it moves the ball faster. On a rebound, the outlet pass is slightly different because the teammate receiving the outlet pass will not yet be positioned downcourt. Instead, the player in possession of the ball turns to the outside of the court and looks for a guard to pass to. When the guard receives the ball, he immediately advances the ball downcourt using a dribble or another pass. If the rebounder is trapped or is in a congested area and unable to make the outlet pass, he can use one or two power dribbles up the middle and then look to pass. A point guard who sees that the rebounder is unable to make the outlet pass should come back to the rebounder to receive a short pass or handoff. The player who receives the pass will then be responsible for moving the ball to the middle of the court by either passing or dribbling. Other teammates will fill the lanes on either side as they proceed down the court. When the ball reaches the middle, the player with the ball will want to get to the free-throw line under control before passing to either lane for a shot or short drive (see figure 5.8).

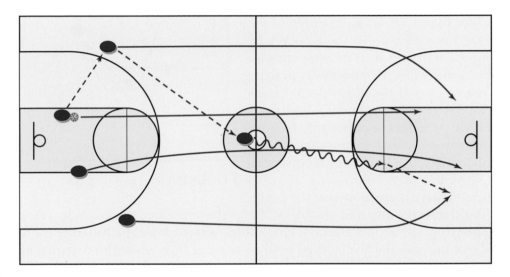

FIGURE 5.8   A typical fast break.

COACHING TIP   The fast break is not started until the defensive team gains possession of the ball and then becomes the offensive team. Players must not anticipate possession and start the fast break early, because this may leave the team shorthanded on defense. Younger players often get in the habit of anticipating that a teammate will gain possession and running away from the ball to start the fast break before possession is really obtained.

Players should stay spread out and run at top speed under control during the fast break. The last two players down the floor are called *trailers* and are typically the bigger forward and the center (the 4 and 5 positions). They cut directly to the blocks on either side, looking for a pass from one of the outside lanes. Trailers often get passes on the blocks from the right- or left-lane cutters when the defense moves out to cover them on the wings.

Basic Offensive Plays

There are several basic offensive plays that every team should learn, including the give-and-go, the pick-and-roll, and inbounds plays.

Give-and-Go

The give-and-go is the most basic play in basketball and exemplifies what team play is all about. The name is derived from the action where one player gives (passes) the ball to a teammate and goes (cuts) to the basket, looking to receive a return pass for a layup (see figure 5.9 for an example of the movement made for a give-and-go play). By passing the ball and then moving without it, the player creates an opportunity to score on a return pass. If the player does not get open on the cut, the movement at least gives the teammate a better opportunity to initiate a one-on-one move, because the cutter's defender will be in a less advantageous position to give defensive help.

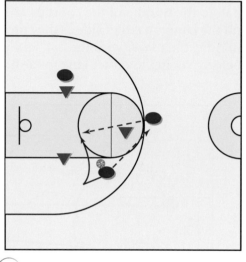

FIGURE 5.9 Give-and-go.

When a player is positioned at the point, she should start the give-and-go at least a step above the free-throw circle. When she is on the wing, she should start the give-and-go a step above the foul line extended. The player initiates the give-and-go with a pass and then reads the defender's position before cutting to the basket. If the defender moves with the passer, continuing to guard closely, the passer should simply make a hard cut to the basket. However, if the defender drops off, moving toward the ball on the pass, the passer should set the defender up with a fake before cutting. The passer should fake by taking a step or two away from the ball, and then, as the defender moves with the passer, the passer should make a sharp cut in front of the defender toward the basket. The passer can also fake by taking a step or two toward the ball, then make a sharp cut behind the defender. This is the backdoor cut, which was discussed previously on page 58 of chapter 4. The key is for players to read their defenders to know which type of cut will be most effective (see Cuts on page 56 of chapter 4).

Pick-and-Roll

The pick-and-roll is another basic play whose name, like that of the give-and-go, comes from the action of the play. A player sets a pick (screen) for a teammate, who dribbles by it for an outside shot or a drive. The screener then rolls toward the basket, looking for a pass from the dribbler for a layup (see figure 5.10 for the movement made for a pick-and-roll play).

The player with the ball must wait until a legal pick is set before she starts the dribble. She then dribbles her defender into the screen that her teammate has set. The screener turns so she can see the dribbler and may receive a pass. The dribbler should take at least two dribbles beyond the screen to create space for the pass to the screener, who rolls to the basket.

FIGURE 5.10 Pick-and-roll.

> **COACHING TIP** After making a roll or cut, players should work to get their lead hand up for a target. This will help the passer identify where the ball should be passed. It also helps the passer know that players are looking to receive the ball as they are cutting to the basket.

Inbounds Plays

Inbounds plays are used to get the ball into the playing area from out of bounds—for example, after a turnover, after a made basket, or when the other team touches the ball last before it goes out of bounds. The primary goal of your inbounds plays should be to get the ball inbounds safely, to score off the inbounds play, or both.

Design most of your inbounds plays to create easy scoring opportunities when your team puts the ball in play from underneath your basket, but keep the plays simple and limit them to just a few. The key is to always have a good passer inbound the ball and for the rest of the team to cut hard to their designated spots.

> **COACHING TIP** When creating inbounds plays for your team, consider aligning players in the same manner for each play so that your players aren't confused about where to position themselves and the defense isn't tipped off by a change in formation.

Types of Offenses

When planning an offense that best suits the needs of the team, coaches must take into consideration their players' skill level, size, quickness, maturity level, and desire compared to other players.

Basic Offenses

For the team's main offense, the coach should choose an offense that is very simple and involves good court spacing. For example, the offense can use a set with a point guard, two wings, and two posts (1-2-2) or a set with a point guard, two wings, a high post, and a low post (1-3-1). Another typical set includes two guards, two wings, and one post player (2-2-1). From all of these sets and the others discussed in this section, the players can set screens and run give-and-go plays.

Fast Break Offense

If the team is quick and small, the fast break offense would be a good option as the initial offense, enabling the team to try to score quickly against teams that are slower. In this offense, the team should try to use the fast break (see page 82) off turnovers and blocked shots with the goal of getting an easy basket. If you want to be a fast-breaking offensive team, you must spend time in practice working on the concepts of filling the lanes and getting the ball up the court as quickly as possible, which involves using the pass rather than the dribble.

5-Out Offense

Regardless of whether you are a fast-breaking team or one that is slower and works to set up the half-court offense, you will need to decide what works best in the half court for your team. A smaller, quicker team will want to spread the court and create opportunities for drives to the basket. A 5-out offense allows for good spacing that will be effective for such drives. The 5-out offense is considered a spread offense in which the middle of the court is open. This offense is a 1-2-2 set with the two baseline players positioned 12 to 15 feet from the basket (see figure 5.11).

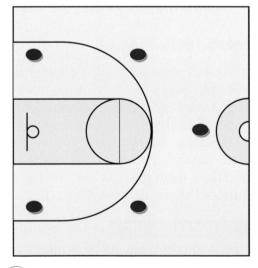

FIGURE 5.11 5-out offensive setup.

1-4 Offense

In addition to the 5-out offense, a 1-4 set can be quite effective for a fast but smaller team. This offense includes a point guard along with four players across the free-throw line and free-throw line extended—two wings and one post player at each of the free-throw elbows (see figure 5.12). Again, the spacing is away from the basket, which allows for open cuts to the basket and screens by the post players on the ball.

Double Low-Post Offense

If you have players with some size on your team, you may want to look for more of a power game, such as a double low-post set with three perimeter players. In the double low-post offense, two players are posting

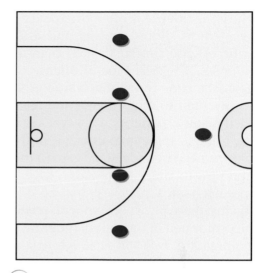

FIGURE 5.12   1-4 offensive setup.

up on each of the low-post blocks (see figure 5.13). This power offense is great for teams with two big players. By having your players in the low post set screens for one another, this offense allows your big players to stay near the basket for good low-post shots and good rebounding position.

1-3-1 Offense

A 1-3-1 set is also a good combination for teams with two good post players. In this offense, one player is positioned at the high post and one at the low post; two wings and a point guard are also included (see figure 5.14). A big player who is also a good passer is great for the high-post position.

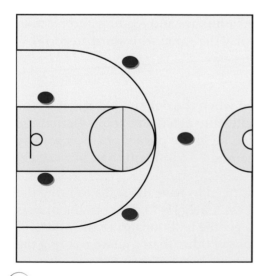

FIGURE 5.13   Double low-post offensive setup.

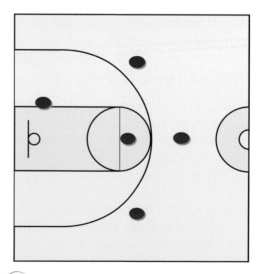

FIGURE 5.14   1-3-1 offensive setup.

Zone Offense

The zone offense is often overlooked; how-ever, teams should practice and drill their zone offense similar to their man-to-man offenses. The best type of offense to play against a zone is one that is similar to your team's man-to-man offense and has many of the same patterns. However, attacking the zone is somewhat different in that the players need to understand gaps in the zone and how to attack these gaps.

Most teams play a 2-3 zone defense. Against this type of zone, your players should be positioned in the gaps of the zone, with a point guard, two wings, a high-post player, and a low-post player (see figure 5.15). This will force the defenders to decide who to guard and will create some confusion for them.

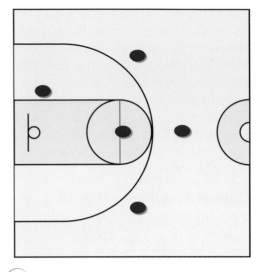

FIGURE 5.15 Zone offensive setup.

A fast-breaking team has some advantage when playing against a zone defense, because the quicker the ball can be advanced, the more difficult it is for the zone to set up and defend the fast break. This is another reason why the fast break should be used to some extent by all teams.

Whatever type of offense you decide on, you must spend time working on it in practice so the players can run your sets without thinking too much. When the play-ers are thinking too much, this slows them down and does not allow them to run the offense easily. If you have too many sets and play calls, this will not allow the players to learn how to play the game. Once your basic offense is established, have the players spend time practicing screening for teammates and reading and reacting to the defense. This teaches the players how to play the game with some freedom.

Press Break Offenses

A press break offense is a full-court offense used when the defense plays some type of full-court, three-quarter-court, or half-court pressure defense to try to disrupt the offensive team. You must prepare your players to be in the proper position so they don't panic when they see a press. You want them to be confident that they can get an easy basket against the press.

If the press is a man-to-man press, the guards need to have the skills to bring the ball up against the press using the dribble. The best strategy is to clear out the players except for the guard, who can use the dribble to get the ball upcourt to the offensive end. Sometimes the offense may want to use a player other than a guard to bring the ball upcourt against man pressure if that player is the best ball handler.

Anytime your opponents use a zone press at any level on the court—full, half, or three-quarter court—your players should use an offensive set that enables them to get the ball in the middle of the court. This can be done by placing a player in the middle of the press to start with or by having a player cut to the middle of the press from the weak side. Once the ball gets to the middle of the court, the offense should attack the defense by dribbling the ball to the basket; an offensive player should be on each side of the basket to create good passing situations.

Special Offenses

As a coach, you must also have some special offenses available when needed. These include last-second shot offenses from full, half, and quarter court; a delay offense when ahead in the last minutes of the game; and quick-hitter offenses for three-point shots or two-point shots.

These special offenses need to be practiced each week so the players know what to run in key situations. Working on these special offenses will give your players confidence; the players will know that they are well prepared for any situation that may arise during the game.

6

Offensive Drills

The following offensive drills can be used to help players develop the skills and tactics that will enable them to become better on the offensive end of the court. Although most of the drills emphasize one or two main goals, players should be developing several offensive skills at the same time. For example, although shooting may be emphasized in one drill, the coach should also give attention to passing or dribbling in the same drill. In this way, players will get the most out of each drill they perform.

For access to some of these drills online, visit the following website: www.Human Kinetics.com/CoachingYouthBasketball5E-OffensiveDrills. Such drills are indicated by this symbol in the outside margin of the text:

Additional offensive drills are provided in chapters 10 to 14; refer to the practice sessions there for even more options.

➤ FOUR-LINE JUMP STOPS

Goal   To learn how to make proper jump stops without traveling after running.

Description   Players divide into four groups and line up along the baseline. When the coach blows the whistle, the first players in line sprint forward. The coach blows a second whistle (after approximately five or six steps by the players), and the players use a jump stop to stop quickly with both feet simultaneously hitting the floor. The coach blows another whistle, and the next players in line begin. Repeat in this manner until all players have reached the opposite baseline. This drill can also be done with the players performing forward and reverse pivots, rebounding technique without the ball, jump shots without the ball, or imaginary tipping.

Variations

- Place a cone on the floor to indicate where the players should execute the jump stop.
- Have each player use a ball and perform the jump stop after dribbling.

➤ DRIBBLE–PIVOT–PASS

Goal   To learn to execute a jump stop and pivot correctly without traveling.

Description   Players divide into four groups and line up along the sideline. The first players in line each have a ball, and on the coach's command, they move forward, dribbling three times, and jump stop. After the jump stop, the players execute a reverse pivot (a front pivot may also be used), pass the ball to the next player in line, and return to the end of the line. Repeat until all players have had a turn.

Use this drill to work on passing as well. The pass back to the next player in line can be a chest pass, bounce pass, two-hand overhead pass, step-out pass (the player steps out to avoid the imaginary defensive player), or step-through pass (the player steps out, fakes a pass, and then crosses over with the same leg to make a pass on the opposite side from which he originally stepped out).

Variations

- Place a cone on the floor to indicate where the player should dribble and perform the pivot.
- Add a pass fake after the pivot and before the player makes the pass to the next player in line.

➤ JAB STEPPING

Goal   To learn how to perform a jab step to create space between the offensive and defensive player.

Description   Players divide into three groups and line up at the top of the key. The first players in line each have a ball, and on the coach's command, they spin the ball out 3 or 4 feet (91 or 122 cm) in front of them. The players take their first step with the nonshooting foot, which will be the pivot foot, to grab the ball, and with the shooting foot, they take a jab step. After the jab step, the players shoot the ball, rebound it, and pass it to the next player in their lines. Repeat until all players have had a turn.

Variations

- Have the players perform the jab steps without the ball to learn the proper footwork before adding the ball.
- Add a defender to the drill so the offensive player must perform the jab step in a live situation.

➤ PARTNER PASSING

Goal   To learn the correct techniques for passing and catching the ball.

Description   Players divide into groups of two and position anywhere on the court, 12 to 15 feet (3.6 to 4.5 m) apart and facing each other. Each pair of players has a ball, and the players pass back and forth to their partner, using proper technique. The coach specifies the type of passes to be made (chest, bounce, or overhead). Continue for 5 to 10 minutes, depending on the age group.

Variations

- Start with the players closer together (6 to 8 feet [183 to 244 cm] apart) so the passes are easier to pass and catch.
- Have the players perform the drill with the weak hand only. To make the drill more competitive, you can also add one or two stationary dribbles before each pass.

➤ TARGET TWO-LINE PASSING

Goal   To learn how to pass the ball to a specific target and how to provide a target for a passer.

Description   Players divide into two groups and line up on the court, approximately 12 to 15 feet apart, facing each other. The first player in one line has a ball, and on the coach's command of "left," "right," or "both," the first player in the other line raises the appropriate hand (or both hands) to act as the passer's target. Once the pass is caught, the two players take a position at the end of the opposite line. Repeat until all players have had a turn.

Variations

- Start with the players closer together (6 to 8 feet apart) so the passes are easier to pass and catch.
- Work on all types of passes to the target—chest, bounce, overheard, and so on.

➤ DRIBBLING LINES

Goal To learn the various dribbling techniques that are necessary to advance the ball against defensive players.

Description Players divide into eight groups and line up across from each other, four lines on each side, along the sidelines on both sides of the court. The first players in each line have a ball, and on the coach's command, they dribble forward toward the middle of the court, using a type of dribble specified by the coach (see the upcoming list). When the players meet in the middle, they execute a crossover dribble (or another dribble specified by the coach) and continue to the opposite sideline, giving the ball to the next player in line. Repeat until all players have had a turn.

In addition to the crossover dribble (see page 64), the players should work on the following dribbles:

- Power dribble (see page 63)
- Speed dribble (the player dribbles as fast as he can without losing control of the ball)
- Control dribble (the player dribbles deliberately under control)
- Hesitation dribble (the player advances forward with a speed dribble, then takes one dribble backward before advancing forward again)
- A combination of the various types of dribbles

Variations
- Place cones where the players should perform each specified dribble, such as the crossover.
- Add a defender so the drill becomes more gamelike.

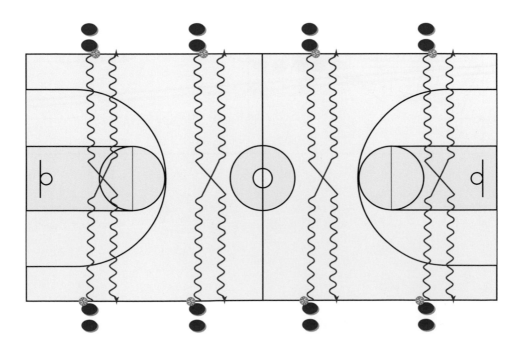

➤ TWO-BALL SHOOTING

Goal To learn to shoot the ball after moving to a spot and squaring up to face the basket.

Description Players line up in two groups at the top of the key on both ends of the court. The second and third players in line each have a ball. The first player in line runs and touches the baseline and then moves to an appropriate place (the coach specifies the type of shot to be made) in order to receive a pass from the second player in line. The player catches the pass, pivots, and shoots the ball using proper form. The player rebounds his own shot, takes a position at the end of the line, and passes the ball up the line. The second player in line, who made the pass previously, now runs to the baseline and moves to an appropriate place in order to receive a pass from the third player in line. Repeat in this manner for 5 to 10 minutes or until all players in line have executed a shot. Make sure the players take shots within their range. Also, remind the players to keep all 10 toes pointed toward the basket.

Variations

- Do not use a ball to start the drill; have each player shoot an imaginary ball after performing the movement.
- Have the players take one dribble either right or left before the shot.

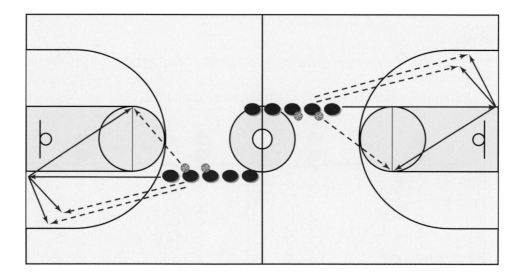

➤ TWO-BALL CUTTING

Goal To practice making cuts to get open to receive a pass and then making a move to score.

Description Players line up in groups of five at the top of the key on both ends of the court. The second and third players in line each have a ball. The first player in line executes a cut (V-cut, L-cut, or backdoor cut) to get the ball, which the second player in line will pass. Once the player receives the pass, he turns and shoots. He then rebounds his own shot, takes a position at the end of the line, and passes the ball up the line. The second player in line, who made the pass previously, now acts as the cutter and executes a cut to get the ball, which the third player in line will pass. Repeat in this manner for 5 to 10 minutes or until all players in line have executed a cut.

Variations

- Have each player begin with the V-cut, followed by the L-cut, and then the backdoor cut. Perform the drill from the left side and then from the right side of the court.
- Ask each player to perform various moves off the cut—for example, executing a crossover dribble before the shot after catching the pass off the V-cut.

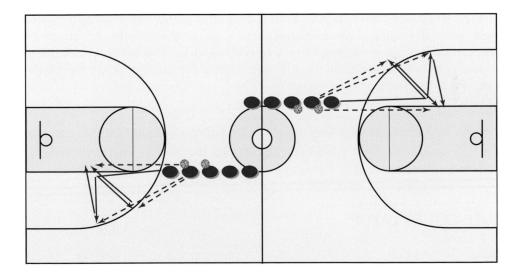

➤ OFFENSIVE REBOUNDING

Goal   To learn how to get into position and grab an offensive rebound.

Description   Players line up in a single-file line at the block on one side of the basket. The coach takes a shot, and the first player in line executes a V-cut or spin move to get into the proper position to rebound the ball at the basket. (The coach should take shots from different areas of the court to practice the rebounds for different types of shots.) Once the player gets the rebound, she passes the ball back to the coach and takes a position at the end of the line. Repeat until all players have had a turn.

Variations
- Have the players perform the offensive rebounding footwork without a shot.
- Add a defensive player to the drill.

➤ ON THE LINE

Goal   To practice making free throws in game-winning situations.

Description   Players divide into two even teams and line up on each sideline on one half of the court. The first player in team A's line shoots two free throws, then the first player in team B's line shoots two free throws. Continue in this fashion, alternating between team A and team B, until all players have shot. The team with the most total points is the winner. If the game is tied after all players from both teams have shot, keep the same order of players and have a "sudden-death" shoot-off—the first player from team A shoots one free throw, then the first player from team B shoots one free throw, and so on. The first time the tie is broken after both teams have shot, the game is over.

Variations
- To make the game easier, move the free-throw line up one to three feet.
- To make the game more difficult, require the winning team to make at least four consecutive free throws in addition to making more free throws than its opponent.

➤ FULL-COURT LAYUPS

Goal   To practice making layups after performing the speed dribble.

Description   Divide players into two groups, one group under each basket. The first three players in each line have a ball. On command, the first player in each line uses a right-handed speed dribble the length of the court and shoots a right-handed layup. The second and third players under each basket will follow on command. After each layup is shot, the first player in line without a ball rebounds the shot taken on his end and then follows the player in front of him down the court for a layup. The drill continues for one minute. Begin by asking the players to make 15 to 20 layups in that time period; you can adjust this goal depending on the players' skill level.

Variations

- Ask the players to speed dribble from half-court to the basket. In this variation, the player shooting the layup will rebound his own ball, giving it to the next player in line without one.
- Have players perform a left-handed speed dribble for a left-handed layup.

➤ FULL-COURT JUMPERS

Goal To work on making jump shots after receiving a pass.

Description Divide players into four groups, with one group in each corner of the court. Start with two basketballs in opposite corners. On command, the first player in each line with a ball will take a few dribbles forward, passing the ball to the other end of the court. Each player follows her pass to the other end of the court for a return pass for a jump shot. This player then goes to the end of the line, while the passer on the same end rebounds the ball and continues the drill going the opposite way. Start with a goal of five to seven made baskets in one minute; you can adjust this according to skill level.

Variations

- Allow players to take several dribbles before passing the ball to the opposite end of the court.
- Ask players to add a dribble to either the right or the left before each jump shot.

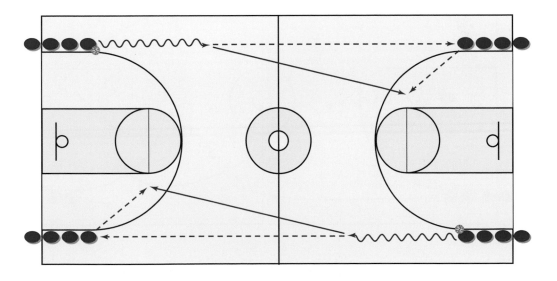

➤ FIVE BALL

Goal   To learn how to catch the ball on the move and come to a stop to shoot.

Description   Divide players into four groups, with one group in each corner of the court. On one end of the court, the first player in each group has a ball. On the opposite end of the court, one player is positioned with a ball under, or just in front of, the basket in between the two groups; from this end of the court, three players make two passes while moving down the court for a layup at the opposite end. The third player and the passer will then each receive a ball from the corners at the opposite end for a jump shot. The player making the layup will grab his ball from the net, turn, and pass in the opposite direction to one of the two corner players who made passes for jumpers. These three players then travel to the opposite end, making two passes for a layup along with two jump shots, and the drill continues. For older age groups, start with a goal of 20 to 25 baskets in one minute; for younger players, adjust the goal to 10 to 12 baskets.

Variations

- Allow players to dribble the ball several times before passing to a teammate for the layup.
- Ask players to add a dribble to either the right or the left before each jump shot.

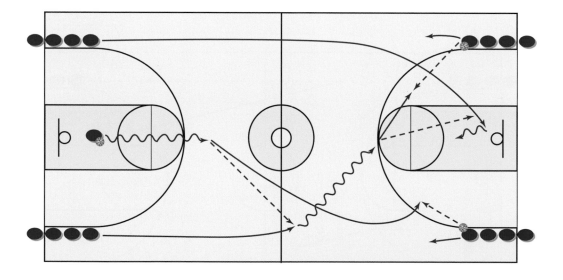

➤ PERFECT LAYUPS

Goal To learn how to pass the ball while moving and to practice making layups.

Description Begin with three lines of players along the baseline. The first player in the left line should have a ball (alternatively, the line on the right can begin with the ball). The first three players move down the court while passing the ball. The player on the left passes to the player in the middle, who passes back to the player on the left; then, the player on the left once more passes to the player in the middle, who this time makes a bounce pass to the player on the right for a layup. The player on the left rebounds the ball and makes a two-hand overhead outlet pass to the middle player, who has moved to the side of the player making the layup. This player continues the other way, making a baseball pass back to the next person in the right line, who continues the drill. For older players, the goal is to make 25 points in one minute; players get 2 points for a perfect layup (meaning the ball does not touch the rim) and 1 point for a made layup. For younger players, adjust the goal to 10 to 12 points.

Variations

- Use only one ball to start the drill and add a second ball later.
- Ask the players to use bounce passes instead of chest passes.

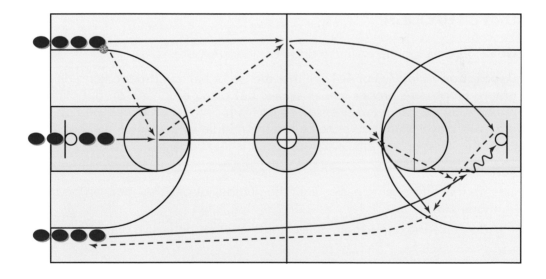

➤ TWO-STEPPIN'

Goal   To use pivots, drop steps, and jab steps to get free for shots.

Description   Play 3v3 in either the full or half court depending on the age group. When a player on the wing receives a pass, the player does either of the following:

1. Dribbles to the defender, stops, pivots, and shoots.
2. Uses a jab or drop step, then dribbles around a defender for a layup.

Two points are awarded if the player performs the pivot, jab, or drop step correctly and gets a shot off; an additional point is given for a made basket. One point is awarded for any made basket, whether made off a pivot or jab or drop step. Play to three points for the 5 to 6 age group, four points for the 7 to 8 age group, five points for the 9 to 10 age group, six points for the 11 to 12 age group, and seven points for the 13 to 14 age group.

Variations

- To make the game easier, use a chair or other object in place of the defender so that the offensive player can get accustomed to the moves.
- To make the game more difficult, award the two "performance" points only on made baskets, or don't award any points for made baskets that did not come off a pivot or jab or drop step.

➤ DRIVE-THROUGH

Goal   To develop the ability to dribble under pressure.

Description   Play 3v3 or 4v4 in either the full or half court depending on the age group. Emphasize proper fundamentals, but place emphasis on dribbling under pressure by awarding the offense two points for scores off drives, one point if the offensive player can dribble the ball to the middle of the lane for a shot, and one point for all other baskets.

Variations

- To make the game easier, limit the number of dribbles that can be made by one player.
- To make the game more difficult, add another defensive player.

➤ IN MY DUST

Goal   To use power dribbles and crossover dribbles to attack the basket.

Description   Play 3v3 or 4v4 in either the full or half court depending on the age group. Emphasize proper fundamentals, but place a special emphasis on effective dribbling by awarding one point each for made baskets, power dribbles, and crossover dribbles. Players should use these types of dribbles only as appropriate within the game situation. Points should not be awarded for ineffective or inappropriate use.

Variation   To make the game more challenging, award points for only one specified move. For example, to focus on the crossover dribble, award one point to players for proper use of the crossover dribble, but require that they pass or shoot before they can be awarded another point.

➤ PASSING CONTEST

Goal   To set up good shots through passing.

Description   Play 3v2 or 4v3 in either the full or half court depending on the age group. To place the emphasis on setting up good shots, award the offense one point for each successful pass and one point for each basket.

Variations
- To make the game easier, play 3v1 or 4v2.
- To make the game more difficult, do any of the following: Play 3v3 or 3v4; award two points for a particular pass of your choosing; require that players use only a certain type of pass (i.e., chest, bounce, or overhead); or allow no dribbling.

➤ CLEANING THE GLASS

Goal   To rebound using proper technique.

Description   Play 2v2 in either the full or half court depending on the age group. Each play begins with the coach shooting at the basket, intentionally missing the shot. The two offensive players try to rebound and score, and the defensive players also try to rebound. If the offense makes a basket or the defense gets the ball, the play is over. Each basket or rebound is worth one point. Switch offense and defense after five plays.

Variations
- To make the game easier, award two points for an offensive rebound.
- To make the game more challenging, require the offensive players to immediately shoot the ball, without a dribble, when they get the rebound.

➤ BUCKETMANIA

Goal   To score as many baskets as possible using proper technique.

Description   Play 3v2 in the half court. Give the three offensive players five minutes to score as many baskets as possible against the two defensive players. After each made basket, a defensive player will rebound the ball and return it to the offense. After five minutes, switch the offense and defense, keeping one of the offensive players on offense so that play remains 3v2. The new offense will have five minutes to score as many baskets as possible.

Variations

- To make the game easier, play 3v1 or 4v2.
- To make the game more difficult, do any of the following: Play 3v3 or 4v4; award two points for a particular type of shot of your choosing; or require that players only take a certain type of shot (e.g., jump shot, layup, shot off a dribble).

➤ ROOM TO MOVE

Goal   To create passing lanes and move to open space for better ball movement.

Description   Play 3v2 in the half or full court depending on the age group. The offense has the ball, and players pass and then move to a place on the court—point, wing, baseline, or low post—that is adjacent to the ball. This emphasizes spacing by allowing the players to get to an open spot so one defender cannot guard two offensive players. Players can dribble, but the emphasis should be on little dribbling and crisp passing. Offensive players must make 10 passes; after the 10th pass, they can shoot and continue to shoot until they score or the defense rebounds.

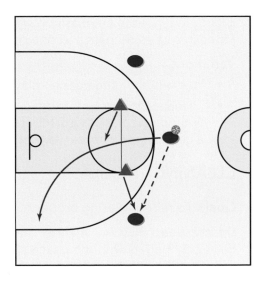

   Award one point for each pass successfully received and one point for a basket. Once a basket is made or the defense rebounds, begin again, this time with the two defenders moving to offense.

Variations

- To make the game easier, play 3v1.
- To make the game more difficult, play 3v3 or allow no dribbling.

➤ LIFE IN THE FAST LANE

Goal   To convert fast break opportunities into baskets.

Description   Play 2v4 using a full court specific to the age group. One of the two offensive players takes a shot, but purposely misses it, to begin the game. The defense rebounds and runs a fast break, making the outlet pass and filling the lanes. The defense (which just converted from offense) attempts to stop the fast break. Award two points for a well-executed break and one additional point for finishing it off with a basket. Switch teams and repeat at the other end of the court.

Variations

- To make the game easier, play 1v4 or 1v3.
- To make the game more difficult, play 3v4 or 4v4, or allow no dribbling.

➤ SCREEN DOOR

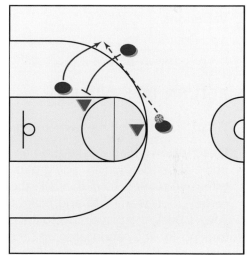

Goal   To set effective screens to free up teammates.

Description   Play 3v2 in either the full or half court depending on the age group. The player with the ball should be positioned out on top (top of the key or circle above the three-point line); one teammate sets a screen for the other teammate, who cuts around the screen and looks for a pass from the player with the ball. The player with the ball can call out "PR" (which signals to set a pick on the right side) or "PL" (which signals to set a pick on the left side), or the teammates can move on their own without the call.

The offense has five turns and is awarded two points for each successful screen and one point for each basket scored directly off the screen. (A screen is successful if it frees the teammate from her defender.) Reset the play after a shot is taken, whether the ball goes in or not.

Variations

- To make the game easier, play 3v1.
- To make the game more difficult, play 3v3.

➤ PICKIN' FOR POINTS

Goal   To score off the pick-and-roll.

Description   Play 3v2 in the half or full court depending on the age group. The player with the ball positions out on top (top of the key or circle above the three-point line), while one offensive player sets a screen for the other offensive player. The player who set the screen then rolls to the basket, hand up, to receive the return pass for the shot. Award the offense two points for each successful pick-and-roll that results in a made basket. Reset the play after a shot is taken, whether the ball goes in or not. Switch teams after five plays.

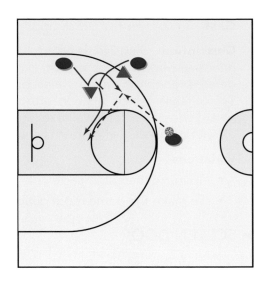

Variations

- To make the game easier, play 3v1.
- To make the game more difficult, play 3v3.

➤ RETURN TO SENDER

Goal   To score off the give-and-go play.

Description   Play 3v3 in the half or full court depending on the age group. When offensive players have the ball, they look for an open teammate and make a pass. After a pass, the player cuts to the basket, looking for the return pass and the shot. Shots must be taken within five feet of the basket. Baskets scored directly off the give-and-go count for two points; other baskets count for one point. Reset the offense after each play. The offense has five turns, then offense and defense are switched.

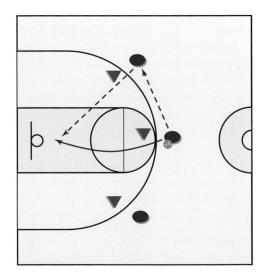

Variations

- To make the game easier, play 3v2.
- To make the game more difficult, award one point for offensive rebounds, which emphasizes blocking out by the defenders.

➤ SECONDS TO GO

Goal To score off an inbounds play.

Description Play 5v3 in the half court. Five seconds are placed on the clock, and an inbounds play is run. Award the offense one point for each basket scored before five seconds elapse.

Variations

- To make the game easier, play 5v2.
- To make the game more difficult, play 5v4 or 5v5.

➤ CUTTHROAT

Goal To learn how to move, square up, and thank the passer in a gamelike situation.

Description This is a very intense and fast 4v4 drill. Four players set up on offense against four defenders; a third group of four is waiting on the sidelines. To stay on offense, players must follow these three rules:

1. Every player must square up on each catch; this means the player must assume a triple-threat position with the ball on the hip and the shooting foot ahead. If the defense is playing very tight, be more lenient; even an attempt to square up is accepted.
2. Every player must move after each pass—cutting to the basket, screening away, and screening on the ball are all acceptable, but the player cannot just stand.
3. When a player makes a basket, she must thank the passer; if the coach made the pass that resulted in a basket, the player must thank the coach.

If a rule is broken, that offensive team must leave the court. The defensive team goes to offense, and the new team comes in on defense. Play for a set period of time (four minutes is appropriate) or to a certain number of points.

Variations

- Begin with just the square-up part of the drill before adding the other two rules.
- To make the drill more difficult, add other rules, such as limiting each player to two dribbles, dictating that all players must touch the ball before a shot is taken, or not allowing the offense to shoot until a ball screen occurs.

7

Defensive Skills

Playing defense is part instinct, part effort, and part technique. Players can improve their instincts by learning technique, practicing plays, and getting repetition. This chapter focuses on the defensive techniques that your players must learn in order to succeed in youth basketball. Again, remember to use the IDEA approach to teaching skills—introduce, demonstrate, and explain the skill, and attend to players as they practice the skill. Also, if you aren't familiar with basketball skills, you may want to watch a video about this subject so you can see how to perform the skills correctly.

Individual defensive skills are sometimes less appreciated than individual offensive skills, but they are just as important. To compete successfully, your players need to learn the basics of player-to-player defense.

Defensive Stance

The defensive stance—commonly referred to as the *ready* or *basketball* position—is the most basic of all defensive skills. It is the positioning that defensive players should strive to maintain at all times. In the ready position, the feet are shoulder-width apart or wider, and the knees are bent and out from the body (see figure 7.1). The hands and arms are above the waist to make the player seem as big as possible. This makes it tougher for offensive players to maneuver around the defender.

FIGURE 7.1 Basic defensive stance.

Defensive Footwork

From the defensive stance, a defender must be able to slide his feet and maintain an arm's distance from an opponent who is attempting to drive or cut to the basket. Players should stand in the ready position, with the knees bent, the rear down, and the back erect; the arms should be held out above the waist. The player should move the leg nearest the intended direction about 2 feet (61 cm) to that side (see figure 7.2a) and then slide the other foot until the feet are once again shoulder-width apart (see figure 7.2b). The player should use short, quick steps, with his weight evenly distributed on the balls of the feet. Remind the player to keep the toes pointed forward and to never cross the feet.

FIGURE 7.2 Defensive slide.

COACHING TIP Younger players tend to cross their feet when attempting to move sideways on a slide. To help prevent this, you can have your players visualize holding a broomstick between their feet that will not allow the feet to cross.

Defensive Body Positioning

To guard a player with the ball effectively, the defensive player's stance and body positioning are the most important elements. When guarding an opponent with the ball, the defensive player should maintain the defensive stance, as described previously, with one hand down to help protect against the crossover dribble and the other hand up in the passing lane to deflect a pass attempt (see figure 7.3 on page 108).

FIGURE 7.3 Defender's body positioning when guarding an opponent with the ball.

FIGURE 7.4 Defender's body positioning when turning an opponent with the ball.

> **COACHING TIP** Teach your players not to reach toward the dribbler. Reaching will cause defensive players to get off balance and allow the dribbler to easily get around them. Reaching may also cause the defender to foul the dribbler.

When the defender is in a situation where he must turn the offensive player, such as when the offensive player is working to dribble the ball up the court, the defender's foot positioning will change. The player must position the foot closest to the rim line (the imaginary line that runs down the center of the court from rim to rim) at least an arm's length away from the offensive player's inside foot to help force the dribbler to the baseline (see figure 7.4). This will force the dribbler to go to the outside or to the baseline. The defensive player's eyes should stay focused on the waist area of the dribbler so that the defender does not get faked out of position by watching the ball or the head and shoulders of the offensive player.

Steals

Stealing refers to intercepting the ball when a pass is made or knocking the ball away from the dribbler. Most often, a steal occurs when a pass is made from one offensive player to another and the defender steps in the path of the pass. When attempting to steal the ball, the defensive player must anticipate where and when the pass will be thrown and get the hand in the passing lane. Stealing the ball from dribblers is often difficult because they can protect the ball using their body. Dribblers also commonly draw a foul on the defender because the defender's reach on the dribbler will often create contact with the offensive player. This also produces a poor defensive stance because the defender's balance is poor when reaching for the ball.

Deflections

Deflections are a big part of the defensive game. A deflection can be a batted ball, kicked ball, or partially blocked shot (see Blocking Shots on page 111)—anytime the defensive player gets a touch on the ball in any form. To create a deflection, the defender needs to be in the proper defensive position when guarding the offensive player with the ball; the defender should have one hand up in the passing lane and one hand down to stop the dribble. The defender should avoid fouling. Deflections are crucial to the defense because they can disrupt the offense even if a steal does not occur. A deflection is often the result of outstanding hustle by a player; in fact, the coach can define "playing hard" in terms of deflections. Be sure to chart and keep track of deflections throughout a game so you have an idea of how many deflections your team is getting. This will enable you to associate those deflections with playing well or winning the game.

Drawing the Charge

Drawing a charge is a momentum changer and is another great example of the defender playing hard. A charge occurs when an offensive player drives hard into the body of a nonmoving defender. The defender has a right to take the space in front of an offensive player if he gets to that space before the offensive player. When the defender moves into the path of the offensive player (see figure 7.5a), he must establish a set position (see figure 7.5b). If the offensive player fails to stop and runs into the defender, a charge should be called by the officials, and the ball will be rewarded to the defensive team.

FIGURE 7.5   Drawing the charge.

The help-side defender is usually the player in position to take a charge by sliding into the path of the offensive player advancing to the basket. The defender may need to sell the charge to the officials by falling backward and landing on his rear (keeping his hands up as he falls back in order to avoid wrist injuries).

Closing Out

Closing out is an instrumental part of the defensive game. A closeout is simply defined as making the shooter shoot the ball with some defensive pressure. A closeout is performed when the defender comes forward (or from the help side or off her player) to guard the shooter. The defender sprints about two-thirds of the distance to the shooter (see figure 7.6a) and then moves into the shooter by taking short, choppy steps while keeping her hands high and her rear down for a low center of gravity (see figure 7.6b). In this position, the defender is also prepared if the shooter decides to ball fake and then put the ball on the floor to dribble.

FIGURE 7.6   Closing out.

Defenders use two types of closeouts—the long closeout and the short closeout. The difference between these two types relates to how close the defender gets to the player he's guarding. The long closeout should be used on a good shooter; in this case, the defender is trying to get the offensive player to put the ball on the floor rather than shoot. On the long closeout, the defender advances close enough to the shooter to force the shooter to either take a difficult shot or put the ball on the floor. The short closeout is performed when the defender is guarding a player who may be a better driver than shooter. In this instance, the defender does not get as close to the shooter because the defender needs to guard against the drive more than the outside shot.

Blocking Shots

Blocking a shot is when a defensive player jumps up and stops a shot in the air taken by the offensive team. This is a skill that not all players, especially those in younger age groups, should use because a foul is often called on this action if the defensive player cannot execute it properly. The defensive player's size, jumping ability, and the ability to properly time the jump are the main factors in determining the quality of this skill. When going for a block (or a deflection), the defender should maintain the defensive stance until the ball leaves the shooter's hand (see figure 7.7*a*). If the defender jumps too soon, the offensive player can easily draw the foul. When going for the block, the defender should do so with an open hand and work to keep the ball in bounds (see figure 7.7*b*).

FIGURE 7.7   Going for a block.

The best player to block a shot is the player on the help side, not the player guarding the ball. This help-side defender has a much better chance to block the shot because he can more easily time her jump to the release of the ball. This player also has a much better chance of blocking the shot without having a foul called on him.

Defensive Rebounding

When the offensive team shoots the ball, the defensive team will try to gain possession by rebounding the missed shot. The technique for rebounding defensively is similar to offensive rebounding in that the player must always first be in the ready position. When preparing to go for the rebound, the player's hands should be above the shoulders so that the player can achieve maximum height on the jump.

However, for defensive rebounds, players must locate their opponents first (see figure 7.8a), achieve an inside position (see figure 7.8b), and box out their opponent (see figure 7.8c)—using a front or rear pivot to get into a position between their opponent and the basket and putting their rear in contact with the opponent. This is done to ensure that the offensive player is behind the defensive player and so that the defensive player can see the flight of the ball when the shot is taken. A front pivot allows the defensive rebounder to turn while watching the offensive player move toward the rebound. A rear pivot is used to move into the path of the offensive player without the same visual contact. Encourage defenders to use whichever method gets them in position in front of the offense, sealing the offensive player away from the basket. Once contact is established with an opposing player, the defensive rebounder wants to maintain that contact until releasing to jump for the rebound.

For rebounding free throws on defense, you should place your best rebounders in the positions closest to the basket because this is where these rebounds generally go. Defenders should be in a balanced stance with the knees bent; the hands should

FIGURE 7.8 Defensive rebounding.

be held above the waist in anticipation of the missed free throw. As the ball hits the rim, the defenders should step toward the free-throw line to block out the offensive rebounder next to them. You should also designate a player to block out the shooter.

Communication

Communication on the basketball court is an essential part of the game, especially on defense, and you need to address this topic with your team. Communication involves talking to teammates in a positive and helpful manner while the game is being played. Most players have a difficult time communicating while playing. However, communication among teammates helps your team play at a higher intensity level and play harder than they would normally.

Communication on defense is constant. Here are some examples of instances in which communication is key:

- Defensive players should call out "Shot!" when the shooter shoots the ball so that all their teammates know to block out and go for the ball.
- Defenders should call out "Ball!" when guarding the ball on the defensive transition, indicating that the next player should guard the next available offensive player closest to the basket.
- Defensive players should call out "Help!" when they are the help-side defender, offering help to the defender guarding the ball if the offensive player gets around him.
- Defensive players should call out "Screen!" when they are guarding the player setting the screen. This lets everyone (especially the teammate being screened) know that a screen is coming.
- Defenders should call out "Switch," "Slide through," "Double team," or "Go behind" to describe how the screen should be defended.
- Players should call out "Man," "Zone," or "Press" after their team has made a basket and is setting up the defense.

Awareness

Awareness is simply anticipation of what might happen next on the court. Although somewhat intuitive, awareness can be taught and is a great skill for each player to have. Defensively, awareness is thinking about what the offensive team might do next and being prepared for this action. For example, guarding a player on the opposite side of the court from the ball puts a defender in help-side position; being aware of this and taking away the player's path to the ball could lead to a steal or a deflection. In other instances, awareness may also lead to taking a charge, closing out on the shooter, or establishing good rebounding position. As a coach, make sure you stress awareness, citing such examples whenever the opportunity presents itself on the court.

8

Defensive Tactics

Good defensive play inhibits the opponent by limiting the number of uncontested shots. Good defense not only reduces scoring opportunities for the opponent, but also opens them up for your own team. For your team to have an effective defense, your players must use correct defensive *technical* skills as discussed in the previous chapter. In addition, your players must work together with teammates to use sound defensive *tactical* skills based on the game situation.

In this chapter, we focus on several aspects of defensive tactics: coordinating a team defense, playing on and off the ball, playing the post, helping out, defending against screens, cutting off passing lanes, and using specific defenses.

Coordinating a Team Defense

The two main types of defenses played in youth basketball are man-to-man defense and zone defense. In man-to-man defense, the defensive player is responsible for a specific offensive player (see figure 8.1), while at the same time, the player must be alert to situations where he can help his teammates and stop the offensive team from scoring. In zone defense, each defender covers an area instead of a specific offensive player—for example, in the commonly used 2-3 zone, two players cover the wings and high-post area, and three players cover the baseline and middle areas (see figure 8.2). Younger players should primarily be taught man-to-man defense. This type of defense provides players with the basic skills necessary for learning zone defense as they move into older age groups or progress in skill.

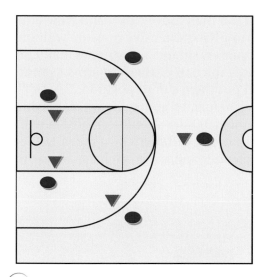

FIGURE 8.1   Man-to-man defense.

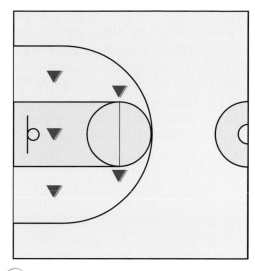

FIGURE 8.2   2-3 zone defense.

Jump Ball Strategies

The defensive jump ball situation can provide your team with a possession if played correctly. If you know that there is little chance to get the tip, then your team must attempt to force the opponent to tip the ball to the tipper's weak side—the side of the court where it would be the most difficult to tip the ball (this would be to the right and to the back for right-handed players). To help do this, you should position a player on each side of the offensive player where the tipper can most easily tip the ball. This will force the tipper to tip the ball at another player in a more difficult position.

Playing On and Off the Ball

When using a man-to-man defense, playing "off the ball" and playing "on the ball" are two basic concepts that your players must be aware of. Certain rules apply when guarding a player with the ball versus guarding players without the ball.

On the Ball

Playing "on the ball" simply refers to defending the offensive player with the ball. When playing on the ball, as the offensive player begins to dribble, the defender should react by sliding the feet and maintaining an arm's distance from the opponent (see figure 8.3a on page 116). The defender should try to beat the offensive player to the spot that the player wants to reach. Moreover, if the defender can get the offensive player to stop and pick up the ball, the defender can then move closer and crowd the offensive player, blocking the passing lanes and applying extensive pressure with the arms (see figure 8.3b). When playing on the ball, players should also strive to maintain focus on the opponent's midsection; if they watch the ball or their opponent's head or feet, they are likely to react to a fake that will put them out of position.

More advanced defenders can focus on four defensive strategies when playing defense on the ball. In each of these strategies, the defender should establish a half-body position against the dribbler in order to dictate the dribbler's next move. Rather than squaring up against his opponent, the defender splits the offensive player in half (see figure 8.4).

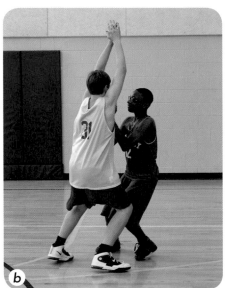

FIGURE 8.3   On-the-ball defense.

FIGURE 8.4   Defensive half-body position.

Turning the dribbler   Defenders who establish a half-body position to either side ahead of the dribbler can force the dribbler to turn or reverse direction. This makes it much more difficult for the dribbler to find an open teammate for the pass because the dribbler is concerned with the defender.

Forcing the dribbler to the sideline   When a defensive player forces the dribbler to dribble toward the sideline, the dribbler can pass in only one direction. A defender can do this by working for position a half body to the inside of the court, with the inside foot (the one closer to the middle of the court) forward and the outside foot back. This technique limits the offensive player to one side of the court and makes the offensive team work much harder to score.

Forcing the dribbler to the middle   By taking position a half body to the outside of the court, a defender can force a dribbler to the middle. This strategy will move the dribbler toward one of the defender's teammates off the ball.

Forcing the dribbler to use the weak hand   By overplaying the strong hand, defenders can force the dribbler to use the weak hand. Defenders can overplay the strong hand by being a half body to the dribbler's strong-hand side.

Off the Ball

Playing "off the ball" simply means guarding an offensive player who does not have the ball. Defending an opponent without the ball is just as important as guarding a player with the ball, but it is a bit more complicated. When playing off the ball, defensive players need to apply the defensive concept of ball-you-man, as shown in figure 8.5, which simply means that a triangle is created between the offensive player with the ball, you (the defender), and the offensive player whom you are guarding.

FIGURE 8.5   Ball-you-man positioning.

Defenders should also position themselves so that they can see the ball (and know if they need to come and help a teammate on a pass or drive), and they must keep track of a moving opponent (their player), who may be trying to get open to receive a pass. The closer an opponent is to the ball, the closer the defender should be to that opponent. The farther the ball is from an opponent, the farther away a defender can play that opponent and be able to give help to the teammate guarding the ball. Defenders must also be able to move quickly as the ball is passed from one offensive player to another and must be able to adjust their position in relationship to the ball and the player they are guarding.

Denial Position

A player should use the denial position when his opponent is one pass away from the ball. The space between two offensive players where a pass can be made is called the *passing lane*. A defender wants to have an arm and leg in the passing lane when guarding a player who is one pass away (see figure 8.6). This denial position allows the defender to establish the ball-you-man relationship and discourages the offensive player with the ball from attempting a pass.

FIGURE 8.6   Denial position.

Open Position

When offensive players are two or more passes away from the ball, the defensive player wants to establish an open position that still maintains the ball-you-man relationship. In the open position, the defender points to the ball with one hand and to the opponent with the other hand (see figure 8.7). Using peripheral vision, the defender moves to react as the ball penetrates toward the basket (to help out on the drive) or moves into denial position if the offensive player cuts hard to receive a pass.

FIGURE 8.7 Open position.

Defensive Techniques On and Off the Ball

Players must remember that court position and defensive stance are two of the most important techniques when playing defense regardless of whether the player they are guarding has the ball. However, there are some things that your players should be aware of and should ask themselves when they are playing specifically on or off the ball.

On the Ball

- Am I in ready position and alert?
- Am I an arm's distance from my player (the ball handler) and able to put pressure on his ability to shoot, pass, or drive?
- Is my player close enough to attempt a good shot?
- Am I close enough to the player to prevent an easy shot?
- Am I too close, so the opponent can drive around me?
- Will a teammate be able to help me if the player beats me with the dribble?

Off the Ball

- Am I in proper position on the help side so that I can see both the ball and the player I am guarding?
- Is my player in a position to cut to the ball side and receive a pass?
- Can I get to my player if the ball is passed to him for a shot?
- Am I too close, so the opponent can make a cut to the ball?
- Am I in proper position so I can help my teammate guarding the offensive player with the ball in case he attempts to drive to the basket?

119

Playing the Post

The post area refers to anywhere in the free-throw lane area; the high post is the area near the free-throw line, the mid post is the area halfway down the lane, and the low post is the area located closest to the basket. Playing defense in the post area is different than playing defense on the perimeter (the area outside the lane). The defense will usually try to keep the ball out of the post area because it is much easier for the offensive team to score in this area. Players should defend the post offensive player based on her position and her ability. The first method is to front the offensive post player to completely deny the pass into the offensive post (see figure 8.8*a*). To do this correctly, the help-side defensive player must be in a position to stop the lob pass over the defensive player who is in the fronting position. The second method is to play directly behind the post player (see figure 8.8*b*). This method will allow the ball to be thrown into the post player but is intended to prevent that player from getting a shot in front of the basket. This is the best method to use when the offensive post player is not a good turnaround shooter, and it is an effective method for blocking out the offensive player. The third way is to play on one side or the other of the offensive player in a partial fronting position (see figure 8.8*c*). This will keep the ball from entering the post and still allow a good position for boxing out.

Helping Out

No matter how well your players position themselves on the court and communicate with each other on defense, an offensive player will at times be open. When this occurs, your players must know how to respond based on what kind of help is needed, and each player must be in a position to help when and where needed. For example, if one of your players spots an opponent wide open under the basket waving for a teammate to pass the ball, that defender should leave an assigned opponent who is farther from the basket and sprint to try to prevent the pass. On the other hand, if a dribbler gets by a defender and is headed for a layup, the defensive player closest to the dribbler between the dribbler and the basket should immediately move in to cut off the lane to the hoop. This can cause the offensive player to commit a charging foul, throw the ball away, or travel. The most important thing for defenders to know is where the ball is located so they can be in a position to help stop the ball, if needed. Whatever the case, the defender who has been beaten, or who loses an offensive player and sees that recovery is impossible, should shout, "Help!" All four teammates should be ready to respond if you have effectively taught them this very important defensive tactic.

On a related note, each player must also know how to properly cover gaps in the defense. Everywhere on the floor, whether it be a man-to-man defense or a zone defense, there are gaps—spaces between two defensive players—that must be covered by the defense. A good offense will try to dribble the ball in those gaps. The defenders must react quickly to this and cover the gaps by sliding the feet and trying to take the charge on the dribbler or causing a turnover.

FIGURE 8.8 Defending the post: (a) denying, (b) playing behind, and (c) partially fronting.

Defending Against Screens

A screen is used by an offensive player to free up a teammate by obstructing the path of the defender. Screens can be used on defenders playing on the ball or on defenders who are guarding an offensive player away from the ball. Defensive players must be able to defend the screening action in order to stop a score. Three ways to defend against a screen are to fight over the top of the screen, to slide behind it, and to switch.

> **COACHING TIP** Players need to communicate and help one another when defending against screens. The defender on the opponent who is setting the screen must alert the defender being screened by calling out the direction of the screen: "Screen right!" or "Screen left!"

Fight Over the Top

A player should fight over the top of a screen when there is room for the defender to get between the screener and the screener's teammate (see figure 8.9). The defender whom the screen was set on should let the teammate guarding the screener know to stay with that opponent by shouting, "Through!" or "Over!" The defender being screened should work to get through the screen by first getting a foot over the screen and then the remainder of the body.

Slide Behind

Sliding behind the screen should be used when guarding a poor shooter or a quick driver, or when the screen is set too far away from the basket for the offensive player to shoot the ball. When an opponent sets a screen on a player guarding a quick driver or when the action is outside the opponent's shooting range, the player being screened should slide behind the screen by moving under the opponent on the basket side, rather than on top (see figure 8.10).

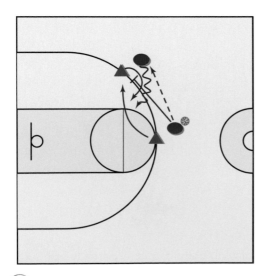

FIGURE 8.9 Fighting over the top of a screen.

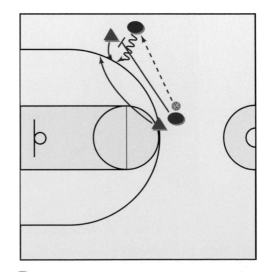

FIGURE 8.10 Sliding behind a screen.

Switch

When teammates are of equal size and defensive ability, the easiest defensive move against a screen is to switch opponents. As the offensive player dribbles around the screen, the defender guarding the screener will switch to guarding the dribbler, and the defender guarding the dribbler will now guard the screener (see figure 8.11). This is the best method for stopping the dribbler from going to the basket; however, it does open up the court for the pass to the screener. If size and defensive ability differ, switching should be the last option because it allows the offense to take advantage of a mismatch. Players who switch should call out the screen by yelling, "Switch!" As players switch, one player must aggressively get in position to deny a pass to the cutter (the screener who rolls to the basket) while the other player gets in position on the ball side of the screener.

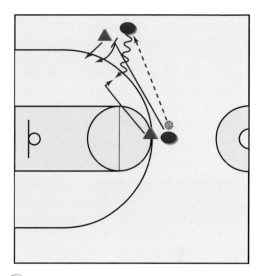

FIGURE 8.11   Switching on a screen.

Switching Defenses

Although teams typically play either a standard man-to-man or zone defense (described on page 114) throughout a game, switching your defense is a good way to cause some problems for the opponent's offense. For example, if the offense has a certain rhythm going against your man-to-man defense, you may want to change what you are doing defensively. This may mean changing to a zone defense or a press (see Pressing Defenses below) in an attempt to take the offense out of their rhythm against your man-to-man defense. Or it may mean doing something different against the screens that the offense sets. For example, you may want to try using a double team on all screens instead of switching on screens, because this will be something that the offense may not be ready to play against. Or you might change the way your defenders are guarding the players in the post or at the wings. Fronting the post players to prevent the quick pass inside or denying the pass to the wings may disrupt the offense. All of these adjustments can be made without too much difficulty and without causing too much confusion for your players.

Pressing Defenses

Regardless of the type of defensive team you are coaching, you must have some type of pressing defense available in case your team is behind in the late stages of a game and needs to force the action in an effort to score some quick points. Pressing defenses are usually a gamble; they involve using traps to disrupt the offense and steal the ball. Many times the press will not lead to steals immediately, but if given a chance to work, over time the press will have some effect on the offense. Depending on your personnel, some pressing defenses that you may choose to run include the following:

- **1-2-1-1 or diamond zone press.** This is a full-court press with one player on the ball, one player at each free-throw elbow, one player at midcourt, and one player back in the opposite lane. The player on the ball and a player at one elbow will set a trap when the ball is inbounded.

- **Man-to-man press.** This is a man-to-man defense starting in the full court; each player guards his offensive player from one end to the other.

- **Various types of three-quarter and half-court presses.** For example, the 1-2-1-1 can be condensed to three-quarter court; the player on the ball moves back to the top of the key, the two players at the elbows move back to the half-court line, and so on. A 2-2-1 three-quarter zone press—with two players at the free-throw elbows, two players at half-court, and one player back in the opposite lane—can also be quite useful. In this zone press, traps occur at the half-court sidelines and corner baselines. Finally, an example of a half-court zone press is the 1-3-1, with one player at half-court, three players along the free-throw line and free-throw line extended, and one player in the lane.

The best strategy is to choose one type of press for your team rather than try to teach too many presses. If you have a shorter, quicker team, the diamond press or a full-court man press should be a good fit for your players' abilities. If you have a slower team, you may want to use a three-quarter zone press that is less of a gamble, such as a 2-2-1 or a 1-2-2. The 2-2-1 is one of the more common presses used at the youth level (see figure 8.12).

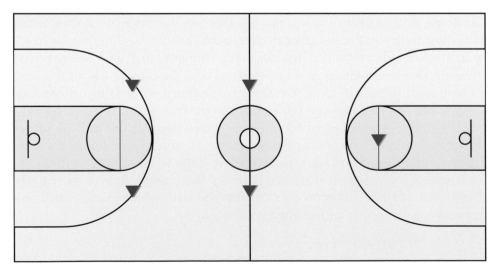

FIGURE 8.12 The 2-2-1 three-quarter zone press.

Defense in Special Situations

Defending special situations such as out-of-bounds plays is something that your team needs to learn and practice. Using a zone defense to defend the out-of-bounds play is usually the best strategy because it helps defenders avoid being caught off guard by multiple screens set by the offense. If the ball is taken out of bounds on the side, your regular defense may be the best route; however, you must ensure that your players communicate screens and always know where the inbounder is located when the ball is taken out of bounds underneath the basket or on the sideline. Defenders sometimes forget about the inbounder, and this player is often left open after inbounding the ball.

Another special situation that a team should be prepared for is when the offense goes into a delay game. In this situation, the defense should know when to foul in order to stop the clock and how to double-team the ball at any place on the court. Communication on the floor is imperative so that all defenders know what to do in such situations.

9

Defensive Drills

Defensive drills are the basis for developing a good defensive team. Defense is the one skill that will remain constant during a game, regardless of whether that game is on the road or at home. Defense is not dependent on the ball going through the basket—rather, defense depends on the effort of each player. The foundation for good defense is the defensive stance and slide, which should be worked on daily. As you progress with your team, two-on-two, three-on-three, and four-on-four drills can be used to bring the defense together in team defense situations.

For access to some of these drills online, visit the following website: www.Human Kinetics.com/CoachingYouthBasketball5E-DefensiveDrills. Such drills are indicated by this symbol in the outside margin of the text:

Additional defensive drills are provided in chapters 10 to 14; refer to the practice sessions there for even more options.

➤ DEFENSIVE SLIDE, SIDELINE TO SIDELINE

Goal   To learn how to slide effectively in a defensive stance.

Description   Players line up perpendicular to the sideline, and on the coach's command, they assume the basic defensive stance and use slides to move across the floor. Players' arms are held out wide, and the players slap the floor on each slide to help emphasize staying low. Once all players have reached the opposite sideline, repeat the drill. Continue for three to seven minutes, depending on the age group.

Points of emphasis include pointing the foot in the direction of the slide (for example, when sliding to the right, the right foot should be pointed to the opposite sideline), moving the foot that is closer to the direction of the slide first (for example, when sliding to the right, the right foot should move first), and making the first step a big step.

Variations

- Start with only one or two slides so players get the idea of how to execute a proper slide.
- Work on the defensive slides while incorporating a slide-run-slide technique.

➤ DEFENDING SHOTS

Goal   To learn the best method for putting pressure on the shooter.

Description   Players divide into two groups and line up at the baseline at one end of the court. The first player in one line has a ball, and on the coach's command, this player dribbles to the basket at the opposite end of the court while the first player in the other line defends him. (The coach designates what type of shot will be taken.) When the player with the ball takes a shot, the defender uses proper technique to block or deflect the shot. The defender rebounds the ball, and both players jog back up the court along the sidelines. The defender gives the ball to the first player in his original line, and both players take a place at the end of their original lines. Repeat until all players have had a turn at defending the shot.

Variations

- Begin the drill at half-court.
- Add crossover dribbles so the defender also works on drop-stepping against the dribbler before the shot is taken.

DEFENSIVE SKILLS

➤ DEFENDING THE DRIBBLE

Goal   To learn to defend a dribbler in a full-court situation.

Description   Players divide into two groups and line up at the baseline at one end of the court. One player has the ball and acts as the offensive player, and the other player acts as the defender. The offensive player moves down the court in a zigzag pattern, using the sidelines as boundaries. The player dribbles the ball at half speed so that the defender can practice the proper mechanics of guarding. Once players reach the opposite baseline, the offensive player rolls the ball back to the next player in line, and two more players move down the court. Repeat until all players have had a turn.

Throughout the drill, the defender must keep his head lower than the offensive player's shoulders. Also, the defender's hand on the same side as his lead foot should be down to discourage the crossover; the other hand should be above his waist to defend the passing lanes.

Variations
- Have players switch offensive and defensive positions at half-court.
- Keep track of the number of times the defender can make the offensive dribbler change directions.

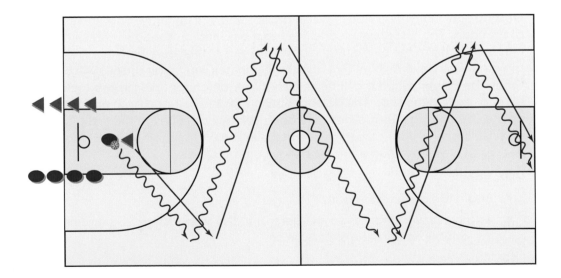

➤ DEFENSIVE REBOUNDING

Goal To learn the technique for blocking out against an offensive player.

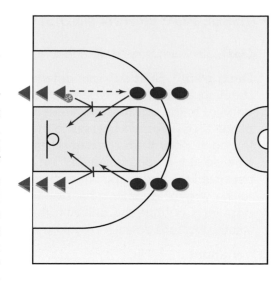

Description Players divide into four groups; two groups are positioned at the baseline on both sides of the basket, and the other two groups are positioned at the free-throw line directly in front of the other lines. The first player in one of the lines under the basket has a ball and passes it to the first player in the line directly in front of him. This player shoots the ball; then, the shooter and the first player in the other line at the free-throw line both go for the rebound. The first two players in the lines at the baseline act as defensive rebounders; they screen out and go for the ball. After the rebound is secured, the ball is returned to the line along the baseline where the drill was originally started, and all players take a position at the end of their lines. Repeat until all players have had a turn at defensive rebounding.

Variations

- To increase the focus on learning proper technique, start with just two groups, one line on the baseline and one line at the free-throw line.
- Allow the offensive players to take one dribble right or left before the shot.

➤ FOUR-ON-FOUR BLOCKOUT

Goal To learn how to block out both on the ball and away from the shooter.

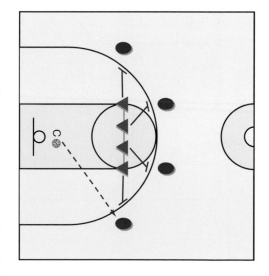

Description Four defenders huddle at the free-throw line with their hands draped over one another's shoulders. Four offensive players—two guards and two wings—are positioned on the court within shooting range. On a count of "1, 2, 3," the defenders yell "Box out!" three times for emphasis. The coach passes the ball to one of the offensive players, who immediately takes a shot. The defenders then concentrate only on blocking out and getting the rebound. The sequence is then repeated. After a designated amount of time, offense and defense switch.

Variations

- Start with two-on-two, then three-on-three, before finally moving to four-on-four.
- Allow the offensive players to take one dribble right or left before the shot.

➤ THREE-PLAYER RUN AND SLIDE

Goal   To learn how to defend a quicker player who is dribbling the ball.

Description   Start with one defensive player guarding one offensive player at the baseline; a third player is positioned on the ball side of the rim. The offensive player dribbles to the sideline, and the defender slides to cut the dribbler off. The offensive player then pivots and passes to the third player, who is a step behind the passer at this point. After the ball is passed, the new ball handler dribbles hard to the opposite sideline at a 45-degree angle. The defender turns and sprints to get in front of this new dribbler at the opposite sideline. At this point, the new dribbler passes back to the original dribbler, who is on the ball side of the rim and one step behind the dribbler. Continue the drill with the same defender for four sideline cutoffs; then rotate positions so each player has an opportunity to be the defender.

Variations

- Begin with just a one-on-one situation in which the dribbler dribbles hard to the opposite sideline and the defender must run and slide to catch the offensive dribbler.
- Once the dribbler has reached half-court, have the offensive player try to score a basket.

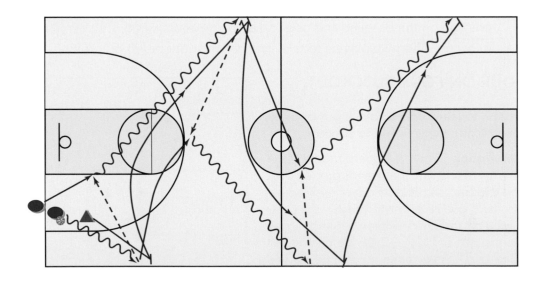

➤ FOUR-PLAYER RUN AND TRAP

Goal   To learn to trap the dribbler.

Description   Start with one defensive player guarding one offensive player at the baseline; a second offensive player and his defender are positioned on the ball side of the rim. The offensive player dribbles to the sideline, and his defender slides to cut the dribbler off. At this point, the second defender leaves his own opponent to trap the dribbler. The offensive player pivots and attempts to break the trap by passing to his teammate, who is a step behind the passer at this point. After the ball is passed, the new ball handler dribbles hard to the opposite sideline at a 45-degree angle. The defenders turn and sprint to get in front of and trap this new dribbler at the opposite sideline. At this point, the new dribbler passes back to the original dribbler, who is on the ball side of the rim and one step behind the dribbler. The drill continues with the same defenders for four sideline traps. Each player should have a turn on defense to work on the trap.

Variations

- Work on the trap in a two-on-one situation with two defenders trapping one offensive player on the sideline.
- Once the ball has crossed the half-court line, have the two offensive players try to score against the two defensive players.

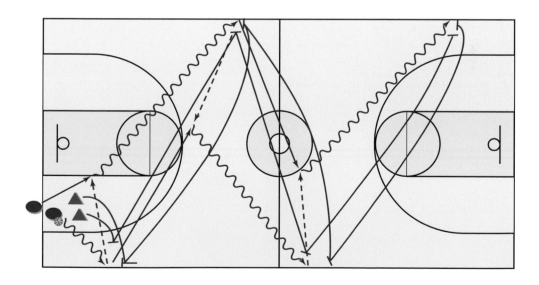

➤ CHAMPIONS

Goal   To learn to close out on the shooter from the help position.

Description   One defensive player starts in good help-side position at the elbow (the gap) with an offensive player on the wing. The coach has the ball at the top of the key. The coach passes to the wing, and the defensive player closes out. The wing passes the ball back to the coach, and the defensive player reacts by jumping back to the gap at the elbow *(a)*. The coach then dribbles to the wing as the offensive player cuts to the block. The defensive player denies and then fronts the offensive player when the ball is on the wing. The coach then reverses the ball to a new player who has stepped in at the top of the key. As the ball is reversed, the defensive player jumps out and up to deny it to the post *(b)*. The offense should make these passes from the top of the key to the wing, and so on, a couple of times until the coach slaps the ball; then the offensive player on the block sprints to the opposite wing as the player at the top of the key steps back out of the drill. The defensive player stays on the help side until the coach skips the ball to the opposite wing. At this point, the defensive player closes out on the player who receives the ball *(c)*. The coach and the opposite wing pass back and forth a couple times as the defender adjusts until the coach slaps the ball once more; then the offensive player on the wing cuts to the middle of the lane and up to the top of the key. The defensive player denies the offensive player cutting *(d)*. When the coach throws the ball to the offensive player at the top of the key, the drill becomes a live one-on-one. The defensive player must close out on the opponent and work to contain and contest the shot.

Variations

- Perform this drill in segments before putting all the defensive techniques together.
- Make this a live drill throughout.

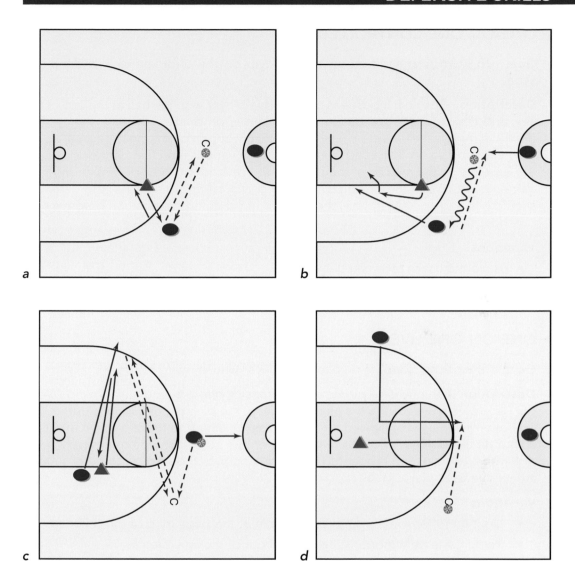

a

b

c

d

➤ ONE-ON-ONE CONTROLLED

Goal   To learn to defend an offensive player on the dribble and in a dead-ball situation.

Description   The coach poses as an offensive player with the ball at the top of the key, and the defender guards the coach in an appropriate defensive stance. The defender mirrors the basketball while the coach sweeps it below the kneecaps, above the head, and so on. The coach then dribbles in various directions (for example, to the baseline or the middle of the floor) as the defender makes defensive slides at game speed. When the defender cuts the coach off at the sideline, the defender should once again trace (follow) the ball in a good defensive position before a new defender takes his place.

Variations
- Have the coach take one dribble only.
- Replace the coach at the top of the key with another player, who will try to score against the defender.

➤ ONE-ON-ONE LIVE

Goal   To work on stopping an offensive player who is trying to score.

Description   An offensive player and a defensive player set up at one wing. When the defensive player hands the offensive player the ball, the drill is considered live. The offensive player is allowed three dribbles maximum to make a move and take a shot as the defender tries to make a defensive stop. The defender finishes the drill with a box-out and rebound. The offensive player then moves to defense, and a new offensive player steps in.

Variations
- Limit the offensive player to one dribble at the beginning of the drill.
- Require the defender to keep the ball out of the lane area.

➤ ONE-ON-ONE LIVE FROM CLOSEOUT

Goal   To learn to close out and then stop the dribbler from reaching the basket.

Description   An offensive player and a defensive player begin on the court. The defensive player begins with the ball on the block in front of the rim. He passes the ball to the offensive player at the elbow to start the drill. On the pass, the defender breaks down (moves into good defensive position) and closes out on his opponent. On the catch, the offensive player is looking to score. He is allowed two dribbles maximum to make a move and take a shot as the defender tries to make a defensive stop. The defender finishes the drill with a box-out and rebound.

Variations
- Limit the offensive player to no dribbles or one dribble at the beginning of the drill.
- Allow the offensive player to take up to three dribbles to score.

➤ ONE-ON-ONE LIVE FROM CLOSEOUT IN HELP POSITION

Goal To learn how to close out on the shooter when guarding another player.

Description Along with the coach, an offensive player and a defensive player begin on the court. The defensive player is in the help position at the elbow. The offensive player is at the top of the key. The coach has the ball on the wing. (Note that the offensive player could instead be on the wing, and the coach with the ball could be at the top of the key.) On the pass from the coach to the offensive player, the defender must close out against the offensive player while staying low. On the catch, the two opponents play one-on-one. The defender ends the drill with a box-out and rebound.

Variations

- Limit the offensive player to no dribbles or one dribble, or limit the offensive player to dribbling either to the right or to the left.
- Allow the offensive player to use unlimited dribble options and let her go either direction with the dribble.

➤ TWO-ON-TWO

Goal To learn ball-side and help-side responsibility.

Description One offensive player is positioned at the top of the key, and one offensive player is positioned on the wing. A defender will guard each player. When the ball is at the top of the key, one defender is on the ball, and the help defender guarding the wing is at the elbow. At this point, play becomes live. As the offense moves the ball, the defenders must keep them from scoring. If the offense scores, defenders will run a down-and-back.

Variations

- Limit the number of dribbles by the offense, or restrict the movement of the offensive players.
- Allow the offensive players to take multiple dribbles and make movements to any location on the court.

➤ THREE-ON-THREE

Goal To work with two other defenders in a three-on-three situation to stop the offense from scoring.

Description The coach starts with the ball under the basket. Three offensive players set up around the perimeter (two at the wings and one at the top of the key). Three defensive players begin in the lane. On the coach's pass out to the offense, one defender closes out on the ball, and the other two go to their help-side positioning (a). From here, the defense practices reacting to the following:

1. **Weak-side interchange.** From the top of the key, the ball is passed to the wing. The offensive players at the top of the key and the wing opposite the ball will interchange (switch positions), and the two defensive players must rotate to their help positions (b).

2. **Paint touches.** From the top of the key, the ball is passed to the wing. The offensive players then try to break down the defense by cutting into the lane (c) or by driving the ball baseline past the defenders. The defense must adjust to all passes, drives, and cuts accordingly.

3. **Baseline rotations.** From the top of the key, the ball is passed to the wing. The offensive player on the wing catches the ball, sweeping it from one side to the other. The weak-side defender must rotate outside of the lane and cut the dribble off as the defender at the top of the key drops to the hole (d). On a skip pass from the dribbler out to the offensive player on the opposite side of the court, the player who rotated over will stay with the ball. The player in the hole defends the first pass out, and the defender who was guarding the ball rotates to the next available offensive player.

4. **Baseline rotations with weak-side interchange.** From the top of the key, the ball is passed to the wing. The two offensive players on the weak side (away from the ball) exchange positions. The defenders must be in position to stay with their offensive players as they exchange places but must also be in position to stop the baseline drive that may occur on the ball side of the floor (e).

Variations

- Teach one part of the drill to the players before adding the other parts.
- Add this rule to the drill: When the coach says "Live," the offensive players can make any moves to try to score against the defenders in a three-on-three situation.

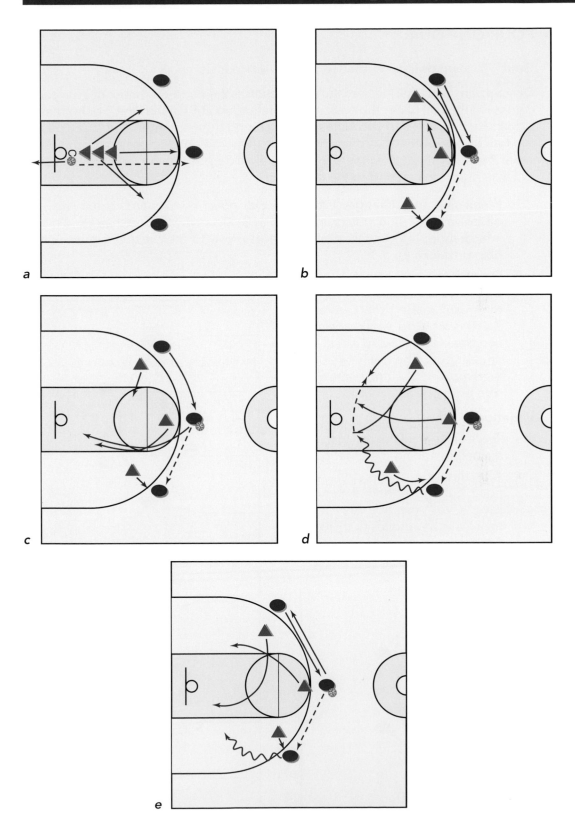

➤ FOUR-ON-FOUR

Goal   To learn defensive rotation in a four-on-four situation.

Description   This drill involves the same action as the three-on-three drill. The coach starts with the ball under the basket. Four defenders start in the lane. Four offensive players, two guards and two wings, set up around the perimeter. The coach passes the ball to one of the four offensive players. One defender closes out on the ball while the other three defenders move to help-side positioning (a). From here, the defense practices reacting to the following:

1. **Weak-side interchange.** When the ball goes from guard to forward, the offensive weak-side guard and weak-side forward will interchange. On that interchange, the defensive players must move to their respective weak-side help positions (b).

2. **Defend the basket cut.** When the ball goes from guard to forward, the guard making the pass cuts to the basket. The weak-side guard and weak-side forward rotate to the empty spots. The defensive players then move to their respective help-side positions (c).

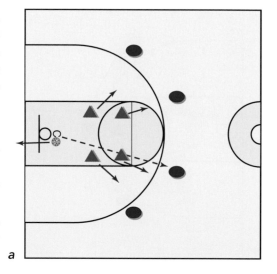

Variations

- Teach one part of the drill to the players before adding the other parts.

- Add this rule to the drill: At any point during the drill, if the coach says "Live," the offensive players may make any moves to try to score against the defenders.

a

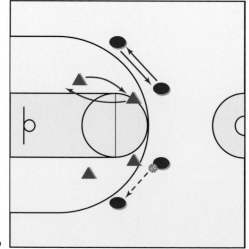

b

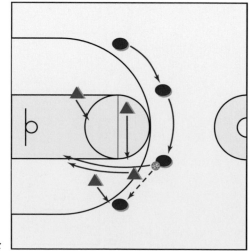

c

➤ HELPING HANDS

Goal   To provide help for a teammate.

Description   Play 3v3. Tape off a 3-foot-by-3-foot area about 15 to 20 feet from the basket from any angle on the court. This area is the "freeze zone"—that is, when a defender enters this zone, the defender must freeze. Instruct the offense to dribble so that the player guarding the dribbler enters the freeze zone. When this happens, the dribbler should dribble toward the basket (the other offensive players should not be clustered around this freeze zone or in the dribbler's path), and the "frozen" defender should call, "Help!" The teammate nearest to this defender should respond appropriately, trying to cut off the dribbler and defend against passes to the dribbler's teammates. If the defense successfully provides help, it gets one point.

   Note: If help is not provided well but the offense misses its shot, the defense does not get a point. Successful help means cutting off the dribbler and not allowing an easy scoring opportunity.

Variations

- To make the game easier, play 3v4 or make the freeze zone farther away from the basket.
- To make the game more challenging, eliminate the freeze zone.

➤ CUTTING OFF

Goal   To defend against screens.

Description   Play 2v2, 3v3, or 4v4. The offense must use screens in setting up plays. If the defense defends well against a screen (that is, no advantage is gained), the defense is awarded one point. If the offense gains an advantage on the screen, the defense loses one point. If the offense scores directly off the screen, the defense loses two points. A play ends after the screen is set (the offense can shoot directly off the screen). From that point, the play is reset, and the offense begins again. After five plays, switch sides.

Variations

- To make the game easier, play 2v3 or 3v4, or allow defenders to call out "Switch!" and then switch players on screens.
- To make the game more difficult, require defenders to fight through or slide behind screens—no switching.

➤ NO PASSING ZONE

Goal   To cut off passing lanes and intercept passes.

Description   Play 3v3. The defense tries to cut off the passing lanes and intercept the ball. Each player on offense can dribble no more than three times before passing. Offensive players move to open spaces to receive passes and then look to hit open teammates with passes. The offense controls the ball for one minute. Then the teams switch sides. Within each one-minute period, the defense returns the ball to the offense if the defense steals it. Each steal counts for one point. Give each team five one-minute periods on defense.

Variations
- To make the game easier, play 3v4 or don't use dribbling.
- To make the game more difficult, play 4v3.

➤ PICKING POCKETS

Goal   To create turnovers by stealing the ball.

Description   Play 3v4 or 2v3 in either the full or half court depending on the age group. The offense must complete four passes before attempting to shoot. The defense must use their defensive positioning to force a turnover or steal. Award two points to the defense for each turnover. As an option, you may also award one point for any of the following: forcing a dribbler to a sideline, funneling a dribbler to the middle (assuming defensive teammates are in the middle to help out), or forcing a dribbler to use the weak hand. Switch offense and defense after five minutes of play.

Variations
- To make the game easier, play 3v5 or 2v4.
- To make the game more difficult, play 3v3 or 4v4.

➤ SCRAMBLE

Goal   To quickly find an offensive player when the team moves from offense to defense.

Description   This drill starts with two offensive guards and two offensive wings spread out along the perimeter against their defenders. The ball is passed around the perimeter, and the defensive players adjust accordingly in their help-side positioning. The coach then blows a whistle, and whoever has the ball places it on the floor. At this point, the defensive players move out to the offensive positions, and the offensive players move to defense. The new defensive players need to guard someone on the opposite side of the floor. When the ball is picked up, the offense makes one more pass; then the drill becomes a live four-on-four drill.

Variations
- Start with a 2v2 and build the drill to a 4v4. You can also limit how many times the offense can dribble when they move from defense to offense.
- Allow unlimited dribbling as soon as the ball goes from defense to offense.

Practicing

Part III

The practice time you spend with your team is the most important time for you and your players. Practice should be fun for the players as well as the coaches. When you step into the practice area, you should know the answers to these questions: (1) What am I going to teach? (2) How am I going to teach it? and (3) Why am I going to teach it? Each practice should have little wasted time; the coach should move quickly from one part to the next. No part of the practice schedule should last any longer than 10 minutes. Practices should go quickly; you will find that the players stay interested in each practice session if they are kept busy and moving.

Warming Up

Warm-ups are extremely important in reducing injuries and allowing the muscles to be ready for more strenuous competition. The warm-up should take approximately 10 to 15 minutes at the start of each practice and should include both stretching and conditioning. The ball can be used in the warm-up to help players develop skills such as dribbling and passing. Have players start at one baseline and perform various warm-up drills (both passing and dribbling related) while moving from one baseline to the other and back again. Stretching can be mixed in on the baselines as players wait their turns.

Drill Work

In each practice session, you should emphasize a few skills and then drill on these skills. The drill work needs to be an extension of your offense and defense; try to develop drills that directly develop parts of your offenses and defenses in addition to individual skills.

Keep in mind the whole–part–whole theory when teaching a new offense or defense. The whole–part–whole method of teaching involves showing and demonstrating the basketball skill and then breaking down the whole into parts for teaching. After teaching the parts of the skill, the coach puts the entire whole back together. The advantage of the whole–part–whole method is that the players will see what they are working toward first. This will make the broken-down drills more effective because the players will already know how the drill fits in with the big picture.

Here are some key points to consider when it comes to preparing and executing drills:

- Make sure every drill has a name.
- Make sure every drill is timed.
- Build a portfolio of drills that specifically relate to your system of play and fundamental concepts.
- Occasionally ask yourself these questions: (1) Why do we do this drill? (2) How often do we do this drill? and (3) Are we receiving the desired results?
- Sell the value of drill work to your players. Most players do not like drills, viewing them as conditioning.

- Vary the use of drills to protect against boredom; the biggest challenge for players during drill work is to consistently concentrate on performance.
- Remember that coaches are teachers, and drill work requires constant teaching.
- Stress enthusiasm. Be a vocal coach, letting players know that you are watching every drill.
- Remember your responsibilities during drill work: to teach, to motivate, and to discipline (not punishing, but stressing correctness and concentration).
- Be sure to balance criticism with praise—praising at least twice for every one criticism.
- Keep in mind that two of the most neglected aspects of drill work are passing and cutting.
- Try to place every drill at the most advantageous time during the practice period.
- Always introduce new drills early in the practice period—when player concentration levels are still high.
- Make sure that physically difficult drills are followed by more fun drills and vice versa.
- Include drill stations; stations allow for more variety (while maintaining emphasis on the same subject matter), protect against monotony, leave fewer players standing around, and give assistant coaches the opportunity to teach.
- For teaching purposes, use small, carefully organized groups of three to five players in each drill.
- Remember that each player will not require the same amount of work or attention on each fundamental in a drill.
- Guard against ending practice with a drill that causes the players to feel as if they are being punished. Instead, end each practice with a drill that players enjoy so that players (and coaches) leave practice with a positive feeling.

Short-Sided Games

Short-sided games are games or drills involving players in situations other than five on five. These are games that break down the offense or defense so players can work on related skills. By using a short-sided game, the coach places the players into a gamelike drill that will help them develop their skills while making the learning fun and second nature (in most cases, short-sided games will be the "part" method of teaching before a whole offense or defense is again worked on in a five-on-five setting).

Short-sided games can also be very valuable in developing the skills of younger players. The players will focus on winning the short-sided game and working with their teammates without thinking too much about the individual skills being used. This is a great opportunity for you to stop the game during a dead-ball situation and explain why a team or player has succeeded by using a skill you've recently taught.

Cooling Down

Every practice should end with cool-down drills that are competitive in nature. These drills should leave the players with a positive feeling about practice and make them want to come back to the next practice. Cool-down drills can include free-throw shooting drills, shooting contests from various spots, and stretching. This is also a time for team bonding, where you may ask players to cheer for one another during a competition. The cool-down may also provide a chance for the coach to visit with individual players (for example, while stretching).

Creating Practice Schedules

Practice schedules are extremely important because they allow the coach to be well organized within each practice session. As a coach, you should first make a list of everything that you want to cover with your team during the year, such as offenses, defenses, out-of-bounds plays, and special situations. You should then create practice schedules containing drills that will be used to develop each of these main parts of the game.

In each practice, remember to stick to your practice schedule. The drills need to stay between 5 to 10 minutes in length; regardless of how the drill is going for the players, move on to the next drill when the time is up according to the practice schedule. If a drill is not going well, don't extend the time for the drill. Review why it did not go well and then perhaps use it again in another practice. Maybe the drill was too complicated for players in your team's age group and you need to adjust the drill for their skill level. You may be tempted to continue working on a drill when it is not going well, but most of the time, the longer you spend on the drill, the worse it gets. The same may happen if a drill is going extremely well.

Practice schedules also give the players the idea that you are very organized and know how to prepare them for competition. This can add to their respect and admiration for you as a coach and teacher.

Coaching in the Practice Setting

Coaching during practices can be intense and stressful for both the coach and players. The coach should try to make each practice as stress free as possible so the players can play a relaxed and confident game. As a coach and teacher, you should remember to

- tell the players what you want,
- show the players what you want (diagram),
- demonstrate to the players what you want (drill),
- clean up the demonstration, and
- use repetition with competition.

Most players will listen to you for only a short period of time, so keep your comments short—preferably a minute or less. Teaching in sound bites, or short phrases, is better than giving long-winded speeches that cause players to lose interest and stand around too long.

If you keep your tone positive when instructing the players, they will react to you in a much better way. Also, try to give feedback as soon as possible to a player. This enables you to provide proper teaching of the skill, and the player can make the adjustments immediately. Finally, don't forget to let your players know when they have done something right.

The following chapters provide practice plans for each age group (5 and 6, 7 and 8, 9 and 10, 11 and 12, and 13 and 14), including one early-season practice, three midseason practices, and one late-season practice. Note that these practice plans are examples only. As a coach, you should put together the practice plan that works best for your team.

10

Practices for Ages 5 and 6

For players who are 5 or 6 years old, basketball is a new activity. Players who are this young often know the sport of basketball through parents, siblings, friends, or media but usually have no idea about any of the skills involved in playing the game. When coaching this age group, your main goal is to establish that basketball is a fun game to play.

Coaching this age group takes a lot of patience and repetition. Patience involves allowing the young players to have fun in a slightly structured atmosphere. You want your young players to have a desire to come back to practice, and over the course of the season, you want them to develop a passion for the game and to continue to improve their skills. Remember that raising your voice or punishing the players by making them do sprints or push-ups will not help them develop a good attitude for the game.

Practice sessions should be no more than an hour and a half and preferably an hour or less. You should change drills every 5 to 10 minutes so the players can keep on task. The biggest challenge with this age group is keeping the players interested and focused while working on a skill. Children this age love competition in drills—for example, counting the number of dribbles they can do in a minute with each hand or the number of times their team can dribble around a cone and back. Be innovative with the players in order to hold their attention and make practice fun.

A variety of skill levels will exist in this age group, and your practice plans should take these differences into account. For example, practices should always include both beginner and advanced skills, and players should be divided into groups according to their skill levels for certain drills. Players who are not as skilled may decide to pout or sit out of a drill because they don't think they are any good or not as good as another player. The coach will need to use some psychology to coax these players back into the drill. Always be positive with these young players, because they need to feel good about their development on the court and with their friends. Do not tolerate any bullying behavior on your team.

Remember to have fun with these players!

Considerations When Coaching Females
Annie Byrne, Marian Catholic High School girls' basketball coach

Coaching 5- and 6-year-old girls requires patience and understanding. The coach must have the patience to teach the fundamentals in a way that these players can relate to. The coach must also understand that most activities that girls participate in at this age are for fun. When attempting to teach the basics of basketball to 5- or 6-year-old girls, a coach will want to develop a practice plan that includes work on the fundamentals and defensive drills; however, practices should also include a lot of fun and enthusiasm while outlining the principles for the youngsters. This is a very rewarding age to coach because the players' progress is so evident and the players show a lot of excitement in their progress. Players will have plenty of energy, so one of your tasks will be to manage that energy while keeping attention. Scores of games are often low, and when someone scores, you may find that everyone claps. This is part of the learning process. Enjoy it. As the players get older, they will need a base to build on, and you are a key component in the beginning stages. Keep in mind, the more fun the players are having, the more they will want to continue to learn and continue to participate in basketball. Teach them in ways they will enjoy. At this age, the more the players enjoy what they are doing, the more you will be able to teach them.

5-6 years old

Early-Season Practices

Early-season practice sessions should establish that basketball is a fun game. Limit the time for each drill to 10 minutes or less. Try to keep players moving during drills and moving from one drill to another, allowing time for them to get a drink between drills.

Early-Season Practice Plan

Date: _____   Time: _____   Practice number: _____

Warm-Up (10 minutes)
Warm-up time should involve activities such as running, pivoting, executing jump stops, and performing V-cuts up and down the court. Players may use basketballs at some point during the warm-up if their skill level is high enough.

COACHING POINTS

- Players need to be lined up and organized for warm-ups. Using the same format for warm-ups each practice will enhance the discipline of the group.
- The coach can have a different player lead warm-ups each day; this will help the players develop leadership.

Four-Line Jump Stops and V-Cuts (10 minutes)

Organize the team into four lines on the baseline with no more than four players in each line. On the coach's command (whistle), the first player in each line runs and comes to a stop at the free-throw line (or free-throw line extended). The players should be in balance when executing the jump stop. On the next command, the first group of four runs to the half-court line and stops, while the next group of four runs to the free-throw line and stops in balance. On the next command, the first group goes to the opposite free-throw line, the second group goes to the half-court line, and the third group of four goes to the free-throw line. The drill continues up and down the court on the coach's command. Once all groups have performed jump stops down and back, the drill is performed using continuous V-cuts; the players run and change direction in a V-cut pattern down the floor.

COACHING POINT

Players tend to have a difficult time stopping in balance, so check that the feet are shoulder-width apart, the hands are above the waist, the head is not leaning forward, and the chin is up.

Freeze Tag With Proper Jump Stops (10 minutes)

Have one player be *It*. This player chases the other players around the court. When touched by the *It* player, the other players must jump stop (freeze) in a proper ready position. The coach can unfreeze a player by touching him when that player shows good ready position.

COACHING POINT

After one or two minutes, the coach should choose a new player to be *It*.

Stationary Dribbling, Right- and Left-Handed (10 minutes)

Each player has a basketball (if this is not possible, players can be split up into two groups, and the drill can be performed by one group at a time). The players begin the drill by dribbling with the right hand first. On the coach's command, the players switch hands, now dribbling with the left hand. In this drill, players can work up to alternating hands with each dribble.

COACHING POINTS

- These young players may try to dribble with the palm of their hand instead of the pads of the fingers and hand.
- The elbow should stay in close to the hip and should not be away from the body.

Form Shooting While Sitting Cross-Legged (10 minutes)

Have players sit cross-legged on the floor in pairs facing each other, with one ball per pair. Instruct the players on how to hold the ball when shooting; the shooting hand should be underneath the ball, and the guide hand should be on the side. On command, the player with the ball shoots or pushes the ball to his partner, releasing it above the eyes and snapping the wrist down goose-neck style.

COACHING POINTS

- This drill can be done with the players shooting against a wall if there are enough basketballs for each player to have one.
- Emphasize that the hand below the ball should be the only hand that shoots the ball.

Pair Passing, Air and Bounce (10 minutes)

Players pair up, and each pair stands about 6 to 8 feet (183 to 244 cm) from each other. On command, the player with the ball passes to her partner using an air pass (a pass that does not touch the floor) or a bounce pass. Both hands and arms should be used to make the pass; the elbows should be close to the body, and the thumbs should be down with palms out after the pass.

COACHING POINTS

- Show the players that a bounce pass should be caught by the partner at the same level that the ball was passed from.
- Note that young players tend to bring the ball above the head to pass; emphasize that each pass should be made from the waist.

Mass Defensive Slide (5 minutes)

All players set up in a scattered formation around the coach, who is in position for all the players to see. On command or by following the coach, players move in a defensive slide to the right and left, keeping the knees bent and the hands above the waist.

COACHING POINTS

- This is a good time to play follow the leader. Have one player positioned in front of the group to lead the other players in the defensive slide drill.
- The coach should make sure that players' feet do not cross or come together during the slide; players should instead use a step and push action with the legs and feet.

Defensive Mirror (10 minutes)

Ask players to pair up, with one player on each side of a line on the court (such as the free-throw line or baseline). One player is designated as the offensive player; this player will move in a quick manner back and forth on her side of the line. The other player is the defender and must slide her feet and try to stay with the offensive player as she moves. The offensive player should remain in a 6- to 8-foot space as she moves back and forth.

COACHING POINT

Tell defenders to keep their eyes on the waist of their offensive player as they move to stay with her. Also teach defenders to avoid crossing their legs.

One-on-One No-Ball Tag (10 minutes)

Ask players to pair up. Start with one player at the free-throw line and the other player in the middle of the lane. On the coach's command, the player at the free-throw line (the offensive player) tries to get to the baseline without getting touched by the other player. The offensive player must stay inside the sidelines and cannot go out of bounds.

COACHING POINT

This drill teaches the players to move their feet and stay in proper ready position, keeping their knees bent for better balance.

Dribble Freeze Tag (10 minutes)

Each player has a basketball (if this is not possible, players can be split up into two groups, and the drill can be performed by one group at a time). One player is designated as Michael Jordan, LeBron James, or any other star your players may know. On command, all players begin dribbling, and this player tries to touch the other players (all players are still maintaining their dribble). Once touched, a player must freeze, still dribbling while stationary. After a specified number of dribbles (to be determined by the coach), the player may be unfrozen.

COACHING POINT

Limit the area for the game to one half of the court or even from free-throw line to baseline so the designated player has more success.

Announcements: _____

Midseason Practices

Midseason practices take on a different look because the players now know some of the drills and may perform certain skills well for their age. Keep the practice sessions fresh by introducing some new drills. A good way to keep the players' interest high is to add some competition to the drills. You will start to see some separation among player skill levels, so account for this in your practice sessions by using a combination of both beginning and advanced drills and dividing players up accordingly.

Midseason Practice Plan 1

Date: _____   Time: _____   Practice number: _____

Warm-Up (10 minutes)

Warm-up time should involve activities such as running, pivoting, executing jump stops, and performing V-cuts up and down the court. Players may use basketballs at some point during the warm-up if their skill level is high enough.

COACHING POINTS

- Players need to be lined up and organized for warm-ups. Using the same format for warm-ups each practice will enhance the discipline of the group.
- The coach can have a different player lead warm-ups each day; this will help the players develop leadership.

Mass Shooting and Layups, Form Only (10 minutes)

Players spread out on the floor and face the coach. On command, the players shoot an imaginary ball, working on proper form for shooting as instructed by the coach. Players should also practice performing layups with an imaginary ball, taking one step and bringing the right knee up with the right hand on the right-handed layup (or bringing the left knee up with the left hand on the left-handed layup).

COACHING POINT

This is the first step in learning how to correctly perform shots and layups. Performing the shooting action with no ball allows the players to focus on using the correct form without worrying about whether the ball goes in the basket.

Dribble Layups (10 minutes)

Players begin in a line starting at the free-throw line elbow. Each player has a basketball. One at a time, players dribble to the basket and perform a layup. The coach rebounds for each player and hands the ball back to him; the player then goes to the back of the line to wait for another turn.

COACHING POINT

You may also want to start this drill without basketballs. Have the players use an imaginary dribble for a layup before adding the ball.

Form Shooting to Partner (10 minutes)

Players pair up, facing each other; each pair has a ball. The player with the ball shoots the ball to his partner using correct shooting form—the elbow is pointed to the target, the shooting hand is underneath the ball, and the guide hand is on the side. The player should lift the ball up and toward his partner.

COACHING POINT

You may want players to begin this drill without using basketballs (players take imaginary shots to their partner) so that form is emphasized before the basketball is added.

Two-Line Passing, Chest and Bounce (10 minutes)

Divide the squad into two lines facing each other; the first person in one line should have a basketball. This player passes the ball using a chest pass to the first person in the opposite line. The passer follows his pass and goes to the end of the opposite line. The drill continues as the players pass the ball and follow it. Once players have practiced the chest pass, they should perform the same drill using the bounce pass.

COACHING POINT

Make sure the receiving player has his hands up and is in ready position, with his knees bent, to catch the pass.

Dribble and Shoot Contest (10 minutes)

Divide players into two or more teams, depending on the number of players. Each team should be limited to three or four players and should have their own basket, if possible. You can have the players start at any place on the court—for example, the free-throw line. The first player on each team dribbles to the basket for a shot, gets her own rebound, and passes back to the next player in line. Each team should count their made baskets. Continue for a specified amount of time and count the made baskets for each group.

COACHING POINT

This shooting drill can also be used for layups or bank shots.

Mass Defensive Slide (5 minutes)

All players set up in a scattered formation around the coach, who is in position for all the players to see. On command or by following the coach, players move in a defensive slide to the right and left, keeping the knees bent and the hands above the waist.

COACHING POINTS

- This is a good time to play follow the leader. Have one player positioned in front of the group to lead the other players in the defensive slide drill.
- The coach should make sure that players' feet do not cross or come together during the slide; players should instead use a step and push action with the legs and feet.

Defensive Mirror (10 minutes)

Ask players to pair up, with one player on each side of a line on the court (such as the free-throw line or baseline). One player is designated as the offensive player;

this player will move in a quick manner back and forth on her side of the line. The other player is the defender and must slide her feet and try to stay with the offensive player as she moves. The offensive player should remain in a 6- to 8-foot space as she moves back and forth.

COACHING POINT

Tell defenders to keep their eyes on the waist of their offensive player as they move to stay with her. Also teach defenders to avoid crossing their legs.

Three-on-Three Half Court (10 minutes)

Divide players into three lines on the baseline. The first player in each line is an offensive player. These players start on the court, facing the basket. The second player in each line is a defensive player. These players defend the offensive players. The rest of the players remain on the baseline. The offensive team tries to score by dribbling, passing, and cutting to the basket. The defensive players work to stay with the offensive player they are assigned to guard. When a basket is made or the defense gets the ball, the defensive team goes to offense, and the next three players in line become the defensive team. Play for a certain amount of time or to a specified score.

COACHING POINT

Depending on the ability of your team, you can put restrictions on the players, such as no stealing the ball from the dribbler on defense, one dribble only for the offense, or the offense must make three passes before a shot is taken.

Dribble Freeze Tag (10 minutes)

Each player has a basketball (if this is not possible, players can be split up into two groups, and the drill can be performed by one group at a time). One player is designated as Michael Jordan, LeBron James, or any other star your players may know. On command, all players begin dribbling, and this player tries to touch the other players (all players are still maintaining their dribble). Once touched, a player must freeze, still dribbling while stationary. After a specified number of dribbles (to be determined by the coach), the player may be unfrozen.

COACHING POINT

Limit the area for the game to one half of the court or even from free-throw line to baseline so the designated player has more success.

Pair Shooting Contest (10 minutes)

Divide players into pairs; each pair has a ball. One player shoots the ball from a specified position on the floor (for example, the right elbow), gets his own rebound, and gives the ball to his partner for the same shot. The drill continues back and forth with the two players taking turns shooting until time is called or until one pair makes a specified number of baskets.

COACHING POINTS

- Try to organize the pairs so the two best shooters are not together.
- Once players have finished shooting from one specified position, ask them to shoot from another (for example, the left elbow).

Announcements: _____

Midseason Practice Plan 2

Date: _____   Time: _____   Practice number: _____

Warm-Up (10 minutes)

Warm-up time should involve activities such as running, pivoting, executing jump stops, and performing V-cuts up and down the court. Players may use basketballs at some point during the warm-up if their skill level is high enough.

COACHING POINTS

- Players need to be lined up and organized for warm-ups. Using the same format for warm-ups each practice will enhance the discipline of the group.
- The coach can have a different player lead warm-ups each day; this will help the players develop leadership.

Mass Ballhandling, Weak-Hand Dribble (10 minutes)

This drill is designed specifically to get players to work on the weak hand. Each player has a basketball. On command, the players dribble with only their weak hand. The coach can allow players to change hands on a whistle. Making a contest out of how many dribbles a player can do in a certain amount of time is a good way to keep players interested.

COACHING POINT

For advanced players, the coach may add some other basic ballhandling instructions (for example, dribbling the ball around the right leg).

Layups, Weak-Hand Dribble (10 minutes)

Players start at the free-throw line elbow on the right side of the court; each player has a ball. The players dribble to the basket using their weak hand and then shoot a right-handed layup. The coach rebounds each ball and gives it back to the player, who then returns to the end of the line. After an appropriate amount of time, players move to the left-side elbow, dribbling to the basket with their weak hand for a left-handed layup.

COACHING POINT

The coach may want players to start the drill using an imaginary basketball so they can get the proper steps and shooting stroke down before adding the ball.

Pair Shooting Contest, Bank Shots (10 minutes)

Divide players into pairs; one partner is at the block facing the basket. This player shoots the ball and must use the backboard for the shot. The player gets his own rebound and gives the ball to his partner for the same shot. The drill continues back and forth with the two players taking turns shooting until time is called or until one pair makes a specified number of baskets.

COACHING POINTS

- Try to organize the pairs so the two best shooters are not together.
- Once the players have shot from one side of the basket, they can move to the other block and shoot bank shots from that side.

Pair Passing, Chest and Bounce (10 minutes)

Players pair up, and each pair of partners stand about 6 to 8 feet from each other. On command, the player with the ball passes to his partner using a chest pass or a bounce pass. Both hands and arms should be used to make the pass; the elbows should be close to the body, and the thumbs should be down with palms out after the pass.

COACHING POINT

Emphasize that each pass should be made from the waist.

Dribble and Shoot Contest (10 minutes)

Divide players into two or more teams, depending on the number of players. Each team should be limited to three or four players and should have their own basket, if possible. You can have the players start at any place on the court—for example, the free-throw line. The first player on each team dribbles to the basket for a shot, gets her own rebound, and passes back to the next player in line. Each team should count their made baskets. Continue for a specified amount of time and count the made baskets for each group.

COACHING POINT

This shooting drill can also be used for layups or bank shots.

Defensive Slide, Sideline to Sideline (5 minutes)

Players line up on one sideline, facing the coach at the end of the court. On command, the players step and push in a defensive slide to the opposite sideline and back again.

COACHING POINT

The players should start slowly by taking a big step with the foot in the direction they are going, pushing off the opposite foot in a defensive slide motion.

Defensive One-on-One, No Ball (10 minutes)

Divide the team into pairs. Players start at the baseline; one partner is designated as the offensive player, and the other partner is designated as the defensive player. The offensive player does not have a ball. On command, the offensive player proceeds down the court using V-cuts in a designated third of the court. The defender slides with the offensive player, performing drop steps with each V-cut.

COACHING POINT

The defender should try to maintain an arm's length of space between himself and the offensive player.

Three-on-Three Half Court, No Dribble (10 minutes)

Divide players into three lines on the baseline. The first player in each line is an offensive player. These players start on the court, facing the basket. The second player in each line is a defensive player. These players defend the offensive players. The rest of the players remain on the baseline. The offensive team tries to score without dribbling the ball; they do this by passing and cutting to the basket. The defensive players work to stay with the offensive player they are assigned to guard. When a basket is made or the defense gets the ball, the defensive team goes to offense, and the next three players in line become the defensive team. Play for a certain amount of time or to a specified score.

COACHING POINT

The defensive team may not steal the ball from the offensive player. This drill encourages the players to cut and move to get open because no dribble can occur.

Dribble Tag Inside Lane (10 minutes)

All players have a ball in the lane. On command, all players start to dribble. While dribbling, each player tries to knock another player's ball out of the lane. When a player's ball is knocked out of the lane, that player is out of the game. The game continues until only one player is left dribbling.

COACHING POINT

Ask players to perform this drill using both strong-hand and weak-hand dribbling.

Pair Shooting Contest, First to 10 (10 minutes)

Players are divided into pairs; each pair has a ball. One player shoots the ball from a specified position on the floor (for example, the right elbow), gets his own rebound, and gives the ball to his partner for the same shot. The drill continues back and forth with the two players taking turns shooting from the same spot until one pair makes 10 baskets.

COACHING POINTS

- Try to organize the pairs so the two best shooters are not together.
- The coach can mix up the drill with dribble shots, layups, and so on.

Announcements: _____

Midseason Practice Plan 3

Date: _____   Time: _____   Practice number: _____

Warm-Up (10 minutes)

Warm-up time should involve activities such as running, pivoting, executing jump stops, and performing V-cuts up and down the court. Players may use basketballs at some point during the warm-up if their skill level is high enough.

COACHING POINTS

- Players need to be lined up and organized for warm-ups. Using the same format for warm-ups each practice will enhance the discipline of the group.
- The coach can have a different player lead warm-ups each day; this will help the players develop leadership.

Follow the Leader Dribbling Work (10 minutes)

One player is the leader, and the rest of the players are in a position on the court where they can see the leader. The leader performs ballhandling movements (dribbling with the weak hand, dribbling around the leg, and so on), and the rest of the players imitate the leader's ballhandling movements.

COACHING POINT

The leader may move while doing the ballhandling movements using various dribbling techniques such as crossover moves and between-the-legs moves.

Two-Line Give-and-Go With Layup (10 minutes)

Arrange players in two lines at the free-throw elbows. The first player in one line starts with the ball, makes a pass to the player in the opposite line, and gets the ball back for a layup on a give-and-go play. The shooter then goes to the end of the passing line, and the passer gets the rebound and goes to the shooting line.

COACHING POINT

You can also use this as a jump shot drill. On the give-and-go cut, the player can stop and shoot a short jump shot instead of a layup.

Pass and Screen for Layup (10 minutes)

Divide players into three lines, one line at the top of the three-point line and one line at each wing. The player at the top of the key starts with the ball, passing it to one of the wings. After the pass, the player at the top of the key sets a screen on an imaginary opponent for the opposite wing, who cuts off the screen for a pass and a layup. Rotate the lines from left wing to top, top to right wing, and right wing to left wing.

COACHING POINT

Use a chair as the defensive player so the screener can set the screen on the chair. The coach can also act as the defender. Eventually, use another player as the defender to be screened.

Three-on-Three Pass, Cut, and Replace (10 minutes)

Organize players into teams of three. One team is the offensive team, and one is the defensive team; the remaining teams stay on the baseline ready to come onto the court. The offensive players should be arranged with a player at the top of the key and two wings. The player at the top of the key begins by making a pass to one of the wings. After the pass, the player makes a cut to the basket. The opposite wing then fills the top position, and the cutter fills the vacated wing position. The ball is then reversed to the top of the key and passed to the other wing; the player at the top of the key cuts to the basket to repeat the process. The coach designates how many ball reversals must take place before the ball can be passed to the cutter for a shot.

COACHING POINT

Do not allow the defenders to intercept the passes. This will enable the offense to have success with the cuts and passes.

Dribble and Shoot Contest, Top of Key (10 minutes)

Divide players into two or more teams, depending on the number of players. Each team should be limited to three or four players and should have their own basket, if possible. Have players start at the top of the three-point line. The first player on each team must dribble toward the basket and stop and shoot a shot inside the lane area; the player then gets her own rebound and passes back to the next player in line. Each team should count their made baskets. Continue for a specified amount of time and count the made baskets for each group.

COACHING POINT

The drill can also be used to practice layups or bank shots.

Mass Rebounding Pivots (5 minutes)

Players are scattered around the court; they are all in a position where they can see the coach. On command, the players pivot so their back is to the coach with their hands up in rebounding position. The players then jump to get the imaginary rebound.

COACHING POINT

Ask the players to tip the imaginary rebound several times before grabbing it.

One-on-One Rebounding With Ball on Floor (10 minutes)

Have the players pair up around the center circle. The first pair takes position along the outside of the circle; the inside player is facing his partner. The ball is in the middle of the circle. On command, the inside player pivots in front of his partner to prevent him from getting to the ball in the middle of the circle. Both players try to get the ball. The inside player has the advantage.

COACHING POINTS

- Players should stay low in good basketball position.
- As the inside player makes a pivot, his hands should go up.

Two-on-Two With Coach (10 minutes)

Divide the team into lines starting at the half-court line. The first two players in line are the defenders, and the next two are the offensive players. The coach is positioned at the free-throw line as a passer. One of the offensive players starts the drill by passing to the coach. Both offensive players then cut and move to get open for a pass from the coach. The offensive players may pass the ball at any time to the coach, who always stays at the free-throw line. Players rotate from offense to defense and from defense to the end of the line.

COACHING POINT

The offensive players can cut to the basket for a pass from the coach, or they can screen for each other.

Team Shooting Competition, 20 in 3 (10 minutes)

Divide the players into three lines on each baseline. A player in the first row on one baseline has a ball, and a player in the second row on the opposite baseline has a ball. The first row of players on the baseline without a basketball run straight down the court and receive a pass from the player on that baseline with a ball. Whoever receives the ball shoots it, rebounding her own shot. She and the other two players then go to the end of each line at that end as the row of players from which the ball was passed run to the other baseline and receive a pass for a shot. The drill continues in this fashion for three minutes; the goal is 20 made baskets.

COACHING POINT

Emphasize footwork on each shot as the ball is passed to the shooter.

Free Throws, Two in a Row (10 minutes)

Pair up players at each free-throw line. Partners take turns shooting one free throw until the pair makes two in a row.

COACHING POINT

The coach can also ask each player to shoot two free throws until the pair makes four in a row.

Announcements: _____

Late-Season Practices

As the season progresses, most of the practice time should still focus on skill development for this age group. However, some drills can progress to team drills that emphasize several skills in one drill. Keep the lines as short as possible so that each player gets more repetitions.

Late-Season Practice Plan

Date: _____   Time: _____   Practice number: _____

Warm-Up (10 minutes)

Warm-up time should involve activities such as running, pivoting, executing jump stops, and performing V-cuts up and down the court. Players may use basketballs at some point during the warm-up if their skill level is high enough.

COACHING POINTS

- Players need to be lined up and organized for warm-ups. Using the same format for warm-ups each practice will enhance the discipline of the group.
- The coach can have a different player lead warm-ups each day; this will help the players develop leadership.

Two-Line Full-Court Passing (10 minutes)

Players line up in two lines on the baseline. Beginning with the first two in each line, players pass the ball back and forth while running down the court. Initially, air passes (passes that do not touch the floor) should be used in this drill; as the team progresses, the coach can ask players to also perform the drill using bounce passes.

COACHING POINT

Players can also perform a defensive slide down the length of the court as they pass the ball to each other.

Full-Court Layups With Dribble (10 minutes)

Divide the team into two groups, forming one line at the baseline under each basket. The first three players in each line should have a basketball. On command, the first player in each line dribbles to the other end and shoots a layup. After each layup is shot, the first player in line without a ball rebounds the shot taken as the shooter goes to the end of the line. Each time a player reaches the half-court line, the next player in line follows.

COACHING POINT

Remind the players to keep their heads up as they dribble the ball.

Defensive Slides, One-on-Zero and One-on-One (10 minutes)

Divide the players into three lines on the baseline. The first player in each line performs defensive slides to the other baseline, making a drop step after every three slides. Once players get the hang of the drill, divide the players into pairs. One partner now dribbles a basketball, using V-cuts and crossover dribbles to change direction, from one baseline to the other; the other partner is the defensive player. The defensive player should slide to stay in front of the dribbler, executing a drop step each time the offensive player changes direction.

COACHING POINTS

- The offensive players should go slowly so the defense can work on footwork.
- Defensive players should remain one arm's length away from the dribbler, keeping their eyes on the dribbler's waist.

Two-on-Two Half Court (10 minutes)

Players begin in two lines at the half-court line. The first two players in line are the defensive players, and the next two are the offensive players. The coach passes a ball to one of the offensive players, and the offensive players dribble, pass, and cut to try to score. The drill is over when the offense scores or the defensive players get the rebound. Players rotate from offense to defense and from defense to the end of the line.

COACHING POINT

Various rules, such as allowing only two dribbles per player, may be implemented in the drill.

Cutthroat, Three-on-Three (10 minutes)

Divide the team into three lines on the baseline; the first players in each line are on offense, and the second players in each line are on defense. The offensive players are facing the basket on the court, and the defenders are in defensive position. The coach starts the drill by passing the ball to one of the offensive players. As a rule, the offensive players must face the basket in the triple-threat position, must move after they pass, and must thank the passer on a pass that results in a basket. If the offense fails to follow one of the rules, the whistle blows, and the offensive players must go to the end of the line. The defense moves to offense, and a new set of three players comes in on defense. Play for a specified period of time or until one team reaches a specified number of points. Each basket counts as a point.

COACHING POINT

Teams must leave and come onto the court quickly.

Freeze Tag With Proper Jump Stops (5 minutes)

Have one player be *It*. This player chases the other players around the court. When touched by the *It* player, the other players must jump stop (freeze) in a proper ready position. The coach can unfreeze a player by touching him when that player shows a good ready position.

COACHING POINT

After one or two minutes, the coach should choose a new player to be *It*.

Pair Shooting Contest, From Four Spots (10 minutes)

Players are divided into pairs; each pair has a ball. In this drill, players shoot from four designated spots chosen by the coach. One player shoots the ball from the first designated position on the floor (for example, the right elbow), gets his own rebound, and gives the ball to his partner for the same shot. Both players must make the shot from this spot before moving to the next spot. The drill continues back and forth with the players taking turns shooting until each player makes all four shots.

COACHING POINTS

- Try to organize the pairs so the two best shooters are not together.
- To make the drill more difficult, the coach can have the players make five shots (or any other specified number) each at every spot before moving to the next.

Two-on-One Half Court (10 minutes)

Divide the team into two lines at half-court; one player is positioned in the middle of the lane as a defender. The first two players in line dribble and pass the ball to try to score against the lone defender.

COACHING POINT

The offensive players should only make one or two passes to try to score.

10-Basket Shooting Contest (10 minutes)

The squad is divided into groups of no more than three per team. The coach designates a shooting spot where the team of players will shoot one shot each until that team makes 10 baskets. Each player rebounds his own shot and passes the ball back to the next person in line.

COACHING POINTS

- Emphasize to players that they should have their feet and hands ready to shoot before the ball is passed.
- The coach can change the specified number of made shots and the shooting spots depending on the players' ability.
- To change up the drill, the coach may specify that the players must shoot bank shots or must dribble and shoot.

Announcements: _____

Practices for Ages 7 and 8

11

Players in the 7- and 8-year age group have more experience than those in the 5- and 6-year age group, but practice sessions will be much the same. You will find that players in this age group have a wide range of ability. Growth spurts take over and cause some players to be taller but less coordinated. Practice sessions should emphasize individual skills such as shooting, passing, dribbling, rebounding, and ballhandling. As the season progresses, the practice sessions can begin to include more offensive and defensive concepts. Plays such as the give-and-go, screen away for teammates, ball screens, and three-player games can be incorporated into these practices. For players at this age group, the man-to-man defense is the only type of defense that should be played. Defensive slides, drop steps, and proper stance are all part of the defensive fundamentals that this age group should be taught. As the season progresses, the players should also be introduced to the concepts of ball-side and help-side defense and defending the ball and their offensive player.

Don't expect these offensive and defensive concepts to be picked up quickly by the players. This will be the first time that many of these players have been exposed to the terminology and fundamental skills related to these concepts. Stay patient and repeat the skills on a consistent basis. Also, keep practices moving quickly from one drill to another with short lines in each drill. Have fun with the players in practice, but work them hard!

Considerations When Coaching Females
Annie Byrne, Marian Catholic High School girls' basketball coach

Coaching 7- and 8-year-old girls should involve a continuation of teaching the fundamentals. All coaches know that the fundamentals are essential when coaching any group of players, especially players at a young age. If these 7- and 8-year-olds did start at age 5 or 6, they may be more familiar with what will be expected of them at a practice session or skills clinic. If they are just beginning at this age, then you will have to go back and reference chapter 10 and start from the beginning. Do not try to speed up the process. Skipping necessary fundamental steps will only hinder your players' development. You must be consistent and must ensure that your players develop a foundation that they can build on.

Items to consider teaching in practice include defensive slides without crossing the feet, the BEEF acronym for shooting (balance, eyes, elbow, follow-through), and ballhandling skills. Also, outlining the rules of the game is helpful for these players. This may include how to line up for free throws, when a player or coach can call a time-out, the procedure for checking in at the scorer's table, how many players are on the floor at one time, taking the ball out of bounds, staying behind the free-throw line when shooting a free throw, what the various positions in basketball are on offense, and how to play a man-to-man and zone defense. This information will be enough to enable the players to compete and begin to understand exactly how the game is played.

Girls at any age need to develop confidence; on the basketball court, this can be done in a variety of ways. Give praise and high-fives as often as you can, and applaud constantly when the effort that you are looking for is given. If players are feeling more confident in their abilities and potential on the court, they will want to spend more time learning and developing their game.

7-8 years old

Early-Season Practices

Early-season practice sessions should be a review of skills previously taught and should include skill development. Introduce new skills early in the season and then review them on a daily basis.

Early-Season Practice Plan

Date: _____   Time: _____   Practice number: _____

Warm-Up (10 minutes)

Players line up on the baseline in four lines. On command, the players run down the court to the opposite baseline. Players work on running, stops, pivots, V-cuts, and jumping during their trips up and down the court.

COACHING POINT

Adjust the skills used in the warm-up based on the ability level of your players.

Four-Line Jump Stops and V-Cuts (10 minutes)

Organize the team into four lines on the baseline with no more than four players in each line. On the coach's command (whistle), the first player in each line runs and comes to a stop at the free-throw line (or free-throw line extended). The players should be in balance when executing the jump stop. On the next command, the first group of four runs to the half-court line and stops, while the next group of four runs to the free-throw line and stops in balance. On the next command, the first group goes to the opposite free-throw line, the second group goes to the half-court line, and the third group of four goes to the free-throw line. The drill continues up and down the court on the coach's command. Once all groups have performed jump stops down and back, the drill is performed using continuous V-cuts; the players run and change direction in a V-cut pattern down the floor.

COACHING POINTS

- On jump stops, check that players' feet are shoulder-width apart, the hands are above the waist, the head is not leaning forward, and the chin is up.
- On V-cuts, confirm that players make a sharp change of direction after planting their outside foot; cuts should not be rounded.

Running Fast Break Lanes (10 minutes)

Players form three lines at one baseline. Cones are spread out from one free-throw line to the other, about five to six feet in from the sideline. On command, the first three players run in three lanes to the other baseline; the players in the outside lanes run outside the cones, and the player in the middle lane runs between the cones (free-throw lanes). No ball is used to start the drill, but depending on player ability, the ball may be added. In that case, the player in the middle lane pushes the ball upcourt and makes a pass to an outside-lane player before that player reaches the offensive lane.

COACHING POINT

Emphasize that the outside players must run wide and outside the cones to establish the outside lanes on the break while the middle player pushes the imaginary ball up the middle.

Stationary Dribbling, Right- and Left-Handed (10 minutes)

Each player has a basketball (if this is not possible, players can be split up into two groups, and the drill can be performed by one group at a time). The players begin the drill by dribbling with the right hand first. On the coach's command, the players switch hands, now dribbling with the left hand. In this drill, players can work up to alternating hands with each dribble.

COACHING POINT

Stress that players need to keep their head up while dribbling.

Form Shooting to Partner (10 minutes)

Players pair up, facing each other; each pair has a ball. The player with the ball shoots the ball to his partner using correct shooting form—the elbow is pointed to the target, the shooting hand is underneath the ball, and the guide hand is on the side. The player should lift the ball up and toward his partner.

COACHING POINT

You may want players to begin this drill without using basketballs (players take imaginary shots to their partner) so that form is emphasized before the basketball is added.

Pair Passing, Air and Bounce (10 minutes)

Players pair up, and each pair stands about 6 to 8 feet (183 to 244 cm) from each other. On command, the player with the ball passes to her partner using an air pass (a pass that does not touch the floor) or a bounce pass. Both hands and arms should be used to make the pass; the elbows should be close to the body, and the thumbs should be down with palms out after the pass.

COACHING POINTS

- Show the players that a bounce pass should be caught by the partner at the same level that the ball was passed from.
- Note that young players tend to bring the ball above the head to pass; emphasize that each pass should be made from the waist.

Mass Defensive Slide (5 minutes)

All players set up in a scattered formation around the coach, who is in position for all the players to see. On command or by following the coach, players move in a defensive slide to the right and left, keeping the knees bent and the hands above the waist.

COACHING POINTS

- This is a good time to play follow the leader. Have one player positioned in front of the group to lead the other players in the defensive slide drill.
- The coach should make sure that players' feet do not cross or come together during the slide; players should instead use a step and push action with the legs and feet.

Defensive Mirror (10 minutes)

Ask players to pair up, with one player on each side of a line on the court (such as the free-throw line or baseline). One player is designated as the offensive player; this player will move in a quick manner back and forth on her side of the line. The other player is the defender and must slide her feet and try to stay with the offensive player as she moves. The offensive player should remain in a 6- to 8-foot space as she moves back and forth.

COACHING POINT

Tell defenders to keep their eyes on the waist of their offensive player as they move to stay with her. Also teach defenders to avoid crossing their legs.

One-on-One No-Ball Tag (10 minutes)

Have players pair up. One partner begins on the baseline, facing the court; this player is the offensive player. The other partner is the defensive player. This player starts at the free-throw line and is facing the offensive player. On command, the offensive player tries to get to the opposite baseline while the defensive player tries to tag or touch him.

COACHING POINT

This is a good drill for working on quickness and change of direction. The defensive player must keep the offensive player in front of him in order to make the tag.

Dribble Freeze Tag (10 minutes)

Each player has a basketball (if this is not possible, players can be split up into two groups, and the drill can be performed by one group at a time). One player is designated as Michael Jordan, LeBron James, or any other star your players may know. On command, all players begin dribbling, and this player tries to touch the other players (all players are still maintaining their dribble). Once touched, a player must freeze, still dribbling while stationary. After a specified number of dribbles (to be determined by the coach), the player may be unfrozen.

COACHING POINT

Limit the area for the game to one half of the court or even from free-throw line to baseline so the designated player has more success.

Announcements: _____

Midseason Practices

Midseason practices will include fewer individual drills and more multiple-player drills. The coach can implement drills that emphasize several skills in one drill. Players will become more comfortable with performing skills in a team setting.

Midseason Practice Plan 1

Date: _____   Time: _____   Practice number: _____

Warm-Up (10 minutes)

Players line up on the baseline in four lines. On command, the players run down the court to the opposite baseline. Players work on running, stops, pivots, V-cuts, and jumping during their trips up and down the court.

COACHING POINT

Adjust the skills used in the warm-up based on the ability level of your players.

Dribble–Pivot–Pass (10 minutes)

Players line up on the sideline with no more than three players per line. The first player takes three right-handed dribbles out and comes to a stop. He then executes a reverse pivot (a front pivot may also be used) and makes a chest pass to the next player in line. The passer goes to the end of the line after the pass, and the next player (the one who caught the pass) dribbles out and makes the pivot and pass.

COACHING POINTS

- Emphasize to players that they should execute the pivot with the knees bent to make the pass.
- Depending on ability, players may instead use bounce passes or one-hand push passes in the drill.

Dribble Layups (10 minutes)

Players begin in a line starting at the free-throw line elbow. Each player has a basketball. One at a time, players dribble to the basket and perform a layup. The coach rebounds for each player and hands the ball back to him; the player then goes to the back of the line to wait for another turn.

COACHING POINT

You may also want to start this drill without basketballs. Have the players use an imaginary dribble for a layup before adding the ball.

Form Shooting to Partner (10 minutes)

Players pair up, facing each other; each pair has a ball. The player with the ball shoots the ball to his partner using correct shooting form—the elbow is pointed to the target, the shooting hand is underneath the ball, and the guide hand is on the side. The player should lift the ball up and toward his partner.

COACHING POINT

You may want players to begin this drill without using basketballs (players take imaginary shots to their partner) so that form is emphasized before the basketball is added.

Two-Line Passing, Chest and Bounce (10 minutes)

Divide the squad into two lines (8 to 12 feet [2.4 to 3.6 m] apart) facing each other; the first person in one line should have a basketball. This player passes the ball using a chest pass to the first person in the opposite line. The passer follows his pass and goes to the end of the opposite line. The drill continues as the players pass the ball and follow it. Once players have practiced the chest pass, they should perform the same drill using the bounce pass.

COACHING POINTS

- The passer's elbows should be close to the body when executing a chest or bounce pass.
- The receiver needs to make sure his hands are up, showing a good target with the fingers and thumb in a W shape.

Dribble and Shoot Contest (10 minutes)

Divide players into two or more teams, depending on the number of players. Each team should be limited to three or four players and should have their own basket, if possible. You can have the players start at any place on the court—for example, the free-throw line. The first player on each team dribbles to the basket for a shot, gets her own rebound, and passes back to the next player in line. Each team should count their made baskets. Continue for a specified amount of time and count the made baskets for each group.

COACHING POINT

This shooting drill can also be used for layups or bank shots.

Mass Defensive Slide (5 minutes)

All players set up in a scattered formation around the coach, who is in position for all the players to see. On command or by following the coach, players move in a defensive slide to the right and left, keeping the knees bent and the hands above the waist.

COACHING POINTS

- This is a good time to play follow the leader. Have one player positioned in front of the group to lead the other players in the defensive slide drill.
- The coach should make sure that players' feet do not cross or come together during the slide; players should instead use a step and push action with the legs and feet.

Defensive Mirror (10 minutes)

Ask players to pair up, with one player on each side of a line on the court (such as the free-throw line or baseline). One player is designated as the offensive player; this player will move in a quick manner back and forth on her side of the line. The other player is the defender and must slide her feet and try to stay with the offensive player as she moves. The offensive player should remain in a 6- to 8-foot space as she moves back and forth.

COACHING POINT

Tell defenders to keep their eyes on the waist of their offensive player as they move to stay with her. Also teach defenders to avoid crossing their legs.

Three-on-Three Half Court (10 minutes)

Divide players into three lines on the baseline. The first player in each line is an offensive player. These players start on the court, facing the basket. The second player in each line is a defensive player. These players defend the offensive players. The rest of the players remain on the baseline. The offensive team tries to score by using cuts and screens. The defensive players work to stay with the offensive player they are assigned to guard. When a basket is made or the defense gets the ball, the defensive team goes to offense, and the next three players in line become the defensive team. Play for a certain amount of time or to a specified score.

COACHING POINTS

- If one player tends to dribble the ball too much, put a limit on the number of dribbles for the offensive team.
- Rules requiring specific techniques—such as pass and cut to the basket or pass and screen away for a teammate—can also be implemented.

Three-on-Two Half Court (10 minutes)

Divide the team into three lines at the half-court line. Two defensive players are in the lane; one player is at the free-throw line, and the other is in the middle of the lane. The coach begins the drill by throwing the ball to the first player in the middle line at half-court. The other two offensive players are wings, positioned out wide on the sides of the court. The middle player makes a pass to one of the wing players, staying to the side of the pass for a possible return pass. The three offensive players try to attack the two defensive players to score. The offensive team should work to get a shot in three passes or less. After the play is over, the two wings move to defense, and the other three players go to the end of the lines.

COACHING POINTS

- Defensive players should be in a tandem position, with the back defender guarding the first pass to the wing and the top defender dropping back to the middle of the lane.
- The middle offensive player must slide to the elbow of the lane to the same side of the pass so that this player is in position to get the ball back for a jump shot.

Five-on-Zero Offense (10 minutes)

Arrange the players in offensive positions based on the offensive set you want to teach. For example, this can be a 1-2-2 set with a point guard, two wings, and two post players or a 2-1-2 set with two guards, a high-post player, and two baseline or post players. In this drill, teach players how they can try to score in the set (including cuts, screens, and so on).

COACHING POINTS

- Teach players proper spacing and how to refill positions after a pass and cut.
- Emphasize that each player should square up to the basket after every catch.

Free Throws, Two in a Row (10 minutes)

Pair up players at each free-throw line. Partners take turns shooting one free throw until the pair makes two in a row.

COACHING POINTS

- The coach can also ask each player to shoot two free throws until the pair makes four in a row.
- As the season progresses, the coach may increase the number of consecutive free throws made from two to three, three to four, and four to five.

Announcements: _____

Midseason Practice Plan 2

Date: _____   Time: _____   Practice number: _____

Warm-Up (10 minutes)

Players line up on the baseline in four lines. On command, the players run down the court to the opposite baseline. Players work on running, stops, pivots, V-cuts, and jumping during their trips up and down the court.

COACHING POINT

Adjust the skills used in the warm-up based on the ability level of your players.

Dribble–Pivot–Pass (10 minutes)

Players line up on the sideline with no more than three players per line. The first player takes three right-handed dribbles out and comes to a stop. He then executes a reverse pivot (a front pivot may also be used) and makes a chest pass to the next player in line. The passer goes to the end of the line after the pass, and the next player (the one who caught the pass) dribbles out and makes the pivot and pass.

COACHING POINTS

- Emphasize to players that they should execute the pivot with the knees bent to make the pass.
- Depending on ability, players may instead use bounce passes or one-hand push passes in the drill.

Layups With Crossover Dribble (10 minutes)

Players set up in one line at the half-court line in the middle of the court. Place a cone at the top of the three-point line. The first player in line dribbles from the half-court line to the cone, performs a crossover dribble at the cone, and then dribbles to the basket for a layup. Players should start with a left-handed dribble and cross over to the right hand for a right-handed layup.

COACHING POINTS

- Start players on the wing or baseline to get a different approach to the basket.
- Once players get the hang of the drill, proceed to having the players start with a right-handed dribble and cross over to the left hand for a left-handed layup.

One-Dribble Shooting From Free-Throw Line (10 minutes)

Players line up in two lines at the free-throw line, one line at each free-throw elbow. The first player in each line takes one dribble and then comes to a good stop for a shot. The player gets his own rebound, passes the ball back to the next player in line, and moves to the end of the line. The drill continues in this fashion for a certain number of baskets or a specified amount of time.

COACHING POINTS

- Take note of each player's footwork in this drill, correcting as necessary.
- Emphasize that players should bend their knees on the stop before shooting.

Two-Line Passing, Chest and Bounce (10 minutes)

Divide the squad into two lines (8 to 12 feet apart) facing each other; the first person in one line should have a basketball. This player passes the ball using a chest pass to the first person in the opposite line. The passer follows his pass and goes to the end of the opposite line. The drill continues as the players pass the ball and follow it. Once players have practiced the chest pass, they should perform the same drill using the bounce pass.

COACHING POINTS

- The passer's elbows should be close to the body when executing a chest or bounce pass.
- The receiver needs to make sure his hands are up, showing a good target with the fingers and thumb in a W shape.

Three-Line Passing Full Court With One Dribble (10 minutes)

Players form three lines on one baseline; the players in the middle line should have a ball. On command, the middle player takes one dribble toward the opposite baseline and then makes a pass to one of the wing players as all three players are running toward the opposite baseline. The wing player catches the ball, takes one dribble, and passes back to the middle player. The middle player then takes one dribble and passes to the opposite wing player. All three players end up on the opposite baseline as the next group of three proceeds downcourt in the same manner.

COACHING POINTS

- Players should rotate lines after they reach the baseline so each player has an opportunity to begin in the middle line.
- Emphasize that passes should be made ahead of the player who is running down the court.

Mass Defensive Slide (5 minutes)

All players set up in a scattered formation around the coach, who is in position for all the players to see. On command or by following the coach, players move in a defensive slide to the right and left, keeping the knees bent and the hands above the waist.

COACHING POINTS

- This is a good time to play follow the leader. Have one player positioned in front of the group to lead the other players in the defensive slide drill.
- The coach should make sure that players' feet do not cross or come together during the slide; players should instead use a step and push action with the legs and feet.

Defensive Mirror (10 minutes)

Ask players to pair up, with one player on each side of a line on the court (such as the free-throw line or baseline). One player is designated as the offensive player; this player will move in a quick manner back and forth on her side of the line. The other player is the defender and must slide her feet and try to stay with the offensive player as she moves. The offensive player should remain in a 6- to 8-foot space as she moves back and forth.

COACHING POINT

Tell defenders to keep their eyes on the waist of their offensive player as they move to stay with her. Also teach defenders to avoid crossing their legs.

Three-on-Three Pass, Cut, and Replace (10 minutes)

Organize players into teams of three. One team is the offensive team, and one is the defensive team; the remaining teams stay on the baseline ready to come onto the court. The offensive players should be arranged with a player at the top of the key and two wings. The player at the top of the key begins by making a pass to one of the wings. After the pass, the player makes a cut to the basket. The opposite wing then fills the top position, and the cutter fills the vacated wing position. The ball is then reversed to the top of the key and passed to the other wing; the player at the top of the key cuts to the basket to repeat the process. The coach designates how many ball reversals must take place before the ball can be passed to the cutter for a shot.

COACHING POINTS

- Ask the offense to focus on proper spacing and filling in each position.
- Restrict the defensive team to intercepting passes only; do not allow them to steal the ball on the dribble.

Three-on-Two, Two-on-One Full Court (10 minutes)

Start with three lines at one end of the court. Two players set up at the opposite end of the court in a defensive position, one player at the free-throw line and one player in the middle of the lane. The first three players in line try to score against the two defenders (three-on-two); the middle player dribbles the ball down the floor and makes a pass to one wing. After the shot, the two defenders become the offensive players, moving to the opposite end of the court with the middle offensive player transitioning to defense (two-on-one). The two wings remain as the defenders in the lane for the next group of three offensive players.

COACHING POINTS

- The three offensive players should work to get a shot after three or fewer passes against the two defenders.
- The two offensive players should work to get a shot after two or fewer passes against the one defender.

Three-on-Three With One Dribble (10 minutes)

Divide players into three lines on the baseline. The first player in each line is an offensive player. These players start on the court, facing the basket. The second player in each line is a defensive player. These players defend the offensive players. The rest of the players remain on the baseline. The offensive team tries to score by using cuts and screens; each player is allowed only one dribble each time she touches the ball. The defensive players work to stay with the offensive player they are assigned to guard. When a basket is made or the defense gets the ball, the defensive team goes to offense, and the next three players in line become the defensive team. Play for a certain amount of time or to a specified score.

COACHING POINTS

- Players should learn to cut after a pass and look to get the ball back for a shot.
- Offensive spacing is crucial.

Free Throws, Two in a Row (10 minutes)

Pair up players at each free-throw line. Partners take turns shooting one free throw until the pair makes two in a row.

COACHING POINTS

- The coach can also ask each player to shoot two free throws until the pair makes four in a row.

- As the season progresses, the coach may increase the number of consecutive free throws made from two to three, three to four, and four to five.

Announcements: _____

Midseason Practice Plan 3

Date: _____   Time: _____   Practice number: _____

Warm-Up (10 minutes)

Players line up on the baseline in four lines. On command, the players run down the court to the opposite baseline. Players work on running, stops, pivots, V-cuts, and jumping during their trips up and down the court.

COACHING POINT

Adjust the skills used in the warm-up based on the ability level of your players.

Two-Line Full-Court Passing, Air (10 minutes)

Players line up in two lines on the baseline. Beginning with the first two in each line, players make air passes (a pass that does not touch the floor) back and forth while running down the court.

COACHING POINT

Players can also perform a defensive slide down the length of the court as they pass the ball to each other.

Two-Line Fast Break With Layup (10 minutes)

The team is arranged in two lines, with one line in the lane facing the opposite basket and the other line at the wing position (players in this line are ready to catch the ball). The first player in the lane line starts with the ball and passes to the player at the wing. The wing player dribbles the ball to the opposite free-throw line and makes a good stop without traveling. The passer runs to the other end in the outside lane to receive a return pass from the wing. After receiving the return pass, this player dribbles in for a layup. These two players stay at this end, switching positions, as the next two players in line take their turn. After all the players have completed the drill going to one basket, they switch positions and complete the drill going back to the original basket.

COACHING POINTS

- Make sure the passer runs wide; to stress this, the coach can place cones on the court and specify that the player must run outside the cones.
- The drill can also be performed with the players executing jump shots off the glass, power shots, or a pass back to the middle player at the free-throw line for a shot.

Seven-Spot Shooting, Two Made Shots From Each Spot (10 minutes)

Pick out seven spots on the floor, marking these spots with tape. Players pair up, and each pair has a ball. The first player shoots the ball at the first spot, gets her own rebound, and passes back to her partner, who shoots at the same spot. After two shots total are made from that spot, the players move to the next spot. Players must make two shots from each spot before they are done with the drill.

COACHING POINTS

- Emphasize that shooters must be ready and must have their feet and hands in good position to shoot when they catch the pass.
- This drill can be changed to require players to make any number of shots before moving to the next spot or require them to make a certain number in a row before moving to the next spot.

Two-Line Give-and-Go With Layup (10 minutes)

Arrange players in two lines at the free-throw elbows. The first player in one line starts with the ball, makes a pass to the player in the opposite line, and gets the ball back for a layup on a give-and-go play. The shooter then goes to the end of the passing line, and the passer gets the rebound and goes to the shooting line.

COACHING POINT

You can also use this as a jump shot drill. On the give-and-go cut, the player can stop and shoot a short jump shot instead of a layup.

Three-on-Three Pass, Cut, and Replace (10 minutes)

Organize players into teams of three. One team is the offensive team, and one is the defensive team; the remaining teams stay on the baseline ready to come onto the court. The offensive players should be arranged with a player at the top of the key and two wings. The player at the top of the key begins by making a pass to one of the wings. After the pass, the player makes a cut to the basket. The opposite wing then fills the top position, and the cutter fills the vacated wing position. The ball is then reversed to the top of the key and passed to the other wing; the player at the top of the key cuts to the basket to repeat the process. The coach designates how many ball reversals must take place before the ball can be passed to the cutter for a shot.

COACHING POINTS

- Ask the offense to focus on proper spacing and filling in each position.
- Restrict the defensive team to intercepting passes only; do not allow them to steal the ball on the dribble.

Two-on-Two Defensive Jump to Ball (5 minutes)

Players form two lines starting at the free-throw lane extended outside the three-point line. One defensive player is guarding each offensive player in a two-on-two situation. The offensive players pass the ball back and forth, moving to any position on the court. With each pass, the defenders must adjust their positioning so they are in good help or on-the-ball position. After a specified amount of time, the next two players in line move to offense, the offensive players move to defense, and the defenders move to the end of each line.

COACHING POINT

The defenders must move as the ball is in the air so they are in correct defensive position when the ball is caught. The coach may need to yell out "Pass!" so the defense can adjust to each pass correctly.

Three-on-Three Defensive Positioning (10 minutes)

The offensive team is set up with a player at the top of the key and players at both wings. A defender is guarding each offensive player for a three-on-three situation; the rest of the team is divided into three lines at half-court. The ball is passed from the top to the wing, back to the top, to the opposite wing, and so on. The defenders move on each pass so that they are in proper position to help or guard the ball. After a specified amount of time, the next three players in line move to offense, the offensive players move to defense, and the defenders move to the end of each line.

COACHING POINT

The defenders must move as the ball is in the air so they are in correct defensive position when the ball is caught. The coach may need to yell out "Pass!" so the defense can adjust to each pass correctly.

Three-on-Three Defending the Pass and Cut (10 minutes)

This drill is a continuation of the previous three-on-three drill. Offensive players are positioned at the top of the key and at each wing, and a defender is guarding each offensive player; the rest of the team is divided into three lines at half-court. The offensive player at the top of the key cuts to the basket every time he makes a pass from the top of the key to a wing. The opposite wing then fills the top, and the cutter goes to the opposite wing. Throughout, the defenders work to move to each pass and defend the cutter going to the basket. After a specified amount of time, the next three players in line move to offense, the offensive players move to defense, and the defenders move to the end of each line.

COACHING POINTS

- The defender on the cutter should be in a position between the ball and the cutter; this takes away the direct pass to the cutter for a shot.
- The defenders must move as the ball is in the air so they are in correct defensive position when the ball is caught. The coach may need to yell out "Pass!" so the defense can adjust to each pass correctly.

Four-on-Four Defensive Shell (10 minutes)

Four players are on offense, and four on defense. The offense is spaced out with one guard above each free-throw lane outside the three-point line and one player at each wing. A defender is guarding each offensive player; the rest of the team is divided into four lines at half-court. One of the guards starts with the ball and passes it to a wing. As the coach observes, the defenders must adjust to each pass so they are in good help position or on-the-ball position. On command, the offense continues to pass the ball from one wing to the other wing, and the defenders adjust their position on each pass. After a specified amount of time, the next four players in line move to offense, the offensive players move to defense, and the defenders move to the end of each line.

COACHING POINTS

- Defenders should be in help position when the ball is on the opposite side of the court. They should point one hand at the ball and one hand at the offensive player they are guarding so that they never lose sight of either.
- Defenders must move as the ball is in the air so they are in correct defensive position when the ball is caught. The coach may need to yell out "Pass!" so the defense can adjust to each pass correctly.

Three-on-Three With One Dribble (10 minutes)

Divide players into three lines on the baseline. The first player in each line is an offensive player. These players start on the court, facing the basket. The second player in each line is a defensive player. These players defend the offensive players. The rest of the players remain on the baseline. The offensive team tries to score by using cuts and screens; each player is allowed only one dribble each time she touches the ball. The defensive players work to stay with the offensive player they are assigned to guard. When a basket is made or the defense gets the ball, the defensive team goes to offense, and the next three players in line become the defensive team. Play for a certain amount of time or to a specified score.

COACHING POINTS

- Players should learn to cut after a pass and look to get the ball back for a shot.
- Offensive spacing is crucial.

Free Throws, Two in a Row (10 minutes)

Pair up players at each free-throw line. Partners take turns shooting one free throw until the pair makes two in a row.

COACHING POINTS

- The coach can also ask each player to shoot two free throws until the pair makes four in a row.
- As the season progresses, the coach may increase the number of consecutive free throws made from two to three, three to four, and four to five.

Announcements: _____

Late-Season Practices

The late-season practice sessions for this group should involve reviewing the skills and ability levels of the team and then working on any areas that are a concern. These practice sessions will also contain more team-oriented drills—three-on-three and four-on-four drills—than in the early-season and midseason practices. Late-season practice sessions also involve more five-player work in gamelike conditions.

Late-Season Practice Plan

Date: _____   Time: _____   Practice number: _____

Warm-Up (10 minutes)

Players line up on the baseline in four lines. On command, the players run down the court to the opposite baseline. Players work on running, stops, pivots, V-cuts, and jumping during their trips up and down the court.

COACHING POINT

Adjust the skills used in the warm-up based on the ability level of your players.

Two-Line Full-Court Passing (10 minutes)

Players line up in two lines on the baseline. Beginning with the first two in each line, players pass the ball back and forth while running down the court. Initially, air passes (passes that do not touch the floor) should be used in this drill; as the team progresses, the coach can ask players to also perform the drill using bounce passes.

COACHING POINT

Players can also perform a defensive slide down the length of the court as they pass the ball to each other.

Full-Court Layups, Right-Handed, 15 per Minute (10 minutes)

Divide the team into two groups, forming one line at the baseline under each basket (on the right side of the baseline). The first three players in each line should have a basketball. On command, the first player in each line dribbles to the other end and shoots a right-handed layup. After each layup is shot, the first player in line without a ball rebounds the shot taken as the shooter goes to the end of the line. Each time a player reaches half-court, the next player in line follows. Ask players to count the number of made layups; the goal is to make 15 by the time a minute has elapsed.

COACHING POINTS

- This is a speed dribbling drill, so the players should dribble the ball out in front of them; always encourage players to keep their head up while dribbling so they can see the court.
- You may need to adjust the goal of 15 made baskets in one minute, depending on your team's skill level.

Defensive Slides, One-on-Zero and One-on-One (10 minutes)

Divide the players into three lines on the baseline. The first player in each line performs defensive slides to the other baseline, making a drop step after every three slides. Once players get the hang of the drill, divide the players into pairs. One partner now dribbles a basketball, using V-cuts and crossover dribbles to change direction, from one baseline to the other; the other partner is the defensive player. The defensive player should slide to stay in front of the dribbler, executing a drop step each time the offensive player changes direction.

COACHING POINTS

- The offensive players should go slowly so the defense can work on footwork.
- Defensive players should remain one arm's length away from the dribbler, keeping their eyes on the dribbler's waist.

Two-on-Two Half Court (10 minutes)

Players begin in two lines at the half-court line. The first two players in line are the defensive players, and the next two are the offensive players. The coach passes a ball to one of the offensive players, and the offensive players dribble, pass, and cut to try to score. The drill is over when the offense scores or the defensive players get the rebound. Players rotate from offense to defense and from defense to the end of the line.

COACHING POINT

Various rules, such as allowing two dribbles, may be implemented in the drill.

Cutthroat, Three-on-Three (10 minutes)

Divide the team into three lines on the baseline; the first players in each line are on offense, and the second players in each line are on defense. The offensive players are facing the basket on the court, and the defenders are in defensive position. The coach starts the drill by passing the ball to one of the offensive players. As a rule, the offensive players must face the basket in triple-threat position, must move after they pass, and must thank the passer on a pass that results in a basket. If the offense fails to follow one of the rules, the whistle blows, and the offensive players must go to the end of the line. The defense moves to offense, and a new set of three players comes in on defense. Play for a specified period of time or until one team reaches a specified number of points. Each basket counts as a point.

COACHING POINT

Teams must leave and come onto the court quickly.

Free Throws, Two in a Row (5 minutes)

Pair up players at each free-throw line. Partners take turns shooting one free throw until the pair makes two in a row.

COACHING POINTS

- The coach can also ask each player to shoot two free throws until the pair makes four in a row.
- As the season progresses, the coach may increase the number of consecutive free throws made from two to three, three to four, and four to five.

Pair Shooting Contest, From Four Spots (10 minutes)

Players are divided into pairs; each pair has a ball. In this drill, players shoot from four designated spots chosen by the coach. One player shoots the ball from the first designated position on the floor (for example, the right elbow), gets his own rebound, and gives the ball to his partner for the same shot. Both players must make the shot from this spot before moving to the next spot. The drill continues back and forth with the players taking turns shooting until each player makes all four shots.

COACHING POINTS

- Try to organize the pairs so the two best shooters are not together.
- To make the drill more difficult, the coach can have the players make five shots (or any other specified number) each at every spot before moving to the next.

Out-of-Bounds Play, Review (10 minutes)

Divide your team into groups of five; one group begins on the court. Have every group of players run your out-of-bounds play without a defense.

COACHING POINTS

- Start with an easy out-of-bounds play for the players; you should not have more than one play at this point, but you can provide many options.
- Most out-of-bounds plays will begin in a box set, with one player in each corner of the lane.

Two-on-One Half Court (10 minutes)

Divide the team into two lines at half-court; one player is positioned in the middle of the lane as a defender. The first two players in line dribble and pass the ball to try to score against the lone defender.

COACHING POINT

The offensive players should only make one or two passes to try to score.

Five-on-Zero Offense (10 minutes)

Arrange the players in offensive positions based on the offensive set you want to teach. For example, this can be a 1-2-2 set with a point guard, two wings, and two post players or a 2-1-2 set with two guards, a high-post player, and two baseline or post players. In this drill, teach players how they can try to score in the set (including cuts, screens, and so on).

COACHING POINTS

- Teach players proper spacing and how to refill positions after a pass and cut.
- Emphasize that each player should square up to the basket after every catch.

10-Basket Shooting Contest (10 minutes)

The squad is divided into groups of no more than three per team. The coach designates a shooting spot where the team of players will shoot one shot each until that team makes 10 baskets. Each player rebounds his own shot and passes the ball back to the next person in line.

COACHING POINTS

- Emphasize to players that they should have their feet and hands ready to shoot before the ball is passed.
- The coach can change the specified number of made shots and the shooting spots depending on the players' ability.
- To change up the drill, the coach may specify that the players must shoot bank shots or must dribble and shoot.

Announcements: _____

12

Practices for Ages 9 and 10

Developing practice plans for players in the 9- and 10-year age group will take some time for the coach. Some of these players may have one to four years of experience, but for others, this may be the first time they have had any organized practice sessions with a coach. The coach will need to do some planning in order to implement drills that will cover the wide range of skill levels that can be present in this age group.

Players in this age group may start to take on specific positions on the court, such as the point guard, wings, or post. However, a coach should not lock players into just one position at this age. Skill development in practice sessions should involve all players working on skills that are used for all positions. General skill development drills will help each young person develop as a player for any position. This is extremely important, because players who are big and tall at this age may end up as guards on a varsity high school team, while smaller players may later become post players or forwards.

Practice sessions should include a good mixture of individual skill development along with team drills that emphasize several skills in one drill. Players in this age group may also be ready for some scrimmage work at the midseason or late-season practice sessions. These scrimmages may range from two-on-two games to five-on-five games. Make these scrimmages controlled; for example, the drill may start with the offensive team working to score, the defensive team converting to offense, and then the teams switching back again. With this format, three possessions take place before players switch out. This gives the coach a chance to bring up any coaching points after every three possessions.

Considerations When Coaching Females
Annie Byrne, Marian Catholic High School girls' basketball coach

When girls reach the age of 9 or 10, their interest in a particular sport, such as basketball, often grows or dissipates. Do all that you can to inspire and motivate your players at this level. Effective motivation can help increase players' skills and accelerate learning. Your motivation alone can drive a good player to continue to excel or can provide a new player with the belief that she can succeed. Your three main points of emphasis at this time should be reassurance, motivation, and teaching.

Again, the coach must start with the fundamentals. To effectively engage the girls at this age, you should include aspects that they enjoy about the game. A good plan is to start with shooting (which everyone loves). Be sure to teach players the correct mechanics of shooting and how to execute a proper follow-through. You can use the traditional concept of BEEF (balance, eyes, elbow, follow-through). Make sure you are encouraging players to shoot with their strong hand, right or left, and help them adjust accordingly. Another idea would be to work on ballhandling and then move to drills in which the players learn that the most important thing when trying to get past a defender is to change speed and direction. You could end with a fun but competitive game of dribble tag.

Other points of emphasis may include footwork and ballhandling, defensive concepts, and the basic rules of the game. At this age, players love to know more about the game itself. They may not truly understand the rules and how to play until they get a bit older or more accustomed to the game, but that is a lot closer than it may seem at this point.

9-10 years old

Early-Season Practices

Early-season practices should be well organized, which will establish the coach's organization for all future practice sessions. Skill development is a high priority for early-season practice sessions. Work on helping your players develop leadership qualities in early-season drills.

Early-Season Practice Plan

Date: _____   Time: _____   Practice number: _____

Warm-Up (10 minutes)

Players line up on the baseline in four lines. On command, the players run down the court to the opposite baseline. Players work on running, stops, pivots, V-cuts, and jumping during their trips up and down the court.

COACHING POINT

Adjust the skills used in the warm-up based on the ability level of your players.

Pair Passing, Two-Hand Chest (10 minutes)

Players pair up, and each pair stands about 6 to 8 feet (183 to 244 cm) from each other. On command, the player with the ball passes to his partner using a two-hand chest pass. Both hands and arms should be used to make the pass; the elbows should be close to the body, and the thumbs should be down with palms out after the pass. The partner then passes the ball back, and so on.

COACHING POINT

Emphasize that each pass should be made from the waist.

Two-Line Passing, Chest and Bounce (10 minutes)

Divide the squad into two lines (8 to 12 feet [2.4 to 3.6 m] apart) facing each other; the first person in one line should have a basketball. This player passes the ball using a chest pass to the first person in the opposite line. The passer follows his pass and goes to the end of the opposite line. The drill continues as the players pass the ball and follow it. Once players have practiced the chest pass, they should perform the same drill using the bounce pass.

COACHING POINTS

- Make sure that players do not travel as they catch the ball or make the pass while moving.
- The receiving player must have his hands up in a ready position to catch the ball.

Stationary Dribbling, Right- and Left-Handed (10 minutes)

Each player has a basketball (if this is not possible, players can be split up into two groups, and the drill can be performed by one group at a time). The players begin the drill by dribbling with the right hand first. On the coach's command, the players switch hands, now dribbling with the left hand. In this drill, players can work up to alternating hands with each dribble.

COACHING POINT

Remind players to keep their head and eyes up while dribbling.

Form Shooting to Partner (10 minutes)

Players pair up, facing each other; each pair has a ball. The player with the ball shoots the ball to his partner using correct shooting form—the elbow is pointed to the target, the shooting hand is underneath the ball, and the guide hand is on the side. The player should lift the ball up and toward his partner.

COACHING POINT

You may want players to begin this drill without using basketballs (players take imaginary shots to their partner) so that form is emphasized before the basketball is added.

Three-Line Passing Full Court, Staying in Lanes (10 minutes)

Players form three lines on one baseline; the players in the middle line should have a ball. On command, the middle player passes to one of the wing players as all three players are running toward the opposite baseline. The wing player catches the ball and passes back to the middle player, who then passes to the opposite wing player, and so on. Players on the wing should stay wide throughout. All three players end up on the opposite baseline as the next group of three proceeds down the court in the same manner.

COACHING POINTS

- While running the court, players should pass the ball across their body as they run forward.
- Players need to keep their hands in and up to call for the ball as they are running.

Mass Defensive Slide (5 minutes)

All players set up in a scattered formation around the coach, who is in position for all the players to see. On command or by following the coach, players move in a defensive slide to the right and left, keeping the knees bent and the hands above the waist.

COACHING POINTS

- This is a good time to play follow the leader. Have one player positioned in front of the group to lead the other players in the defensive slide drill.
- The coach should make sure that players' feet do not cross or come together during the slide; players should instead use a step and push action with the legs and feet.

Defensive Mirror (10 minutes)

Ask players to pair up, with one player on each side of a line on the court (such as the free-throw line or baseline). One player is designated as the offensive player; this player will move in a quick manner back and forth on her side of the line. The other player is the defender and must slide her feet and try to stay with the offensive player as she moves. The offensive player should remain in a 6- to 8-foot space as she moves back and forth.

COACHING POINT

Tell defenders to keep their eyes on the waist of their offensive player as they move to stay with her. Also teach defenders to avoid crossing their legs.

Seven-Spot Shooting, Two Made Shots From Each Spot (10 minutes)

Pick out seven spots on the floor, marking these spots with tape. Players pair up, and each pair has a ball. The first player shoots the ball at the first spot, gets her own rebound, and passes back to her partner, who shoots at the same spot. After two shots total are made from that spot, the players move to the next spot. Players must make two shots from each spot before they are done with the drill.

COACHING POINTS

- Emphasize that shooters must be ready and must have their feet and hands in good position to shoot when they catch the pass.
- This drill can be changed to require players to make any number of shots before moving to the next spot or require them to make a certain number in a row before moving to the next spot.

Dribble Freeze Tag (10 minutes)

Each player has a basketball (if this is not possible, players can be split up into two groups, and the drill can be performed by one group at a time). One player is designated as Michael Jordan, LeBron James, or any other star your players may know. On command, all players begin dribbling, and this player tries to touch the other players (all players are still maintaining their dribble). Once touched, a player must freeze, still dribbling while stationary. After a specified number of dribbles (to be determined by the coach), the player may be unfrozen.

COACHING POINT

Limit the area for the game to one half of the court or even from free-throw line to baseline so the designated player has more success.

Dribble and Shoot Contest (10 minutes)

Divide players into two or more teams, depending on the number of players. Each team should be limited to three or four players and should have their own basket, if possible. You can have the players start at any place on the court—for example, the free-throw line. The first player on each team dribbles to the basket for a shot, gets her own rebound, and passes back to the next player in line. Each team should count their made baskets. Continue for a specified amount of time and count the made baskets for each group.

COACHING POINTS

- This shooting drill can also be used for layups or bank shots.
- The coach may need to limit the number of dribbles to two or three before each shot.

Announcements: _____

Midseason Practices

Midseason practices for this age group will involve a combination of skill development and team drills, as well as some competitive drills. Players will now be ready to learn how to compete and win or lose; however, for competitive drills, coaches should be aware of players who are physically more mature and should match them up accordingly.

Midseason Practice Plan 1

Date: _____   Time: _____   Practice number: _____

Warm-Up (10 minutes)

Players line up on the baseline in four lines. On command, the players run down the court to the opposite baseline. Players work on running, stops, pivots, V-cuts, and jumping during their trips up and down the court.

COACHING POINT

Adjust the skills used in the warm-up based on the ability level of your players.

Dribble–Pivot–Pass (10 minutes)

Players line up on the sideline with no more than three players per line. The first player takes three right-handed dribbles out and comes to a stop. He then executes a reverse pivot (a front pivot may also be used) and makes a chest pass to the next player in line. The passer goes to the end of the line after the pass, and the next player (the one who caught the pass) dribbles out and makes the pivot and pass.

COACHING POINTS

- Emphasize to players that they should execute the pivot with the knees bent to make the pass.
- Depending on ability, players may instead use bounce passes or one-hand push passes in the drill.

Full-Court Layups, Right-Handed, 20 per Minute (10 minutes)

Divide the team into two groups, forming one line at the baseline under each basket (on the right side of the baseline). The first three players in each line should have a basketball. On command, the first player in each line dribbles to the other end and shoots a right-handed layup. After each layup is shot, the first player in line without a ball rebounds the shot taken as the shooter goes to the end of the line. Each time a player reaches half-court, the next player in line follows. Ask players to count the number of made layups; the goal is to make 20 by the time a minute has elapsed.

COACHING POINTS

- This is a speed dribbling drill, so the players should dribble the ball out in front of them; always encourage players to keep their head up while dribbling so they can see the court.
- You may need to adjust the goal of 20 made baskets in one minute, depending on your team's skill level.

Form Shooting to Partner (10 minutes)

Players pair up, facing each other; each pair has a ball. The player with the ball shoots the ball to his partner using correct shooting form—the elbow is pointed to the target, the shooting hand is underneath the ball, and the guide hand is on the side. The player should lift the ball up and toward his partner.

COACHING POINT

You may also ask players to shoot the ball with one hand; this ensures that the elbow is underneath the basketball in proper position.

Two-Line Passing, Chest and Bounce (10 minutes)

Divide the squad into two lines (8 to 12 feet apart) facing each other; the first person in one line should have a basketball. This player passes the ball using a chest pass to the first person in the opposite line. The passer follows his pass and goes to the end of the opposite line. The drill continues as the players pass the ball and follow it. Once players have practiced the chest pass, they should perform the same drill using the bounce pass.

COACHING POINTS

- The passer's elbows should be close to the body when executing a chest or bounce pass.
- The receiver needs to make sure his hands are up, showing a good target with the fingers and thumb in a W shape.

Dribble and Shoot Contest (10 minutes)

Divide players into two or more teams, depending on the number of players. Each team should be limited to three or four players and should have their own basket, if possible. You can have the players start at any place on the court—for example, the free-throw line. The first player on each team dribbles to the basket for a shot, gets her own rebound, and passes back to the next player in line. Each team should count their made baskets. Continue for a specified amount of time and count the made baskets for each group.

COACHING POINTS

- Players should dribble the ball with the outside hand.
- The coach may need to limit the number of dribbles to two or three before each shot.

Mass Defensive Slide (5 minutes)

All players set up in a scattered formation around the coach, who is in position for all the players to see. On command or by following the coach, players move in a defensive slide to the right and left, keeping the knees bent and the hands above the waist.

COACHING POINTS

- This is a good time to play follow the leader. Have one player positioned in front of the group to lead the other players in the defensive slide drill.
- The coach should make sure that players' feet do not cross or come together during the slide; players should instead use a step and push action with the legs and feet.

Two-on-Two Defensive Help (10 minutes)

Players form two lines, one at each wing outside the three-point line. One defensive player is guarding each offensive player in a two-on-two situation. The wing who starts with the ball skip passes it to his teammate on the opposite wing. The first wing's defender moves from guarding the player with the ball to the help-side rim line (the imaginary line running from rim to rim in the center of the floor) as the ball is skipped across to the opposite wing, while his teammate shifts to on-the-ball defense. After a specified amount of time, the next two players in line move to offense, the offensive players move to defense, and the defenders move to the end of each line.

COACHING POINTS

- The first defender must sprint to the rim line in good defensive position so he can see the ball and his player.
- The second defender must sprint to the offensive player catching the ball; the defender's hands should be up as he closes out on the shot.

Three-on-Three Half Court (10 minutes)

Divide players into three lines on the baseline. The first player in each line is an offensive player. These players start on the court, facing the basket. The second player in each line is a defensive player. These players defend the offensive players. The rest of the players remain on the baseline. The offensive team tries to score by dribbling, passing, and using cuts and screens. The defensive players work to stay with the offensive player they are assigned to guard. When a basket is made or the defense gets the ball, the defensive team goes to offense, and the next three players in line become the defensive team. Play for a certain amount of time or to a specified score.

COACHING POINT

Depending on the ability of your team, you can put restrictions on the players, such as no stealing the ball from the dribbler on defense, one dribble only for the offense, or the offense must make three passes before a shot is taken.

Three-on-Two Half Court (10 minutes)

Divide the team into three lines at the half-court line. Two defensive players are in the lane; one player is at the free-throw line, and the other is in the middle of the lane. The coach begins the drill by throwing the ball to the first player in the middle line at half-court. The other two offensive players are wings, positioned out wide on the sides of the court. The middle player makes a pass to one of the wing players, staying to the side of the pass for a possible return pass. The three offensive players try to attack the two defensive players to score. The offensive team should work to get a shot in two passes or less (the offense should try to make no more passes than there are defenders). After the play is over, the two wings move to defense, and the other three players go to the end of the lines.

COACHING POINTS

- Defensive players should be in a tandem position, with the back defender guarding the first pass to the wing and the top defender dropping back to the middle of the lane.
- The middle offensive player must slide to the elbow of the lane to the same side of the pass so that this player is in position to get the ball back for a jump shot.

Five-on-Zero Offense (10 minutes)

Arrange the players in offensive positions based on the offensive set you want to teach. For example, this can be a 1-2-2 set with a point guard, two wings, and two post players or a 2-1-2 set with two guards, a high-post player, and two baseline or post players. In this drill, teach players how they can try to score in the set (including cuts, screens, and so on).

COACHING POINTS

- Teach players proper spacing and how to refill positions after a pass and cut.
- Emphasize that each player should square up to the basket after every catch.

Free Throws, Two in a Row (10 minutes)

Pair up players at each free-throw line. Partners take turns shooting one free throw until the pair makes two in a row.

COACHING POINT

Adjust the number of consecutive free throws made based on the skill level of your players.

Announcements: _____

Midseason Practice Plan 2

Date: _____   Time: _____   Practice number: _____

Warm-Up (10 minutes)

Players line up on the baseline in four lines. On command, the players run down the court to the opposite baseline. Players work on running, stops, pivots, V-cuts, and jumping during their trips up and down the court.

COACHING POINT

Adjust the skills used in the warm-up based on the ability level of your players.

Dribble–Pivot–Pass (10 minutes)

Players line up on the sideline with no more than three players per line. The first player takes three right-handed dribbles out and comes to a stop. He then executes a reverse pivot (a front pivot may also be used) and makes a chest pass to the next player in line. The passer goes to the end of the line after the pass, and the next player (the one who caught the pass) dribbles out and makes the pivot and pass.

COACHING POINTS

- Emphasize to players that they should execute the pivot with the knees bent to make the pass.
- Depending on ability, players may instead use bounce passes or one-hand push passes in the drill.

Full-Court Layups, Left-Handed, 20 per Minute (10 minutes)

Divide the team into two groups, forming one line at the baseline under each basket (on the left side of the baseline). The first three players in each line should have a basketball. On command, the first player in each line dribbles to the other end and shoots a left-handed layup. After each layup is shot, the first player in line without a ball rebounds the shot taken as the shooter goes to the end of the line. Each time a player reaches half-court, the next player in line follows. Ask players to count the number of made layups; the goal is to make 20 by the time a minute has elapsed.

COACHING POINTS

- This is a speed dribbling drill, so the players should dribble the ball out in front of them; always encourage players to keep their head up while dribbling so they can see the court.
- You may need to adjust the goal of 20 made baskets in one minute, depending on your team's skill level.

One-Dribble Shooting From Free-Throw Line (10 minutes)

Players line up in two lines at the free-throw line, one line at each free-throw elbow. The first player in each line takes one dribble and then comes to a good stop for a shot. The player gets his own rebound, passes the ball back to the next player in line, and moves to the end of the line. The drill continues in this fashion for a certain number of baskets or a specified amount of time.

COACHING POINTS

- Players should dribble with the outside hand.
- Once players practice the one-dribble shot, this drill can be made into a contest between the groups.

Dribble and Shoot Contest (10 minutes)

Divide players into two or more teams, depending on the number of players. Each team should be limited to three or four players and should have their own basket, if possible. You can have the players start at any place on the court—for example, the free-throw line or half-court line. The first player on each team dribbles to the basket for a shot, gets her own rebound, and passes back to the next player in line. Each team should count their made baskets. Continue for a specified amount of time and count the made baskets for each group.

COACHING POINTS

- Players should dribble the ball with the outside hand.
- This drill can also combine dribble moves (such as the crossover) before the shot.

Three-on-Two, Two-on-One Full Court (10 minutes)

Start with three lines at one end of the court. Two players set up at the opposite end of the court in a defensive position, one player at the free-throw line and one player in the middle of the lane. The first three players in line try to score against the two defenders (three-on-two); the middle player dribbles the ball down the floor and makes a pass to one wing. After the shot, the two defenders become the offensive players, moving to the opposite end of the court with the middle offensive player transitioning to defense (two-on-one). The two wings remain as the defenders in the lane for the next group of three offensive players.

COACHING POINTS

- The three offensive players should work to get a shot after three or fewer passes against the two defenders.
- The two offensive players should work to get a shot after two or fewer passes against the one defender.

Defensive Slide, Sideline to Sideline (5 minutes)

Players line up on one sideline, facing the coach at the end of the court. On command, the players step and push in a defensive slide to the opposite sideline and back again.

COACHING POINTS

- The players should start slowly by taking a big step with the foot in the direction they are going, pushing off the opposite foot in a defensive slide motion.
- Players need to keep their head level as they slide.

Two-on-Two Defensive Help (10 minutes)

Players form two lines, one at each wing outside the three-point line. One defensive player is guarding each offensive player in a two-on-two situation. The wing who starts with the ball skip passes it to his teammate on the opposite wing. The first wing's defender moves from guarding the player with the ball to the help-side rim line (the imaginary line running from rim to rim in the center of the floor) as the ball is skipped across to the opposite wing, while his teammate shifts to on-the-ball defense. After a specified amount of time, the next two players in line move to offense, the offensive players move to defense, and the defenders move to the end of each line.

COACHING POINTS

- The first defender must sprint to the rim line in good defensive position so he can see the ball and his player.
- The second defender must sprint to the offensive player catching the ball; the defender's hands should be up as he closes out on the shot.

Three-on-Three Pass, Cut, and Replace (10 minutes)

Organize players into teams of three. One team is the offensive team, and one is the defensive team; the remaining teams stay on the baseline ready to come onto the court. The offensive players should be arranged with a player at the top of the key and two wings. The player at the top of the key begins by making a pass to one of the wings. After the pass, the player makes a cut to the basket. The opposite wing then fills the top position, and the cutter fills the vacated wing position. The ball is then reversed to the top of the key and passed to the other wing; the player at the top of the key cuts to the basket to repeat the process. The coach designates how many ball reversals must take place before the ball can be passed to the cutter for a shot.

COACHING POINT

Ask the offense to focus on proper spacing and filling in each position.

Three-on-Three With One Dribble (10 minutes)

Divide players into three lines on the baseline. The first player in each line is an offensive player. These players start on the court, facing the basket. The second player in each line is a defensive player. These players defend the offensive players. The rest of the players remain on the baseline. The offensive team tries to score by using cuts and screens; each player is allowed only one dribble each time she touches the ball. The defensive players work to stay with the offensive player they are assigned to guard. When a basket is made or the defense gets the ball, the defensive team goes to offense, and the next three players in line become the defensive team. Play for a certain amount of time or to a specified score.

COACHING POINTS

- Players should learn to cut after a pass and look to get the ball back for a shot.
- Offensive spacing is crucial.

Four-on-Four Defensive Shell (10 minutes)

Four players are on offense, and four on defense. The offense is spaced out with one guard above each free-throw lane outside the three-point line and one player at each wing. A defender is guarding each offensive player; the rest of the team is divided into four lines at half-court. One of the guards starts with the ball and passes it to a wing. As the coach observes, the defenders must adjust to each pass so they are in good help position or on-the-ball position. On command, the offense continues to pass the ball from one wing to the other wing, and the defenders adjust their position on each pass. After a specified amount of time, the next four players in line move to offense, the offensive players move to defense, and the defenders move to the end of each line.

COACHING POINTS

- Defenders should be in help position when the ball is on the opposite side of the court. They should point one hand at the ball and one hand at the offensive player they are guarding so that they never lose sight of either.
- Defenders must move as the ball is in the air so they are in correct defensive position when the ball is caught. The coach may need to yell out "Pass!" so the defense can adjust to each pass correctly.

Free Throws, Two in a Row (10 minutes)

Pair up players at each free-throw line. Partners take turns shooting one free throw until the pair makes two in a row.

COACHING POINT

Adjust the number of consecutive free throws made based on the skill level of your players.

Announcements: _____

Midseason Practice Plan 3

Date: _____   Time: _____   Practice number: _____

Warm-Up (10 minutes)

Players line up on the baseline in four lines. On command, the players run down the court to the opposite baseline. Players work on running, stops, pivots, V-cuts, and jumping during their trips up and down the court.

COACHING POINT

Adjust the skills used in the warm-up based on the ability level of your players.

Two-Line Fast Break With Layup (10 minutes)

The team is arranged in two lines, with one line in the lane facing the opposite basket and the other line at the wing position (players in this line are ready to catch the ball). The first player in the lane line starts with the ball and passes to the player at the wing. The wing player dribbles the ball to the opposite free-throw line and makes a good stop without traveling. The passer runs to the other end in the outside lane to receive a return pass from the wing. After receiving the return pass, this player dribbles in for a layup. These two players stay at this end, switching positions, as the next two players in line take their turn. After all the players have completed the drill going to one basket, they switch positions and complete the drill going back to the original basket.

COACHING POINTS

- Make sure the passer runs wide; to stress this, the coach can place cones on the court and specify that the player must run outside the cones.
- The drill can also be performed with the players executing jump shots off the glass, power shots, or a pass back to the middle player at the free-throw line for a shot.

Full-Court Layups, Left-Handed, 25 per Minute (10 minutes)

Divide the team into two groups, forming one line at the baseline under each basket (on the left side of the baseline). The first three players in each line should have a basketball. On command, the first player in each line dribbles to the other end and shoots a left-handed layup. After each layup is shot, the first player in line without a ball rebounds the shot taken as the shooter goes to the end of the line. Each time a player reaches half-court, the next player in line follows. Ask players to count the number of made layups; the goal is to make 25 by the time a minute has elapsed.

COACHING POINTS

- This is a speed dribbling drill, so the players should dribble the ball out in front of them; always encourage players to keep their head up while dribbling so they can see the court.
- You may need to adjust the goal of 25 made baskets in one minute, depending on your team's skill level.

Four-Corner Passing and Jump Shots (10 minutes)

Begin this drill with one line of players in each corner of the court, with two balls in opposite corners (four balls total). The first player in each line with a ball (the shooting lines) takes a few dribbles forward, then passes the ball to the first player in line at the other end of the court (the passing lines). The passer follows the pass, receives a return pass, and takes a shot. He then moves to the end of the same line at this end (the passing line), while the player who made the return pass rebounds the ball, passes it to the opposite corner at the same end, and moves to the end of that line (the shooting line).

COACHING POINTS

- Shooters need to have their feet in the proper position for shooting when they catch the ball.
- Rebounders should look to make good outlet passes.

Two-Ball Dribbling (10 minutes)

Players pair up along one sideline. The first player in each pair has two basketballs; this player dribbles both balls simultaneously from one sideline to the other and back. She then hands off the balls to her partner, who continues the drill.

COACHING POINTS

- Players need to keep their head up while dribbling both balls; they should not look at the basketballs.
- After players dribble both balls simultaneously, they can repeat the drill, this time alternating bounces while dribbling both balls.

Three-on-Two Half Court (10 minutes)

Divide the team into three lines at the half-court line. Two defensive players are in the lane; one player is at the free-throw line, and the other is in the middle of the lane. The coach begins the drill by throwing the ball to the first player in the middle line at half-court. The other two offensive players are wings, positioned out wide on the sides of the court. The middle player makes a pass to one of the wing players, staying to the side of the pass for a possible return pass. The three offensive players try to attack the two defensive players to score. The offensive team should work to get a shot in two passes or less (the offense should try to make no more passes than there are defenders). After the play is over, the two wings move to defense, and the other three players go to the end of the lines.

COACHING POINTS

- Defensive players should be in a tandem position, with the back defender guarding the first pass to the wing and the top defender dropping back to the middle of the lane.
- The middle offensive player must slide to the elbow of the lane to the same side of the pass so that this player is in position to get the ball back for a jump shot.

Four-on-Four Defensive Shell, Jump to Ball (5 minutes)

As in the four-on-four defensive shell drill, four players are on offense, and four on defense. The offense is spaced out with one guard above each free-throw lane outside the three-point line and one player at each wing. A defender is guarding each offensive player; the rest of the team is divided into four lines at half-court. One of the guards starts with the ball and passes it to a wing. As the coach observes, the defenders must jump to the ball, adjusting to each pass so they are in good help position or on-the-ball position. On command, the offense continues to pass the ball from one wing to the other wing, and the defenders jump to the ball and adjust their position on each pass. After a specified amount of time, the next four players in line move to offense, the offensive players move to defense, and the defenders move to the end of each line.

COACHING POINTS

- Defenders should be in help position when the ball is on the opposite side of the court. They should point one hand at the ball and one hand at the offensive player they are guarding so that they never lose sight of either.
- Defenders must move as the ball is in the air so they are in correct defensive position when the ball is caught. The coach may need to yell out "Pass!" so the defense can adjust to each pass correctly.

Three-on-Three Defensive Help (10 minutes)

In this three-on-three drill, the defense works on defending dribble penetration by the offensive players, who are trying to get to the basket. The defender who is guarding the player closest to the dribbler must help stop the dribbler, recovering back to his own player once the ball has been passed back out.

COACHING POINTS

- Defenders need to stay in a good defensive stance.
- Defenders need to watch the dribbler as well as the player they are guarding so they can be in a position to help.

Cutthroat, Four-on-Four (10 minutes)

Divide the team into four lines on the baseline; the first players in each line are on offense, and the second players in each line are on defense. The offensive players are facing the basket on the court. The coach starts the drill by passing the ball to one of the offensive players. The defenders run from the baseline to close out on the offense in defensive position. As a rule, the offensive players must face the basket in triple-threat position, must move after they pass, and must thank the passer on a pass that results in a basket. If the offense fails to follow one of the rules, the whistle blows, and the offensive players must go to the end of the line. The defense moves to offense, and a new set of three players comes in on defense. Play for a specified period of time or until one team reaches a specified number of points. Each basket counts as a point.

COACHING POINTS

- Teams must leave and come onto the court quickly.
- Players must perform the action specified by each rule immediately; if not, the team is out.

Five-on-Zero Offense (10 minutes)

Arrange the players in offensive positions based on the offensive set you want to teach. For example, this can be a 1-2-2 set with a point guard, two wings, and two post players or a 2-1-2 set with two guards, a high-post player, and two baseline or post players. In this drill, teach players how they can try to score in the set (including cuts, screens, and so on).

COACHING POINTS

- Teach players proper spacing and how to refill positions after a pass and cut.
- Emphasize that each player should square up to the basket after every catch.

Five-on-Five Scrimmage, Controlled (10 minutes)

Divide the team into two teams of five for a scrimmage that involves using the skills and tactics that the players have learned so far in practices. Have the players go five-on-five half court and transition into a full-court scrimmage after a made or missed basket. They should stop at the other end, then again go five-on-five into a full-court scrimmage. Sub players as necessary.

COACHING POINTS

- The coach should stop play when necessary to explain areas on both offense and defense that need work.
- Offensive players need to sprint back on a change of possession in order to stop the ball first.

Free Throws, Two in a Row (10 minutes)

Pair up players at each free-throw line. Partners take turns shooting one free throw until the pair makes two in a row.

COACHING POINT

Adjust the number of consecutive free throws made based on the skill level of your players.

Announcements: _____

Late-Season Practices

Practice drills during the late season will include team drills that help develop team skills as well as individual skills. The coach should plan carefully in order to account for individual differences in the skill levels on the team.

Late-Season Practice Plan

Date: _____   Time: _____   Practice number: _____

Warm-Up (10 minutes)

Players line up on the baseline in four lines. On command, the players run down the court to the opposite baseline. Players work on running, stops, pivots, V-cuts, and jumping during their trips up and down the court.

COACHING POINT

Adjust the skills used in the warm-up based on the ability level of your players.

Four-Corner Passing and Jump Shots (10 minutes)

Begin this drill with one line of players in each corner of the court, with two balls in opposite corners (four balls total). The first player in each line with a ball (the shooting lines) takes a few dribbles forward, then passes the ball to the first player in line at the other end of the court (the passing lines). The passer follows the pass, receives a return pass, and takes a shot. He then moves to the end of the same line at this end (the passing line), while the player who made the return pass rebounds the ball, passes it to the opposite corner at the same end, and moves to the end of that line (the shooting line). The goal is to make 10 jump shots in one minute.

COACHING POINTS

- Shooters need to have their feet in the proper position for shooting when they catch the ball.
- Rebounders should look to make good outlet passes.

Full-Court Layups, Right-Handed, 30 per Minute (10 minutes)

Divide the team into two groups, forming one line at the baseline under each basket (on the right side of the baseline). The first three players in each line should have a basketball. On command, the first player in each line dribbles to the other end and shoots a right-handed layup. After each layup is shot, the first player in line without a ball rebounds the shot taken as the shooter goes to the end of the line. Each time a player reaches half-court, the next player in line follows. Ask players to count the number of made layups; the goal is to make 30 by the time a minute has elapsed.

COACHING POINTS

- This is a speed dribbling drill, so the players should dribble the ball out in front of them; always encourage players to keep their head up while dribbling so they can see the court.
- You may need to adjust the goal of 30 made baskets in one minute, depending on your team's skill level.

Defensive Slides, One-on-Zero and One-on-One (10 minutes)

Divide the players into three lines on the baseline. The first player in each line performs defensive slides to the other baseline, making a drop step after every three slides. Once players get the hang of the drill, divide the players into pairs. One partner now dribbles a basketball, using V-cuts and crossover dribbles to change direction, from one baseline to the other; the other partner is the defensive player. The defensive player should slide to stay in front of the dribbler, executing a drop step each time the offensive player changes direction.

COACHING POINTS

- The offensive players should go slowly so the defense can work on footwork.
- Defensive players should remain one arm's length away from the dribbler, keeping their eyes on the dribbler's waist.

Three-on-Three Half Court (10 minutes)

Divide players into three lines on the baseline. The first player in each line is an offensive player. These players start on the court, facing the basket. The second player in each line is a defensive player. These players defend the offensive players. The rest of the players remain on the baseline. The offensive team tries to score by dribbling, passing, and using cuts and screens. The defensive players work to stay with the offensive player they are assigned to guard. When a basket is made or the defense gets the ball, the defensive team goes to offense, and the next three players in line become the defensive team. Play for a certain amount of time or to a specified score.

COACHING POINT

Depending on the ability of your team, you can put restrictions on the players, such as no stealing the ball from the dribbler on defense, one dribble only for the offense, or the offense must make three passes before a shot is taken.

Cutthroat, Four-on-Four (10 minutes)

Divide the team into four lines on the baseline; the first players in each line are on offense, and the second players in each line are on defense. The offensive players are facing the basket on the court. The coach starts the drill by passing the ball to one of the offensive players. The defenders run from the baseline to close out on the offense in defensive position. As a rule, the offensive players must face the basket in triple-threat position, must move after they pass, and must thank the passer on a pass that results in a basket. If the offense fails to follow one of the rules, the whistle blows, and the offensive players must go to the end of the line. The defense moves to offense, and a new set of three players comes in on defense. Play for a specified period of time or until one team reaches a specified number of points. Each basket counts as a point.

COACHING POINTS

- Teams must leave and come onto the court quickly.
- Players must perform the action specified by each rule immediately; if not, the team is out.

Free Throws, Two in a Row (5 minutes)

Pair up players at each free-throw line. Partners take turns shooting one free throw until the pair makes two in a row.

COACHING POINT

Adjust the number of consecutive free throws made based on the skill level of your players.

Pair Shooting Contest, From Four Spots (10 minutes)

Players are divided into pairs; each pair has a ball. In this drill, players shoot from four designated spots chosen by the coach. One player shoots the ball from the first designated position on the floor (for example, the right elbow), gets his own rebound, and gives the ball to his partner for the same shot. Both players must make the shot from this spot before moving to the next spot. The drill continues back and forth with the players taking turns shooting until each player makes all four shots.

COACHING POINTS

- Try to organize the pairs so the two best shooters are not together.
- To make the drill more difficult, the coach can have the players make five shots (or any other specified number) each at every spot before moving to the next.

Out-of-Bounds Play, Review (10 minutes)

Divide your team into groups of five; one group begins on the court. Have every group of players run your out-of-bounds play without a defense.

COACHING POINTS

- Start with an easy out-of-bounds play for the players; you should not have more than one play at this point, but you can provide many options.
- Most out-of-bounds plays will begin in a box set, with one player in each corner of the lane.

Two-on-One Half Court (10 minutes)

Divide the team into two lines at half-court; one player is positioned in the middle of the lane as a defender. The first two players in line dribble and pass the ball to try to score against the lone defender.

COACHING POINT

The offensive players should only make one or two passes to try to score.

Five-on-Zero Offense (10 minutes)

Arrange the players in offensive positions based on the offensive set you want to teach. For example, this can be a 1-2-2 set with a point guard, two wings, and two post players or a 2-1-2 set with two guards, a high-post player, and two baseline or post players. In this drill, teach players how they can try to score in the set (including cuts, screens, and so on).

COACHING POINTS

- Teach players proper spacing and how to refill positions after a pass and cut.
- Emphasize that each player should square up to the basket after every catch.

Four-Quarter Shooting (10 minutes)

This is a three-player drill using two balls. Two players have a ball. One player with a ball shoots her ball, rebounds, and passes the ball to the player who does not have a ball. The other player with the ball shoots her ball immediately after the first player, gets the rebound, and passes to the player who now does not have a ball (the first shooter). After the shot, each player repositions for the pass from the next shooter. Play for four minutes, keeping track of made baskets.

COACHING POINT

The shooter must get a rebound, pass the ball, and then immediately look for the pass from the next shooter.

Announcements: _____

13

Practices for Ages 11 and 12

Players in this age group will start to see a lot of improvement in skill development, and they will be anxious to work on team drills along with improving their individual skills. In each practice, the coach should try to include drills that work on several skills at the same time. Though the emphasis in these drills may be on one or two skills, the players are also working on other skills during the drill. The coach should emphasize the skill that needs the most work.

For players at this age, competitive drills are effective for keeping the players' interest as well as enhancing their skill development. Competition may come in the form of player versus player or time and score. Competition during drills will allow players to become acclimated to gamelike conditions and work on performing skills under the same pressure found in game situations.

Particularly with this age group, the coach should remember the six guidelines for shaping skills, as described on page 50 of part II. The coach will now start to use more offensive strategies to attack defenses. Out-of-bounds plays and other special situations should be worked on in practice; the players play more games throughout the season, so they need to practice these situations.

Coaches should start to help players develop leadership qualities. Some ideas for developing leadership qualities in players include asking individual players to demonstrate a new drill, asking individual players to verbalize either strategy or how to perform a drill to the rest of the team, and asking individual players to organize drills themselves.

Considerations When Coaching Females
Annie Byrne, Marian Catholic High School girls' basketball coach

Ages 11 and 12 can be an awkward time for girls because their bodies are growing and changing. Coordination and balance may be a bit of a challenge for some taller girls who are having a difficult time getting their body to do what their brain wants it to do. Encouragement is a key ingredient at this time. At this point, the girls have likely been participating in basketball to some extent through school basketball, camps, skills clinics, and so on. To determine where to start with a particular group, the coach should evaluate their ability to perform basic skills such as correct footwork and the mechanics of shooting. The coach can also evaluate the players' understanding of defensive concepts (man-to-man and zone), rules of the game, and positions (guards, forwards, posts).

Having these girls do ladder work (exercises in which players jump into and out of a rope ladder placed on the floor) and jump rope is a good idea because this helps them with balance and coordination. When incorporating sprints into practice, an effective method is to have the players sprint to half-court and then turn and backpedal to the baseline. This enables the players to work on changing direction and speed while keeping balance and increasing foot speed. Other drills to consider are ones that will increase ability while raising confidence. Some suggestions are three-line passing, one-on-one defensive slides, shell drills, box-out drills, and transition drills (three-on-two, two-on-one).

11-12 years old

Early-Season Practices

Early-season practice sessions should always begin with a review of fundamental skills. Not only is this a good refresher for the players, but it also helps the coach to evaluate the skill levels of his players and plan for future practice sessions.

Early-Season Practice Plan

Date: _____   Time: _____   Practice number: _____

Warm-Up (10 minutes)

Players line up on the baseline in four lines. On command, the players run down the court to the opposite baseline. Players work on running, stops, pivots, V-cuts, and jumping during their trips up and down the court.

COACHING POINT

Adjust the skills used in the warm-up based on the ability level of your players.

Pair Passing, Two-Hand Chest (10 minutes)

Players pair up, and each pair stands about 6 to 8 feet (183 to 244 cm) from each other. On command, the player with the ball passes to his partner using a two-hand chest pass. Both hands and arms should be used to make the pass; the elbows should be close to the body, and the thumbs should be down with palms out after the pass. The partner then passes the ball back, and so on.

COACHING POINTS

- Players should step toward the target as they pass the ball.
- Receivers should have their hands up ready for the catch.

Two-Line Passing: Chest, Bounce, Overhead, and Baseball (10 minutes)

Divide the squad into two lines facing each other; the lines should be at least lane-width apart depending on player ability. The first person in one line should have a basketball. This player passes the ball using a chest pass to the first person in the opposite line. The passer follows his pass and goes to the end of the opposite line. The drill continues as the players pass the ball and follow it. Once players have practiced the chest pass, they should perform the same drill using the bounce pass, overhead pass, and baseball pass.

COACHING POINTS

- Players should step as they pass the ball, making the pass more direct.
- To help communication, players should call out the name of the player they are passing to.

Four-Line Dribbling, Crossover (10 minutes)

Players are in four lines on each sideline, facing each other. The first player in each line starts with a right-handed dribble, dribbling to midcourt, where each player crosses over to the left hand and continues to the opposite line. Each player makes a jump stop and passes to the next player in the opposite line. The drill continues back and forth with players performing the crossover dribble.

COACHING POINTS

- Players must keep their head and chin up on the crossover in order to avoid a collision with the player coming from the opposite direction.
- The crossover dribble should be low, below the knees.

Form Shooting (10 minutes)

Players stand two to three feet from a basket, placing the ball in one hand. Players bend the knees and shoot the ball one handed to the basket. This drill helps the players develop the proper fundamentals of shooting.

COACHING POINTS

- The elbow of the shooting arm should be at shoulder level and should not drop lower when executing the one-hand shot.
- Players must be careful not to grip the ball like a baseball or softball; the ball should rest on the hand.

Three-Line Passing Full Court, Staying in Lanes (10 minutes)

Players form three lines on one baseline; the players in the middle line should have a ball. On command, the middle player passes to one of the wing players as all three players are running toward the opposite baseline. The wing player catches the ball and passes back to the middle player, who then passes to the opposite wing player, and so on. Players on the wing should stay wide throughout. All three players end up on the opposite baseline as the next group of three proceeds down the court in the same manner.

COACHING POINTS

- While running the court, players should pass the ball across their body as they run forward.
- Players need to keep their hands in and up to call for the ball as they are running.

Mass Defensive Slide (5 minutes)

All players set up in a scattered formation around the coach, who is in position for all the players to see. On command or by following the coach, players move in a defensive slide to the right and left and from front to back, keeping the knees bent and the hands above the waist.

COACHING POINTS

- This is a good time to play follow the leader. Have one player positioned in front of the group to lead the other players in the defensive slide drill.
- The coach should make sure that players' feet do not cross or come together during the slide; players should instead use a step and push action with the legs and feet.

Defensive Mirror (10 minutes)

Ask players to pair up, with one player on each side of a line on the court (such as the free-throw line or baseline). One player is designated as the offensive player; this player will move in a quick manner back and forth on her side of the line. The other player is the defender and must slide her feet and try to stay with the offensive player as she moves. The offensive player should remain in a 6- to 8-foot space as she moves back and forth.

COACHING POINT

Tell defenders to keep their eyes on the waist of their offensive player as they move to stay with her. Also teach defenders to avoid crossing their legs.

Seven-Spot Shooting, Two Made Shots From Each Spot (10 minutes)

Pick out seven spots on the floor, marking these spots with tape. Players pair up, and each pair has a ball. The first player shoots the ball at the first spot, gets her own rebound, and passes back to her partner, who shoots at the same spot. After two shots total are made from that spot the players move to the next spot. Players must make two shots from each spot before they are done with the drill.

COACHING POINTS

- Emphasize that shooters must be ready and must have their feet and hands in good position to shoot when they catch the pass.
- This drill can be changed to require players to make any number of shots before moving to the next spot or require them to make a certain number in a row before moving to the next spot.

Two-on-One Fast Break Half Court (10 minutes)

Players form three lines at the baseline. On command, the first three players run to half-court. The middle player then runs back and gets in position to be a defender. The coach passes the ball to one of the players at half-court, and these players attack the basket in a two-on-one situation.

COACHING POINTS

- Offensive players should try to get a good shot with no more than one pass.
- Most of the time, a bounce pass should be thrown in a two-on-one situation.

Three-on-Two Fast Break Half Court (10 minutes)

Players form five lines at the baseline. On command, the first five players run to half-court. The middle player and the two outside players in line will be the offensive players, and the other two players will move back as defenders. The coach passes the ball to the middle player at the half-court line, and the offensive players attack the defenders in a three-on-two situation.

COACHING POINTS

- The offensive team should try to score with only two passes.
- After the middle player passes to one of the wings, this player should go to the side of the pass at the free-throw line elbow for a possible return pass.

Announcements: _____

Midseason Practices

At this level, midseason practices will become more competitive and include more team drills. However, players still need to work on the basic skills of passing, shooting, rebounding, and dribbling during these practice sessions.

Midseason Practice Plan 1

Date: _____   Time: _____   Practice number: _____

Warm-Up (10 minutes)

Players line up on the baseline in four lines. On command, the players run down the court to the opposite baseline. Players work on running, stops, pivots, V-cuts, and jumping during their trips up and down the court.

COACHING POINT

Adjust the skills used in the warm-up based on the ability level of your players.

Dribble–Pivot–Pass (10 minutes)

Players line up on the sideline with no more than three players per line. The first player takes three right-handed dribbles out and comes to a stop. He then executes a reverse pivot (a front pivot may also be used) and makes a chest pass to the next player in line. The passer goes to the end of the line after the pass, and the next player (the one who caught the pass) dribbles out and makes the pivot and pass.

COACHING POINTS

- Emphasize to players that they should execute the pivot with the knees bent to make the pass.
- Depending on ability, players may instead use bounce passes or one-hand push passes in the drill.

Full-Court Layups, Right-Handed, 30 per Minute (10 minutes)

Divide the team into two groups, forming one line at the baseline under each basket (on the right side of the baseline). The first three players in each line should have a basketball. On command, the first player in each line dribbles to the other end and shoots a right-handed layup. After each layup is shot, the first player in line without a ball rebounds the shot taken as the shooter goes to the end of the line. Each time a player reaches half-court, the next player in line follows. Ask players to count the number of made layups; the goal is to make 30 by the time a minute has elapsed.

COACHING POINTS

- This is a speed dribbling drill, so the players should dribble the ball out in front of them; always encourage players to keep their head up while dribbling so they can see the court.
- You may need to adjust the goal of 30 made baskets in one minute, depending on your team's skill level.

Form Shooting (10 minutes)

Players stand two to three feet from a basket, placing the ball in one hand. Players bend the knees and shoot the ball one handed to the basket. This drill helps the players develop the proper fundamentals of shooting.

COACHING POINTS

- The elbow of the shooting arm should be at shoulder level and should not drop lower when executing the one-hand shot.
- Players must be careful not to grip the ball like a baseball or softball; the ball should rest on the hand.

Two-Line Passing: Chest, Bounce, Overhead, and Baseball (10 minutes)

Divide the squad into two lines facing each other; the lines should be at least lane-width apart depending on player ability. The first person in one line should have a basketball. This player passes the ball using a chest pass to the first person in the opposite line. The passer follows his pass and goes to the end of the opposite line. The drill continues as the players pass the ball and follow it. Once players have practiced the chest pass, they should perform the same drill using the bounce pass, overhead pass, and baseball pass.

COACHING POINTS

- Players should step as they pass the ball, making the pass more direct.
- To help communication, players should call out the name of the player they are passing to.

Five-on-Zero Fast Break From Rebound (10 minutes)

Five players are positioned in the lane. The coach shoots the ball, and the players rebound the ball and then move down the court for a five-on-zero fast break on the opposite end. The rebounder makes an outlet pass to a guard; the wings run in both outside lanes, the post runs in the middle lane, and the forward is the trailer, stopping at the free-throw line.

COACHING POINT

The outlet should be to the side of the rebounder, outside the lane.

Mass Defensive Slide (5 minutes)

All players set up in a scattered formation around the coach, who is in position for all the players to see. On command or by following the coach, players move in a defensive slide to the right and left, keeping the knees bent and the hands above the waist.

COACHING POINTS

- This is a good time to play follow the leader. Have one player positioned in front of the group to lead the other players in the defensive slide drill.
- The coach should make sure that players' feet do not cross or come together during the slide; players should instead use a step and push action with the legs and feet.

Two-on-Two Defensive Help (10 minutes)

Players form two lines, one at each wing outside the three-point line. One defensive player is guarding each offensive player in a two-on-two situation. The wing who starts with the ball skip passes it to his teammate on the opposite wing. The first wing's defender moves from guarding the player with the ball to the help-side rim line (the imaginary line running from rim to rim in the center of the floor) as the ball is skipped across to the opposite wing, while his teammate shifts to on-the-ball defense. After a specified amount of time, the next two players in line move to offense, the offensive players move to defense, and the defenders move to the end of each line.

COACHING POINTS

- The first defender must sprint to the rim line in good defensive position so he can see the ball and his player.
- The second defender must sprint to the offensive player catching the ball; the defender's hands should be up as he closes out on the shot.

Four-on-Four Defensive Shell (10 minutes)

Four players are on offense, and four on defense. The offense is spaced out with one guard above each free-throw lane outside the three-point line and one player at each wing. A defender is guarding each offensive player; the rest of the team is divided into four lines at half-court. One of the guards starts with the ball and passes it to a wing. As the coach observes, the defenders must adjust to each pass so they are in good help position or on-the-ball position. On command, the offense continues to pass the ball from one wing to the other wing, and the defenders adjust their position on each pass. After a specified amount of time, the next four players in line move to offense, the offensive players move to defense, and the defenders move to the end of each line.

COACHING POINTS

- Defenders should be in help position when the ball is on the opposite side of the court. They should point one hand at the ball and one hand at the offensive player they are guarding so that they never lose sight of either.
- Defenders must move as the ball is in the air so they are in correct defensive position when the ball is caught. The coach may need to yell out "Pass!" so the defense can adjust to each pass correctly.

Three-on-Two, Two-on-One Full Court (10 minutes)

Start with three lines at one end of the court. Two players set up at the opposite end of the court in a defensive position, one player at the free-throw line and one player in the middle of the lane. The first three players in line try to score against the two defenders (three-on-two); the middle player dribbles the ball down the floor and makes a pass to one wing. After the shot, the two defenders become the offensive players, moving to the opposite end of the court with the middle offensive player transitioning to defense (two-on-one). The two wings remain as the defenders in the lane for the next group of three offensive players.

COACHING POINTS

- The three offensive players should work to get a shot after three or fewer passes against the two defenders.
- The two offensive players should work to get a shot after two or fewer passes against the one defender.

Five-on-Zero Offense (10 minutes)

Arrange the players in offensive positions based on the offensive set you want to teach. For example, this can be a 1-2-2 set with a point guard, two wings, and two post players or a 2-1-2 set with two guards, a high-post player, and two baseline or post players. In this drill, teach players how they can try to score in the set (including cuts, screens, and so on).

COACHING POINTS

- Teach players proper spacing and how to refill positions after a pass and cut.
- Emphasize that each player should square up to the basket after every catch.

Free Throws, Two in a Row (10 minutes)

Pair up players at each free-throw line. Partners take turns shooting one free throw until the pair makes two in a row.

COACHING POINT

Adjust the number of consecutive free throws made based on the skill level of your players.

Announcements: _____

Midseason Practice Plan 2

Date: _____   Time: _____   Practice number: _____

Warm-Up (10 minutes)

Players line up on the baseline in four lines. On command, the players run down the court to the opposite baseline. Players work on running, stops, pivots, V-cuts, and jumping during their trips up and down the court.

COACHING POINT

Adjust the skills used in the warm-up based on the ability level of your players.

Dribble–Pivot–Pass (10 minutes)

Players line up on the sideline with no more than three players per line. The first player takes three right-handed dribbles out and comes to a stop. He then executes a reverse pivot (a front pivot may also be used) and makes a chest pass to the next player in line. The passer goes to the end of the line after the pass, and the next player (the one who caught the pass) dribbles out and makes the pivot and pass.

COACHING POINTS

- Emphasize to players that they should execute the pivot with the knees bent to make the pass.
- Depending on ability, players may instead use bounce passes or one-hand push passes in the drill.

Full-Court Layups, Left-Handed, 30 per Minute (10 minutes)

Divide the team into two groups, forming one line at the baseline under each basket (on the left side of the baseline). The first three players in each line should have a basketball. On command, the first player in each line dribbles to the other end and shoots a left-handed layup. After each layup is shot, the first player in line without a ball rebounds the shot taken as the shooter goes to the end of the line. Each time a player reaches half-court, the next player in line follows. Ask players to count the number of made layups; the goal is to make 30 by the time a minute has elapsed.

COACHING POINTS

- This is a speed dribbling drill, so the players should dribble the ball out in front of them; always encourage players to keep their head up while dribbling so they can see the court.
- You may need to adjust the goal of 30 made baskets in one minute, depending on your team's skill level.

Four-Corner Passing and Jump Shots (10 minutes)

Begin this drill with one line of players in each corner of the court, with two balls in opposite corners (four balls total). The first player in each line with a ball (the shooting lines) takes a few dribbles forward, then passes the ball to the first player in line at the other end of the court (the passing lines). The passer follows the pass, receives a return pass, and takes a shot. He then moves to the end of the same line at this end (the passing line), while the player who made the return pass rebounds the ball, passes it to the opposite corner at the same end, and moves to the end of that line (the shooting line).

COACHING POINTS

- Shooters need to have their feet in the proper position for shooting when they catch the ball.
- Rebounders should look to make good outlet passes.

Two-Line Fast Break With Layup (10 minutes)

The team is arranged in two lines, with one line in the lane facing the opposite basket and the other line at the wing position (players in this line are ready to catch the ball). The first player in the lane line starts with the ball and passes to the player at the wing. The wing player dribbles the ball to the opposite free-throw line and makes a good stop without traveling. The passer runs to the other end in the outside lane to receive a return pass from the wing. After receiving the return pass, this player dribbles in for a layup. These two players stay at this end, switching positions, as the next two players in line take their turn. After all the players have completed the drill going to one basket, they switch positions and complete the drill going back to the original basket.

COACHING POINTS

- Make sure the passer runs wide; to stress this, the coach can place cones on the court and specify that the player must run outside the cones.
- The drill can also be performed with the players executing jump shots off the glass, power shots, or a pass back to the middle player at the free-throw line for a shot.

Five-on-Zero Fast Break From Rebound (10 minutes)

Five players are positioned in the lane. The coach shoots the ball, and the players rebound the ball and then move down the court for a five-on-zero fast break on the opposite end. The rebounder makes an outlet pass to a guard; the wings run in both outside lanes, the post runs in the middle lane, and the forward is the trailer, stopping at the free-throw line.

COACHING POINT

The outlet should be to the side of the rebounder, outside the lane.

Two-on-Two Defensive Help (5 minutes)

Players form two lines, one at each wing outside the three-point line. One defensive player is guarding each offensive player in a two-on-two situation. The wing who starts with the ball skip passes it to his teammate on the opposite wing. The first wing's defender moves from guarding the player with the ball to the help-side rim line (the imaginary line running from rim to rim in the center of the floor) as the ball is skipped across to the opposite wing, while his teammate shifts to on-the-ball defense. After a specified amount of time, the next two players in line move to offense, the offensive players move to defense, and the defenders move to the end of each line.

COACHING POINTS

- The first defender must sprint to the rim line in good defensive position so he can see the ball and his player.
- The second defender must sprint to the offensive player catching the ball; the defender's hands should be up as he closes out on the shot.

Three-on-Three Defensive Help (10 minutes)

In this three-on-three drill, the defense works on defending dribble penetration by the offensive players, who are trying to get to the basket. The defender who is guarding the player closest to the dribbler must help stop the dribbler, recovering back to his own player once the ball has been passed back out.

COACHING POINTS

- Defenders need to stay in a good defensive stance.
- Defenders need to watch the dribbler as well as the player they are guarding so they can be in a position to help.

Four-on-Four Defensive Shell (10 minutes)

Four players are on offense, and four on defense. The offense is spaced out with one guard above each free-throw lane outside the three-point line and one player at each wing. A defender is guarding each offensive player; the rest of the team is divided into four lines at half-court. One of the guards starts with the ball and passes it to a wing. As the coach observes, the defenders must adjust to each pass so they are in good help position or on-the-ball position. On command, the offense continues to pass the ball from one wing to the other wing, and the defenders adjust their position on each pass. After a specified amount of time, the next four players in line move to offense, the offensive players move to defense, and the defenders move to the end of each line.

COACHING POINTS

- Defenders should be in help position when the ball is on the opposite side of the court. They should point one hand at the ball and one hand at the offensive player they are guarding so that they never lose sight of either.

- Defenders must move as the ball is in the air so they are in correct defensive position when the ball is caught. The coach may need to yell out "Pass!" so the defense can adjust to each pass correctly.

Three-on-Two, Two-on-One Full Court (10 minutes)

Start with three lines at one end of the court. Two players set up at the opposite end of the court in a defensive position, one player at the free-throw line and one player in the middle of the lane. The first three players in line try to score against the two defenders (three-on-two); the middle player dribbles the ball down the floor and makes a pass to one wing. After the shot, the two defenders become the offensive players, moving to the opposite end of the court with the middle offensive player transitioning to defense (two-on-one). The two wings remain as the defenders in the lane for the next group of three offensive players.

COACHING POINTS

- The three offensive players should work to get a shot after three or fewer passes against the two defenders.
- The two offensive players should work to get a shot after two or fewer passes against the one defender.

Five-on-Zero Offense (10 minutes)

Arrange the players in offensive positions based on the offensive set you want to teach. For example, this can be a 1-2-2 set with a point guard, two wings, and two post players or a 2-1-2 set with two guards, a high-post player, and two baseline or post players. In this drill, teach players how they can try to score in the set (including cuts, screens, and so on).

COACHING POINTS

- Teach players proper spacing and how to refill positions after a pass and cut.
- Emphasize that each player should square up to the basket after every catch.

Free Throws, Two in a Row (10 minutes)

Pair up players at each free-throw line. Partners take turns shooting one free throw until the pair makes two in a row.

COACHING POINT

Adjust the number of consecutive free throws made based on the skill level of your players.

Announcements: _____

Midseason Practice Plan 3

Date: _____   Time: _____   Practice number: _____

Warm-Up (10 minutes)

Players line up on the baseline in four lines. On command, the players run down the court to the opposite baseline. Players work on running, stops, pivots, V-cuts, and jumping during their trips up and down the court.

COACHING POINT

Adjust the skills used in the warm-up based on the ability level of your players.

Full-Court Layups, Right-Handed, 40 per Minute (10 minutes)

Divide the team into two groups, forming one line at the baseline under each basket (on the right side of the baseline). The first three players in each line should have a basketball. On command, the first player in each line dribbles to the other end and shoots a right-handed layup. After each layup is shot, the first player in line without a ball rebounds the shot taken as the shooter goes to the end of the line. Each time a player reaches half-court, the next player in line follows. Ask players to count the number of made layups; the goal is to make 40 by the time a minute has elapsed.

COACHING POINTS

- This is a speed dribbling drill, so the players should dribble the ball out in front of them; always encourage players to keep their head up while dribbling so they can see the court.
- You may need to adjust the goal of 40 made baskets in one minute, depending on your team's skill level.

Five-Ball Shooting, Layup With Two Jumpers (10 minutes)

Players are in four lines, one line in each corner. One end will include a player at the middle of the baseline with a ball. This player and the first player in each line at that end make two passes as they move to the opposite end for a layup. As the layup is made by the third player, the two passers (including the middle player) each receive a ball from the two lines at the opposite end for a jump shot. The player who has taken the layup rebounds her own shot and turns, making an outlet pass and moving in the opposite direction with the first two players in line (who have just passed for jumpers). These players again make two passes for a layup, followed by two jump shots, and the drill continues. The goal is to make 15 baskets in one minute.

COACHING POINT

At this age, players may need to take several dribbles before passing from one wing to the other for the layup.

Four-Corner Passing and Jump Shots (10 minutes)

Begin this drill with one line of players in each corner of the court, with two balls in opposite corners (four balls total). The first player in each line with a ball (the shooting lines) takes a few dribbles forward, then passes the ball to the first player in line at the other end of the court (the passing lines). The passer follows the pass, receives a return pass, and takes a shot. He then moves to the end of the same line at this end (the passing line), while the player who made the return pass rebounds the ball, passes it to the opposite corner at the same end, and moves to the end of that line (the shooting line). The goal is to make 10 jump shots in one minute.

COACHING POINTS

- Shooters need to have their feet in the proper position for shooting when they catch the ball.
- Rebounders should look to make good outlet passes.

Cutthroat, Four-on-Four (10 minutes)

Divide the team into four lines on the baseline; the first players in each line are on offense, and the second players in each line are on defense. The offensive players are facing the basket on the court. The coach starts the drill by passing the ball to one of the offensive players. The defenders run from the baseline to close out on the offense in defensive position. As a rule, the offensive players must face the basket in triple-threat position, must move after they pass, and must thank the passer on a pass that results in a basket. If the offense fails to follow one of the rules, the whistle blows, and the offensive players must go to the end of the line. The defense moves to offense, and a new set of three players comes in on defense. Play for a specified period of time or until one team reaches a specified number of points. Each basket counts as a point.

COACHING POINTS

- Players must perform the action specified by each rule immediately; if not, the team is out.
- Other rules can be added, such as limiting the offense to two dribbles or not allowing the offense to shoot until a ball screen has occurred or all players have touched the ball.

11-Player Fast Break (10 minutes)

A line of players is set up at each of the four wing areas in the full court. Two defenders are positioned at the free-throw line and lane on both sides of the court, and three offensive players are at half-court with the ball. The drill begins with the offensive players going against two of the defenders. Once the shot is taken by the offense, the defenders rebound the ball either on a make or a miss. Two of the three offensive players remain on the court as defenders, and the other goes to the end of one of the wing lines. The defender who gets the rebound makes an outlet pass to one of the first players in line at the wings. With the other wing and the defender, this wing dribbles down to the opposite court for a three-on-two situation. The drill continues in this fashion for a set amount of time.

COACHING POINTS

- Make sure that outlet players are very vocal in calling for the ball.
- The defender who makes the outlet pass should follow wide to the side, filling the wing on the fast break.

10-Basket Shooting Contest (5 minutes)

The squad is divided into groups of no more than three per team. The coach designates a shooting spot where the team of players will shoot one shot each until that team makes 10 baskets. Each player rebounds his own shot and passes the ball back to the next person in line.

COACHING POINTS

- Emphasize to players that they should have their feet and hands ready to shoot before the ball is passed.
- The coach can change the specified number of made shots and the shooting spots depending on the players' ability.

Four-on-Four Defensive Shell (10 minutes)

Four players are on offense, and four on defense. The offense is spaced out with one guard above each free-throw lane outside the three-point line and one player at each wing. A defender is guarding each offensive player; the rest of the team is divided into four lines at half-court. One of the guards starts with the ball and passes it to a wing. As the coach observes, the defenders must adjust to each pass so they are in good help position or on-the-ball position. On command, the offense continues to pass the ball from one wing to the other wing, and the defenders adjust their position on each pass. After a specified amount of time, the next four players in line move to offense, the offensive players move to defense, and the defenders move to the end of each line.

COACHING POINTS

- Defenders should be in help position when the ball is on the opposite side of the court. They should point one hand at the ball and one hand at the offensive player they are guarding so that they never lose sight of either.
- Defenders must move as the ball is in the air so they are in correct defensive position when the ball is caught. The coach may need to yell out "Pass!" so the defense can adjust to each pass correctly.

Five-on-Four Fast Break With Defensive Trailer (10 minutes)

Divide the team into five lines across the baseline, with five players facing them at the free-throw line. The coach begins the drill by throwing the ball to one of the first players in line at the baseline. The player opposite the pass at the free-throw line runs to touch the baseline while the rest of the players move down the court in a five-on-four situation. The player who touches the baseline is the trailer, catching up to make the drill a five-on-five.

COACHING POINTS

- The offense should attack the four defenders, trying to get a fast break basket before the fifth defender comes into play.
- The defense needs to stop the ball first, slowing the offensive team down until the fifth defender catches up.

Five-on-Zero Offense (10 minutes)

Arrange the players in offensive positions based on the offensive set you want to teach. For example, this can be a 1-2-2 set with a point guard, two wings, and two post players or a 2-1-2 set with two guards, a high-post player, and two baseline or post players. In this drill, teach players how they can try to score in the set (including cuts, screens, and so on).

COACHING POINTS

- Teach players proper spacing and how to refill positions after a pass and cut.
- Emphasize that each player should square up to the basket after every catch.

Five-on-Five Scrimmage, Controlled (10 minutes)

Divide the team into two teams of five for a scrimmage that involves using the skills and tactics that the players have learned so far in practices. Have the players go five-on-five half court and transition into a full-court scrimmage after a made or missed basket. They should stop at the other end, then again go five-on-five into a full-court scrimmage. Sub players as necessary.

COACHING POINTS

- The coach should stop play when necessary to explain areas on both offense and defense that need work.
- Offensive players need to sprint back on a change of possession in order to stop the ball first.

Free Throws, Two in a Row (10 minutes)

Pair up players at each free-throw line. Partners take turns shooting one free throw until the pair makes two in a row.

COACHING POINT

Adjust the number of consecutive free throws made based on the skill level of your players.

Announcements: _____

Late-Season Practices

Late-season practices will be geared more toward team drills, but as always, players will continue to work on skills. The coach should attempt to keep the practice sessions fresh by adding new drills that keep the players interested and enthused about coming to practice. Repetition is the key to skill development.

Late-Season Practice Plan

Date: _____   Time: _____   Practice number: _____

Warm-Up (10 minutes)

Players line up on the baseline in four lines. On command, the players run down the court to the opposite baseline. Players work on running, stops, pivots, V-cuts, and jumping during their trips up and down the court.

COACHING POINT

Adjust the skills used in the warm-up based on the ability level of your players.

Four-Corner Passing and Jump Shots (10 minutes)

Begin this drill with one line of players in each corner of the court, with two balls in opposite corners (four balls total). The first player in each line with a ball (the shooting lines) takes a few dribbles forward, then passes the ball to the first player in line at the other end of the court (the passing lines). The passer follows the pass, receives a return pass, and takes a shot. He then moves to the end of the same line at this end (the passing line), while the player who made the return pass rebounds the ball, passes it to the opposite corner at the same end, and moves to the end of that line (the shooting line). The goal is to make 15 jump shots in one minute.

COACHING POINTS

- Shooters need to have their feet in the proper position for shooting when they catch the ball.
- Rebounders should look to make good outlet passes.

Full-Court Layups, Left-Handed, 40 per Minute (10 minutes)

Divide the team into two groups, forming one line at the baseline under each basket (on the left side of the baseline). The first three players in each line should have a basketball. On command, the first player in each line dribbles to the other end and shoots a left-handed layup. After each layup is shot, the first player in line without a ball rebounds the shot taken as the shooter goes to the end of the line. Each time a player reaches half-court, the next player in line follows. Ask players to count the number of made layups; the goal is to make 40 by the time a minute has elapsed.

COACHING POINTS

- This is a speed dribbling drill, so the players should dribble the ball out in front of them; always encourage players to keep their head up while dribbling so they can see the court.
- You may need to adjust the goal of 40 made baskets in one minute, depending on your team's skill level.

Defensive Slides, One-on-Zero and One-on-One (10 minutes)

Divide the players into three lines on the baseline. The first player in each line performs defensive slides to the other baseline, making a drop step after every three slides. Once players get the hang of the drill, divide the players into pairs. One partner now dribbles a basketball, using V-cuts and crossover dribbles to change direction, from one baseline to the other; the other partner is the defensive player. The defensive player should slide to stay in front of the dribbler, executing a drop step each time the offensive player changes direction.

COACHING POINTS

- The offensive players should go slowly so the defense can work on footwork.
- Defensive players should remain one arm's length away from the dribbler, keeping their eyes on the dribbler's waist.

Cutthroat, Four-on-Four (10 minutes)

Divide the team into four lines on the baseline; the first players in each line are on offense, and the second players in each line are on defense. The offensive players are facing the basket on the court. The coach starts the drill by passing the ball to one of the offensive players. The defenders run from the baseline to close out on the offense in defensive position. As a rule, the offensive players must face the basket in triple-threat position, must move after they pass, and must thank the passer on a pass that results in a basket. If the offense fails to follow one of the rules, the whistle blows, and the offensive players must go to the end of the line. The defense moves to offense, and a new set of three players comes in on defense. Play for a specified period of time or until one team reaches a specified number of points. Each basket counts as a point.

COACHING POINTS

- Players must perform the action specified by each rule immediately; if not, the team is out.
- Other rules can be added, such as limiting the offense to two dribbles or not allowing the offense to shoot until a ball screen has occurred or all players have touched the ball.

Five-on-Five Scrimmage, Controlled (10 minutes)

Divide the team into two teams of five for a scrimmage that involves using the skills and tactics that the players have learned so far in practices. Have the players go five-on-five half court and transition into a full-court scrimmage after a made or missed basket. They should stop at the other end, then again go five-on-five into a full-court scrimmage. Sub players as necessary.

COACHING POINTS

- The coach should stop play when necessary to explain areas on both offense and defense that need work.
- Offensive players need to sprint back on a change of possession in order to stop the ball first.

Free Throws, Two in a Row (5 minutes)

Pair up players at each free-throw line. Partners take turns shooting one free throw until the pair makes two in a row.

COACHING POINT

Adjust the number of consecutive free throws made based on the skill level of your players.

Pair Shooting (10 minutes)

Players are divided into pairs with one ball per pair. One player shoots the ball, rebounds her shot, and passes the ball back to the other player for a shot. Pairs continue in this manner for a specified amount of time.

COACHING POINTS

- The shooter should work to catch the ball in proper shooting position; the knees should be bent, and the player should catch the ball at waist level.
- After the shot, the shooter should run to get the rebound before the ball hits the floor.

Out-of-Bounds Plays, Review (10 minutes)

Divide your team into groups of five; one group begins on the court. Have every group of players run your out-of-bounds plays without a defense. Then practice the out-of-bounds plays in a five-on-five situation, against a defense.

COACHING POINTS

- Most out-of-bounds plays will begin in a box set, with one player in each corner of the lane. Coaches should have the same set for all out-of-bounds plays.
- Teams should practice these plays against both a zone defense and a man-to-man defense.

Three-on-Two, Two-on-One Full Court (10 minutes)

Start with three lines at one end of the court. Two players set up at the opposite end of the court in a defensive position, one player at the free-throw line and one player in the middle of the lane. The first three players in line try to score against the two defenders (three-on-two); the middle player dribbles the ball down the floor and makes a pass to one wing. After the shot, the two defenders become the offensive players, moving to the opposite end of the court with the middle offensive player transitioning to defense (two-on-one). The two wings remain as the defenders in the lane for the next group of three offensive players.

COACHING POINTS

- The three offensive players should work to get a shot after three or fewer passes against the two defenders.
- The two offensive players should work to get a shot after two or fewer passes against the one defender.

Five-on-Zero Offense (10 minutes)

Arrange the players in offensive positions based on the offensive set you want to teach. For example, this can be a 1-2-2 set with a point guard, two wings, and two post players or a 2-1-2 set with two guards, a high-post player, and two baseline or post players. In this drill, teach players how they can try to score in the set (including cuts, screens, and so on).

COACHING POINTS

- Teach players proper spacing and how to refill positions after a pass and cut.
- Emphasize that each player should square up to the basket after every catch.

Four-Quarter Shooting (10 minutes)

This is a three-player drill using two balls. Two players have a ball. One player with a ball shoots her ball, rebounds, and passes the ball to the player who does not have a ball. The other player with the ball shoots her ball immediately after the first player, gets the rebound, and passes to the player who now does not have a ball (the first shooter). After the shot, each player repositions for the pass from the next shooter. Play for four minutes, keeping track of made baskets.

COACHING POINT

The shooter must get a rebound, pass the ball, and then immediately look for the pass from the next shooter.

Announcements: _____

14

Practices for Ages 13 and 14

Players in this age group will obviously have the most experience, but sometimes coaches make the mistake of forgetting about skill development. Coaches should always keep in mind that repetition is key for skill development. Drills performed in practices are the essence of skill and team development.

Following are some points to consider when preparing and executing practice sessions for 13- and 14-year-olds:

- Make sure every drill has more than one purpose.
- Combine as many fundamentals as possible into each drill, even though the emphasis may be on one skill only.
- Express your expectations for each drill at the start; set the tone and don't compromise your standards.
- Perform drills at the full-court level, three-quarter-court level, and half-court level.
- Stress to players the importance of transferring the correct execution of drills to game situations.
- Create competition—against clock, against opponent, or against self—in each drill.
- Be demanding—demand correct execution of basic skills.
- Hold each player to your highest performance standards.

Considerations When Coaching Females
Annie Byrne, Marian Catholic High School girls' basketball coach

Girls who are 13 or 14 years old are at the age right before they enter high school. Ideally, this would be a good time to pick up the pace of the game. After this year, the players will be expected to compete at a high school level. A key word to explore during this time is *versatility*. If a kid is always in the paint, she should come out to the perimeter and experience play facing the basket. If a kid is always on the perimeter, she should experience play in the paint. Guards need to know how to post up, and posts need to be able to face the basket. At this age, girls should be encouraged to step out of their comfort zone because they may be asked to change positions at the next level (depending on surrounding personnel and how they develop individually).

A good drill with multiple purposes for this age group would be a five-on-five, controlled half court, with a third team ready at all times on the baseline. As players begin to understand how to match up, communicate defensively, and play multiple positions, you can move this to a full-court game with the third team on the sideline. Other things that a coach should teach these players include how to set a screen, how to set up a screener and receive the screen, and how to understand options off a screen (e.g., curling, flaring, or a simple catch and shoot) based on how the defense reacts. These concepts should raise the average 14-year-old's basketball IQ, pick up the pace of the game, and increase versatility.

13-14 years old

Early-Season Practices

Early-season practices should involve reviewing the skills that the coach believes are important. Early-season practice sessions will give you an idea of the skill level of your team and what you need to work on in upcoming practice sessions. Take notes during practice to help prepare for the next practice session.

Early-Season Practice Plan

Date: _____   Time: _____   Practice number: _____

Warm-Up (10 minutes)

Players line up on the baseline in four lines. On command, the players run down the court to the opposite baseline. Players work on running, stops, pivots, V-cuts, and jumping during their trips up and down the court.

COACHING POINT
Adjust the skills used in the warm-up based on the ability level of your players.

Dribble–Pivot–Pass (10 minutes)
Players line up on the sideline with no more than three players per line. The first player takes three right-handed dribbles out and comes to a stop. He then executes a reverse pivot (a front pivot may also be used) and makes a chest pass to the next player in line. The passer goes to the end of the line after the pass, and the next player (the one who caught the pass) dribbles out and makes the pivot and pass.

COACHING POINTS
- Emphasize to players that they should execute the pivot with the knees bent to make the pass.
- Depending on ability, players may instead use bounce passes or one-hand push passes in the drill.

Two-Line Passing: Chest, Bounce, Overhead, and Baseball (10 minutes)
Divide the squad into two lines facing each other; the lines should be at least lane-width apart depending on player ability. The first person in one line should have a basketball. This player passes the ball using a chest pass to the first person in the opposite line. The passer follows his pass and goes to the end of the opposite line. The drill continues as the players pass the ball and follow it. Once players have practiced the chest pass, they should perform the same drill using the bounce pass, overhead pass, and baseball pass.

COACHING POINTS
- Players should step as they pass the ball, making the pass more direct.
- To help communication, players should call out the name of the player they are passing to.

Form Shooting (10 minutes)
Players stand two to three feet from a basket, placing the ball in one hand. Players bend the knees and shoot the ball one handed to the basket. This drill helps the players develop the proper fundamentals of shooting.

COACHING POINTS
- The elbow of the shooting arm should be at shoulder level and should not drop lower when executing the one-hand shot.
- Players must be careful not to grip the ball like a baseball or softball; the ball should rest on the hand.

Offensive Wing Moves (10 minutes)

Two lines of players begin on the blocks under the basket; the players are facing the coach, who is at the top of the key with a ball. On command, the first player in one line steps into the lane, performing a V-cut against an imaginary player to get open at the wing position. The coach passes the ball to the outside hand of the player. On the catch, the player squares up to the basket with his nonshooting foot as his pivot foot (for a right-handed shooter, the left foot should be the pivot foot). After squaring up, the player makes a move to the basket, taking one or two dribbles and then a shot. He gets his own rebound and passes the ball out to the coach; the player then goes to the end of the opposite line so that he works on both sides of the court.

COACHING POINTS

- The pivot foot should always be the same.
- A third line of players can replace the coach as the passer.

Three-on-Zero Fast Break (10 minutes)

Players form three lines under the basket. The first player in the middle line has a ball. This player throws the ball off the backboard to begin the drill; she rebounds the ball and makes an outlet to either side of the court. She then moves behind the outlet player, who dribbles to the middle of the floor as the opposite wing runs down the opposite lane for a three-player fast break situation. The dribbler passes to either wing for a layup. Players should rotate lines so that all players play each position.

COACHING POINT

The last pass should be a bounce pass outside the lane area to the wing. This allows for an easier catch and layup.

Mass Defensive Slide (5 minutes)

All players set up in a scattered formation around the coach, who is in position for all the players to see. On command or by following the coach, players move in a defensive slide to the right and left and from front to back, keeping the knees bent and the hands above the waist.

COACHING POINTS

- This is a good time to play follow the leader. Have one player positioned in front of the group to lead the other players in the defensive slide drill.
- The coach should make sure that players' feet do not cross or come together during the slide; players should instead use a step and push action with the legs and feet.

Two-on-Two Defensive Help (10 minutes)

Players form two lines, one at each wing outside the three-point line. One defensive player is guarding each offensive player in a two-on-two situation. The wing who starts with the ball skip passes it to his teammate on the opposite wing. The first wing's defender moves from guarding the player with the ball to the help-side rim line (the imaginary line running from rim to rim in the center of the floor) as the ball is skipped across to the opposite wing, while his teammate shifts to on-the-ball defense. After a specified amount of time, the next two players in line move to offense, the offensive players move to defense, and the defenders move to the end of each line.

COACHING POINTS

- The first defender must sprint to the rim line in good defensive position so he can see the ball and his player.
- The second defender must sprint to the offensive player catching the ball; the defender's hands should be up as he closes out on the shot.

Four-on-Four Defensive Shell (10 minutes)

Four players are on offense, and four on defense. The offense is spaced out with one guard above each free-throw lane outside the three-point line and one player at each wing. A defender is guarding each offensive player; the rest of the team is divided into four lines at half-court. One of the guards starts with the ball and passes it to a wing. As the coach observes, the defenders must adjust to each pass so they are in good help position or on-the-ball position. On command, the offense continues to pass the ball from one wing to the other wing, and the defenders adjust their position on each pass. After a specified amount of time, the next four players in line move to offense, the offensive players move to defense, and the defenders move to the end of each line.

COACHING POINTS

- Defenders should be in help position when the ball is on the opposite side of the court. They should point one hand at the ball and one hand at the offensive player they are guarding so that they never lose sight of either.
- Defenders must move as the ball is in the air so they are in correct defensive position when the ball is caught. The coach may need to yell out "Pass!" so the defense can adjust to each pass correctly.

Two-on-One Fast Break Half Court (10 minutes)

Players form three lines at the baseline. On command, the first three players run to half-court. The middle player then runs back and gets in position to be a defender. The coach passes the ball to one of the players at half-court, and these players attack the basket in a two-on-one situation.

COACHING POINTS

- Offensive players should try to get a good shot with no more than one pass.
- Most of the time, a bounce pass should be thrown in a two-on-one situation.

Three-on-Two Fast Break Half Court (10 minutes)

Players form five lines at the baseline. On command, the first five players run to half-court. The middle player and the two outside players in line will be the offensive players, and the other two players will move back as defenders. The coach passes the ball to the middle player at the half-court line, and the offensive players attack the defenders in a three-on-two situation.

COACHING POINTS

- The offensive team should try to score with only two passes.
- After the middle player passes to one of the wings, this player should go to the side of the pass at the free-throw line elbow for a possible return pass.

Seven-Spot Shooting, Two Made Shots From Each Spot (10 minutes)

Pick out seven spots on the floor, marking these spots with tape. Players pair up, and each pair has a ball. The first player shoots the ball at the first spot, gets her own rebound, and passes back to her partner, who shoots at the same spot. After two shots total are made from that spot, the players move to the next spot. Players must make two shots from each spot before they are done with the drill.

COACHING POINTS

- Emphasize that shooters must be ready and must have their feet and hands in good position to shoot when they catch the pass.
- This drill can be changed to require players to make any number of shots before moving to the next spot or require them to make a certain number in a row before moving to the next spot.
- A time limit can also be enforced; in this case, the players try to make as many shots as possible in a certain period of time.

Announcements: _____

Midseason Practices

Midseason practice sessions are a continuation of early-season practice sessions, but the drills become more competitive. More team drills are added for working on team play as well. At this point, the coach may also add more offensive plays for the team, and the players will need practice time to perfect those plays.

Midseason Practice Plan 1

Date: _____   Time: _____   Practice number: _____

Warm-Up (10 minutes)

Players line up on the baseline in four lines. On command, the players run down the court to the opposite baseline. Players work on running, stops, pivots, V-cuts, and jumping during their trips up and down the court.

COACHING POINT

Adjust the skills used in the warm-up based on the ability level of your players.

Dribble–Pivot–Pass (10 minutes)

Players line up on the sideline with no more than three players per line. The first player takes three right-handed dribbles out and comes to a stop. He then executes a reverse pivot (a front pivot may also be used) and makes a chest pass to the next player in line. The passer goes to the end of the line after the pass, and the next player (the one who caught the pass) dribbles out and makes the pivot and pass.

COACHING POINTS

- Emphasize to players that they should execute the pivot with the knees bent to make the pass.
- Depending on ability, players may instead use bounce passes or one-hand push passes in the drill.

Full-Court Layups, Right-Handed, 50 per Minute (10 minutes)

Divide the team into two groups, forming one line at the baseline under each basket (on the right side of the baseline). The first three players in each line should have a basketball. On command, the first player in each line dribbles to the other end and shoots a right-handed layup. After each layup is shot, the first player in line without a ball rebounds the shot taken as the shooter goes to the end of the line. Each time a player reaches half-court, the next player in line follows. Ask players to count the number of made layups; the goal is to make 50 by the time a minute has elapsed.

COACHING POINTS

- This is a speed dribbling drill, so the players should dribble the ball out in front of them; always encourage players to keep their head up while dribbling so they can see the court.
- You may need to adjust the goal of 50 made baskets in one minute, depending on your team's skill level.

Pair Shooting (10 minutes)

Players are divided into pairs with one ball per pair. One player shoots the ball, rebounds her shot, and passes the ball back to the other player for a shot. Pairs continue in this manner for a specified amount of time.

COACHING POINTS

- The shooter should work to catch the ball in proper shooting position; the knees should be bent, and the player should catch the ball at waist level.
- After the shot, the shooter should run to get the rebound before the ball hits the floor.

Offensive Wing Moves (10 minutes)

Two lines of players begin on the blocks under the basket; the players are facing the coach, who is at the top of the key with a ball. On command, the first player in one line steps into the lane, performing a V-cut against an imaginary player to get open at the wing position. The coach passes the ball to the outside hand of the player. On the catch, the player squares up to the basket with his nonshooting foot as his pivot foot (for a right-handed shooter, the left foot should be the pivot foot). After squaring up, the player makes a move to the basket, taking one or two dribbles and then a shot. He gets his own rebound and passes the ball out to the coach; the player then goes to the end of the opposite line so that he works on both sides of the court.

COACHING POINTS

- The pivot foot should always be the same.
- A third line of players can replace the coach as the passer.

Five-on-Zero Fast Break From Rebound (10 minutes)

Five players are positioned in the lane. The coach shoots the ball, and the players rebound the ball and then move down the court for a five-on-zero fast break on the opposite end. The rebounder makes an outlet pass to a guard; the wings run in both outside lanes, the post runs in the middle lane, and the forward is the trailer, stopping at the free-throw line.

COACHING POINT

The outlet should be to the side of the rebounder, outside the lane.

Mass Defensive Slide (5 minutes)

All players set up in a scattered formation around the coach, who is in position for all the players to see. On command or by following the coach, players move in a defensive slide to the right and left, keeping the knees bent and the hands above the waist.

COACHING POINTS

- This is a good time to play follow the leader. Have one player positioned in front of the group to lead the other players in the defensive slide drill.
- The coach should make sure that players' feet do not cross or come together during the slide; players should instead use a step and push action with the legs and feet.

Two-on-Two Defensive Help (10 minutes)

Players form two lines, one at each wing outside the three-point line. One defensive player is guarding each offensive player in a two-on-two situation. The wing who starts with the ball skip passes it to his teammate on the opposite wing. The first wing's defender moves from guarding the player with the ball to the help-side rim line (the imaginary line running from rim to rim in the center of the floor) as the ball is skipped across to the opposite wing, while his teammate shifts to on-the-ball defense. After a specified amount of time, the next two players in line move to offense, the offensive players move to defense, and the defenders move to the end of each line.

COACHING POINTS

- The first defender must sprint to the rim line in good defensive position so he can see the ball and his player.
- The second defender must sprint to the offensive player catching the ball; the defender's hands should be up as he closes out on the shot.

Four-on-Four Defensive Shell (10 minutes)

Four players are on offense, and four on defense. The offense is spaced out with one guard above each free-throw lane outside the three-point line and one player at each wing. A defender is guarding each offensive player; the rest of the team is divided into four lines at half-court. One of the guards starts with the ball and passes it to a wing. As the coach observes, the defenders must adjust to each pass so they are in good help position or on-the-ball position. On command, the offense continues to pass the ball from one wing to the other wing, and the defenders adjust their position on each pass. After a specified amount of time, the next four players in line move to offense, the offensive players move to defense, and the defenders move to the end of each line.

COACHING POINTS

- Defenders should be in help position when the ball is on the opposite side of the court. They should point one hand at the ball and one hand at the offensive player they are guarding so that they never lose sight of either.
- Defenders must move as the ball is in the air so they are in correct defensive position when the ball is caught. The coach may need to yell out "Pass!" so the defense can adjust to each pass correctly.

Three-on-Two, Two-on-One Full Court (10 minutes)

Start with three lines at one end of the court. Two players set up at the opposite end of the court in a defensive position, one player at the free-throw line and one player in the middle of the lane. The first three players in line try to score against the two defenders (three-on-two); the middle player dribbles the ball down the floor and makes a pass to one wing. After the shot, the two defenders become the offensive players, moving to the opposite end of the court with the middle offensive player transitioning to defense (two-on-one). The two wings remain as the defenders in the lane for the next group of three offensive players.

COACHING POINTS

- The three offensive players should work to get a shot after three or fewer passes against the two defender
- The two offensive players should work to get a shot after two or fewer passes against the one defender.

Five-on-Zero Offense (10 minutes)

Arrange the players in offensive positions based on the offensive set you want to teach. For example, this can be a 1-2-2 set with a point guard, two wings, and two post players or a 2-1-2 set with two guards, a high-post player, and two baseline or post players. In this drill, teach players how they can try to score in the set (including cuts, screens, and so on).

COACHING POINTS

- Teach players proper spacing and how to refill positions after a pass and cut.
- Emphasize that each player should square up to the basket after every catch.

Free Throws, Two in a Row (10 minutes)

Pair up players at each free-throw line. Partners take turns shooting one free throw until the pair makes two in a row.

COACHING POINT

Adjust the number of consecutive free throws made based on the skill level of your players.

Announcements: _____

Midseason Practice Plan 2

Date: _____   Time: _____   Practice number: _____

Warm-Up (10 minutes)

Players line up on the baseline in four lines. On command, the players run down the court to the opposite baseline. Players work on running, stops, pivots, V-cuts, and jumping during their trips up and down the court.

COACHING POINT

Adjust the skills used in the warm-up based on the ability level of your players.

Two-Ball Dribbling (10 minutes)

Players pair up along one sideline. The first player in each pair has two basketballs; this player dribbles both balls simultaneously from one sideline to the other and back. She then hands off the balls to her partner, who continues the drill.

COACHING POINTS

- Players need to keep their head up while dribbling both balls; they should not look at the basketballs.
- After players dribble both balls simultaneously, they can repeat the drill, this time alternating bounces while dribbling both balls. They may also perform low dribbles, perform high dribbles, perform one high and one low dribble, and switch hands.

Full-Court Layups, Left-Handed, 50 per Minute (10 minutes)

Divide the team into two groups, forming one line at the baseline under each basket (on the left side of the baseline). The first three players in each line should have a basketball. On command, the first player in each line dribbles to the other end and shoots a left-handed layup. After each layup is shot, the first player in line without a ball rebounds the shot taken as the shooter goes to the end of the line. Each time a player reaches half-court, the next player in line follows. Ask players to count the number of made layups; the goal is to make 50 by the time a minute has elapsed.

COACHING POINTS

- This is a speed dribbling drill, so the players should dribble the ball out in front of them; always encourage players to keep their head up while dribbling so they can see the court.
- You may need to adjust the goal of 50 made baskets in one minute, depending on your team's skill level.

Weak-Hand Development (10 minutes)

Players divide into pairs along the court. Each pair passes the ball back and forth using the weak hand only. Players should keep their strong hand behind their back.

COACHING POINT

Players should vary the types of passes, using chest, bounce, and baseball passes.

Box With Pivot (10 minutes)

Players begin along the baseline with a ball. On command, the first person in each line spins the ball out to the free-throw line, passing the ball to herself and then performing one of the following moves:

- Drop-step layup: flash, two-foot jump stop, drop step, one-dribble layup.
- Inside pivot and jump shot: flash, two-foot jump stop, fake, drop step and pivot on inside foot, jump shot.
- Inside pivot to fake jump shot and crossover: flash, two-foot jump stop, fake, drop step and pivot on inside foot, fake jump shot, crossover with one dribble.
- Reverse pivot and jump shot: flash, two-foot jump stop, reverse pivot, jump shot.
- Reverse pivot and outside pivot foot rip (moving the ball quickly from one side of the body to the other) to outside: flash, two-foot jump stop, reverse pivot on outside foot, rip to outside.
- Reverse pivot and outside pivot foot fake rip to crossover: flash, two-foot jump stop, reverse pivot on outside foot, fake, rip to crossover.

After each move, players should rebound their own shots and move to the end of the line.

COACHING POINTS

- Players should always perform a jump stop when stopping.
- Players need to stay low and in balance on all pivots.

Five-on-Zero Fast Break From Rebound (10 minutes)

Five players are positioned in the lane. The coach shoots the ball, and the players rebound the ball and then move down the court for a five-on-zero fast break on the opposite end. The rebounder makes an outlet pass to a guard; the wings run in both outside lanes, the post runs in the middle lane, and the forward is the trailer, stopping at the free-throw line.

COACHING POINT

The outlet should be to the side of the rebounder, outside the lane.

Defensive Slides, One-on-One (5 minutes)

Divide players into pairs in three lines on the baseline. One player in each pair is on defense, and the other is on offense. The offensive player dribbles a basketball, using V-cuts and crossovers to change direction, from one baseline to the other against the defensive player. The defensive player should slide to stay in front of the dribbler, executing a drop step each time the offensive player changes direction.

COACHING POINTS

- The defender should keep his head below the offensive player's shoulders and should keep his knees bent to move quickly.
- Defenders should remain one arm's length away from the dribbler, keeping their arms out wide from the body and keeping their eyes on the dribbler's waist.

Three-on-Two Fast Break With Defensive Trailer (10 minutes)

Divide the team into three lines across the baseline, with three players facing them at the free-throw line. The coach begins the drill by throwing the ball to one of the first players in line at the baseline. The player opposite the pass at the free-throw line runs to touch the baseline while the rest of the players move down the court in a three-on-two situation. The player who touches the baseline is the trailer, catching up to make the drill a three-on-three.

COACHING POINTS

- Before the third defender makes it to the ball, the other two defenders must communicate regarding who is defending the ball.
- The offense should try to score while they have the three-on-two advantage.

Four-on-Four Defensive Shell (10 minutes)

Four players are on offense, and four on defense. The offense is spaced out with one guard above each free-throw lane outside the three-point line and one player at each wing. A defender is guarding each offensive player; the rest of the team is divided into four lines at half-court. One of the guards starts with the ball and passes it to a wing. As the coach observes, the defenders must adjust to each pass so they are in good help position or on-the-ball position. On command, the offense continues to pass the ball from one wing to the other wing, and the defenders adjust their position on each pass. After a specified amount of time, the next four players in line move to offense, the offensive players move to defense, and the defenders move to the end of each line.

COACHING POINTS

- Defenders should be in help position when the ball is on the opposite side of the court. They should point one hand at the ball and one hand at the offensive player they are guarding so that they never lose sight of either.
- Defenders must move as the ball is in the air so they are in correct defensive position when the ball is caught. The coach may need to yell out "Pass!" so the defense can adjust to each pass correctly.

Three-on-Two, Two-on-One Full Court (10 minutes)

Start with three lines at one end of the court. Two players set up at the opposite end of the court in a defensive position, one player at the free-throw line and one player in the middle of the lane. The first three players in line try to score against the two defenders (three-on-two); the middle player dribbles the ball down the floor and makes a pass to one wing. After the shot, the two defenders become the offensive players, moving to the opposite end of the court with the middle offensive player transitioning to defense (two-on-one). The two wings remain as the defenders in the lane for the next group of three offensive players.

COACHING POINTS

- The three offensive players should work to get a shot after three or fewer passes against the two defenders.
- The two offensive players should work to get a shot after two or fewer passes against the one defender.

Five-on-Zero Offense (10 minutes)

Arrange the players in offensive positions based on the offensive set you want to teach. For example, this can be a 1-2-2 set with a point guard, two wings, and two post players or a 2-1-2 set with two guards, a high-post player, and two baseline or post players. In this drill, teach players how they can try to score in the set (including cuts, screens, and so on).

COACHING POINTS

- Teach players proper spacing and how to refill positions after a pass and cut.
- Emphasize that each player should square up to the basket after every catch.

Free Throws, Two in a Row (10 minutes)

Pair up players at each free-throw line. Partners take turns shooting one free throw until the pair makes two in a row.

COACHING POINT

Adjust the number of consecutive free throws made based on the skill level of your players.

Announcements: _____

Midseason Practice Plan 3

Date: _____   Time: _____   Practice number: _____

Warm-Up (10 minutes)

Players line up on the baseline in four lines. On command, the players run down the court to the opposite baseline. Players work on running, stops, pivots, V-cuts, and jumping during their trips up and down the court.

COACHING POINT

Adjust the skills used in the warm-up based on the ability level of your players.

Full-Court Layups, Right-Handed, 50 per Minute (10 minutes)

Divide the team into two groups, forming one line at the baseline under each basket (on the right side of the baseline). The first three players in each line should have a basketball. On command, the first player in each line dribbles to the other end and shoots a right-handed layup. After each layup is shot, the first player in line without a ball rebounds the shot taken as the shooter goes to the end of the line. Each time a player reaches half-court, the next player in line follows. Ask players to count the number of made layups; the goal is to make 50 by the time a minute has elapsed.

COACHING POINTS

- This is a speed dribbling drill, so the players should dribble the ball out in front of them; always encourage players to keep their head up while dribbling so they can see the court.
- You may need to adjust the goal of 50 made baskets in one minute, depending on your team's skill level.

Four-Corner Passing and Jump Shots (10 minutes)

Begin this drill with one line of players in each corner of the court, with two balls in opposite corners (four balls total). The first player in each line with a ball (the shooting lines) takes a few dribbles forward, then passes the ball to the first player in line at the other end of the court (the passing lines). The passer follows the pass, receives a return pass, and takes a shot. He then moves to the end of the same line at this end (the passing line), while the player who made the return pass rebounds the ball, passes it to the opposite corner at the same end, and moves to the end of that line (the shooting line). The goal is to make 15 jump shots in one minute.

COACHING POINTS

- Shooters need to have their feet in the proper position for shooting when they catch the ball.
- Rebounders should look to make good outlet passes.

Five-Ball Shooting, Layup With Two Jumpers (10 minutes)

Players are in four lines, one line in each corner. One end will include a player at the middle of the baseline with a ball. This player and the first player in each line at that end make two passes as they move to the opposite end for a layup. As the layup is made by the third player, the two passers (including the middle player) each receive a ball from the two lines at the opposite end for a jump shot. The player who has taken the layup rebounds her own shot and turns, making an outlet pass and moving in the opposite direction with the first two players in line (who have just passed for jumpers). These players again make two passes for a layup, followed by two jump shots, and the drill continues. The goal is to make 22 baskets in one minute.

COACHING POINTS

- The outlet pass needs to be a good, quick pass to start the drill.
- Jump shots should be eight-foot jumpers outside the lane.
- The goal can be adjusted according to players' skill level.

Perfect Layups (10 minutes)

Begin with three lines of players along the baseline. The first player in the left line should have a ball (alternatively, the line on the right can begin with the ball). The first three players make passes while moving down the court. The player on the left passes to the player in the middle, who passes back to the player on the left; then, the player on the left once more passes to the player in the middle, who this time makes a bounce pass to the player on the right for a layup. The player on the left rebounds the ball and makes a two-hand overhead outlet pass to the middle player, who has moved to the side of the player making the layup. This player continues the other way, making a baseball pass back to the next person in the left line, who continues the drill. The goal is to make 25 points in one minute; players earn 2 points for a perfect layup, meaning the ball does not touch the rim, and 1 point for a made layup.

COACHING POINTS

- Passing must be crisp and on target.
- The goal of 25 points can be adjusted depending on skill level.

Two-Line Rebounding (10 minutes)

Players are lined up in two lines at the elbows of the free-throw line. The coach shoots the ball, and the first two players go for the rebound. The player who gets the rebound then tries to make a shot with the other player defending him.

COACHING POINT

The coach should not call fouls unless they are flagrant; the players need to rebound and shoot with pressure.

One-on-One-on-One Rebounding (5 minutes)

Players form one line on the baseline. The coach begins the drill by shooting the ball, and three players go for the rebound. Whoever gets the rebound tries to score. This follow-up shot will be treated as if it were a miss regardless of whether the shot is made. Once again, the three players go for the ball and for a score. Once one player gets three scores, he moves to the end of the line at the baseline, and the first player in the line rotates in. The drill keeps going until all players get three scores.

COACHING POINTS

- Players must go up strong to shoot the ball with pressure from the other two players.
- If the ball hits the floor or goes outside the lane, the ball is dead, and the coach will reshoot.

Five-on-Four Fast Break With Defensive Trailer (10 minutes)

Divide the team into five lines across the baseline, with five players facing them at the free-throw line. The coach begins the drill by throwing the ball to one of the first players in line at the baseline. The player opposite the pass at the free-throw line runs to touch the baseline while the rest of the players move down the court in a five-on-four situation. The player who touches the baseline is the trailer, catching up to make the drill a five-on-five.

COACHING POINTS

- The offense should attack the four defenders, trying to get a fast break basket before the fifth defender comes into play.
- The defense needs to stop the ball first, slowing the offensive team down until the fifth defender catches up.

Four-on-Four With Transition (10 minutes)

Begin this drill with eight players in a half-court four-on-four situation. Three lines of players are set up at the baseline on each end of the court. On a rebound or made shot, the defender who gets the ball along with the first three players in line at the baseline execute a fast break to the opposite end, while the four offensive players transition to defense. The other three defenders go to the end of each line along the baseline. The drill continues in this manner for a designated amount of time.

COACHING POINTS

- Players moving from offense to defense must sprint back in defensive transition, communicating who has the ball and help side.
- Offensive players should fill lanes on the fast break to the opposite end.

Five-on-Five Controlled Half Court (10 minutes)

Players play a five-on-five controlled half-court scrimmage. The offense should work on team offensive sets. Sub players accordingly.

COACHING POINTS

- This drill can transition into the five-on-five scrimmage so the team can work on transitioning from offense to defense, and vice versa.
- The coach can use this drill to make teaching points about the offense.

Five-Possession Five-on-Five (10 minutes)

This is a full-court five-on-five drill in which each team has five possessions. Score is kept; at the end of five possessions, the winning team stays on the court, and the losing team rotates out.

COACHING POINTS

- Start with a jump ball so the players have practice with jump ball situations.
- This drill allows players to practice in gamelike conditions and situations.

Free Throws, Two in a Row (10 minutes)

Pair up players at each free-throw line. Partners take turns shooting one free throw until the pair makes two in a row.

COACHING POINT

Adjust the number of consecutive free throws made based on the skill level of your players.

Announcements: _____

Late-Season Practices

Late-season practices for this age group again need to be skill improvement sessions that include team drills. Team offense and team defense should be a major part of the practice sessions, which should include three-, four-, or five-player drills. Competitive drills are also good for late-season practice sessions for players in this age group.

Late-Season Practice Plan

Date: _____   Time: _____   Practice number: _____

Warm-Up (10 minutes)

Players line up on the baseline in four lines. On command, the players run down the court to the opposite baseline. Players work on running, stops, pivots, V-cuts, and jumping during their trips up and down the court.

COACHING POINT

Adjust the skills used in the warm-up based on the ability level of your players.

Four-Corner Passing and Jump Shots (10 minutes)

Begin this drill with one line of players in each corner of the court, with two balls in opposite corners (four balls total). The first player in each line with a ball (the shooting lines) takes a few dribbles forward, then passes the ball to the first player in line at the other end of the court (the passing lines). The passer follows the pass, receives a return pass, and takes a shot. He then moves to the end of the same line at this end (the passing line), while the player who made the return pass rebounds the ball, passes it to the opposite corner at the same end, and moves to the end of that line (the shooting line). The goal is to make 15 jump shots in one minute.

COACHING POINTS

- Shooters need to have their feet in the proper position for shooting when they catch the ball.
- Rebounders should look to make good outlet passes.

Full-Court Layups, Left-Handed, 50 per Minute (10 minutes)

Divide the team into two groups, forming one line at the baseline under each basket (on the left side of the baseline). The first three players in each line should have a basketball. On command, the first player in each line dribbles to the other end and shoots a left-handed layup. After each layup is shot, the first player in line without a ball rebounds the shot taken as the shooter goes to the end of the line. Each time a player reaches half-court, the next player in line follows. Ask players to count the number of made layups; the goal is to make 50 by the time a minute has elapsed.

COACHING POINTS

- This is a speed dribbling drill, so the players should dribble the ball out in front of them; always encourage players to keep their head up while dribbling so they can see the court.
- You may need to adjust the goal of 50 made baskets in one minute, depending on your team's skill level.

Cutthroat, Four-on-Four (10 minutes)

Divide the team into four lines on the baseline; the first players in each line are on offense, and the second players in each line are on defense. The offensive players are facing the basket on the court. The coach starts the drill by passing the ball to one of the offensive players. The defenders run from the baseline to close out on the offense in defensive position. As a rule, the offensive players must face the basket in triple-threat position, must move after they pass, and must thank the passer on a pass that results in a basket. If the offense fails to follow one of the rules, the whistle blows, and the offensive players must go to the end of the line. The defense moves to offense, and a new set of three players comes in on defense. Play for a specified period of time or until one team reaches a specified number of points. Each basket counts as a point.

COACHING POINTS

- Players must perform the action specified by each rule immediately; if not, the team is out.
- Other rules can be added, such as limiting the offense to two dribbles or not allowing the offense to shoot until a ball screen has occurred or all players have touched the ball.

Five-on-Five Full-Court Press (10 minutes)

This is a controlled five-on-five drill that enables players to work on press defense. The defense is set up in a press defense that the team uses during games. The defenders apply this press against the offense, and the offense works to break the press for a score. Once the press is attacked by the offense and a shot is taken, the drill begins again with the same 10 players. After four or five repetitions, teams are rotated so that all players have a chance to work on the press defense.

COACHING POINT

Between repetitions, the coach can provide specific feedback and teaching points to players.

Five-on-Five Scrimmage, Controlled (10 minutes)

Divide the team into two teams of five for a scrimmage that involves using the skills and tactics that the players have learned so far in practices. Have the players go five-on-five half court and transition into a full-court scrimmage after a made or missed basket. They should stop at the other end, then again go five-on-five into a full-court scrimmage. Sub players as necessary.

COACHING POINTS

- The coach should stop play when necessary to explain areas on both offense and defense that need work.
- Offensive players need to sprint back on a change of possession in order to stop the ball first.

Free Throws, Two in a Row (5 minutes)

Pair up players at each free-throw line. Partners take turns shooting one free throw until the pair makes two in a row.

COACHING POINT

Adjust the number of consecutive free throws made based on the skill level of your players.

Four-on-Four Defensive Shell With Rotation (10 minutes)

Four players are on offense, and four on defense. The offense is spaced out with one guard above each free-throw lane outside the three-point line and one player at each wing. A defender is guarding each offensive player; the rest of the team is divided into four lines at half-court. One of the guards starts with the ball and passes it to a wing. As the coach observes, the defenders must adjust to each pass so they are in good help position or on-the-ball position. On command, the offense continues to pass the ball from one wing to the other wing, and the defenders adjust their position on each pass. After a specified amount of time, the offensive team drives to the baseline on the dribble. The defender opposite the drive should be in position to rotate from the lane area to help stop the dribbler on the baseline. The next four players in line will then move to offense, the offensive players move to defense, and the defenders move to the end of each line.

COACHING POINTS

- Defenders need to stay in a good defensive stance with their knees bent so they can move quickly to the ball.
- Defenders should be in help position when the ball is on the opposite side of the court. They should point one hand at the ball and one hand at the offensive player they are guarding so that they never lose sight of either.

Out-of-Bounds Plays, Review (10 minutes)

Divide your team into groups of five; one group begins on the court. Have every group of players run your out-of-bounds plays without a defense. Then practice the out-of-bounds plays in a five-on-five situation, against a defense.

COACHING POINTS

- Teams should practice these plays against both a zone defense and a man-to-man defense.
- Teams should practice out-of-bounds plays under both sides of the basket, as well as on the sidelines.

Three-on-Two, Two-on-One Full Court (10 minutes)

Start with three lines at one end of the court. Two players set up at the opposite end of the court in a defensive position, one player at the free-throw line and one player in the middle of the lane. The first three players in line try to score against the two defenders (three-on-two); the middle player dribbles the ball down the floor and makes a pass to one wing. After the shot, the two defenders become the offensive players, moving to the opposite end of the court with the middle offensive player transitioning to defense (two-on-one). The two wings remain as the defenders in the lane for the next group of three offensive players.

COACHING POINTS

- The three offensive players should work to get a shot after three or fewer passes against the two defenders.
- The two offensive players should work to get a shot after two or fewer passes against the one defender.

Five-on-Zero Offense (10 minutes)

Arrange the players in offensive positions based on the offensive set you want to teach. For example, this can be a 1-2-2 set with a point guard, two wings, and two post players or a 2-1-2 set with two guards, a high-post player, and two baseline or post players. In this drill, teach players how they can try to score in the set (including cuts, screens, and so on).

COACHING POINTS

- Teach players proper spacing and how to refill positions after a pass and cut.
- Emphasize that each player should square up to the basket after every catch.

Four-Quarter Shooting (10 minutes)

This is a three-player drill using two balls. Two players have a ball. One player with a ball shoots her ball, rebounds, and passes the ball to the player who does not have a ball. The other player with the ball shoots her ball immediately after the first player, gets the rebound, and passes to the player who now does not have a ball (the first shooter). After the shot, each player repositions for the pass from the next shooter. Play for four minutes, keeping track of made baskets.

COACHING POINT

The shooter must get a rebound, pass the ball, and then immediately look for the pass from the next shooter.

Announcements: _____

Appendix

Checklists and Forms

This appendix contains checklists and forms. You may reproduce and use the checklists and forms indicated as needed for your basketball program; these materials may also be found at the following website: www.HumanKinetics.com/CoachingYouthBasketball5E-Forms. They are indicated by this symbol in the outside margin of the text:

Please note that all forms and checklists should be reviewed on an annual basis. All legal forms should be evaluated by your legal counsel and insurance agent to ensure that they properly reflect your program and relevant state and local laws.

Facilities and Equipment Checklist

- ❏ The stairs and corridors leading to the gym are well lit.
- ❏ The stairs and corridors are free of obstruction.
- ❏ The stairs and corridors are in good repair.
- ❏ Exits are well marked and illuminated.
- ❏ Exits are free of obstruction.
- ❏ Uprights and other projections are padded, including the basket standards or poles.
- ❏ Walls are free of projections.
- ❏ Windows are located high on the walls.
- ❏ Wall plugs and light switches are insulated and protected.
- ❏ Lights are shielded.
- ❏ Lighting is sufficient to illuminate the playing area well.
- ❏ The heating and cooling system for the gym is working properly and is monitored regularly.
- ❏ Ducts, radiators, pipes, and so on are shielded or designed to withstand high impact.
- ❏ Tamper-free thermostats are housed in impact-resistant covers.
- ❏ If there is an overhanging track, it has secure railings with a minimum height of 3 feet, 6 inches.
- ❏ The track has direction signs posted.
- ❏ The track is free of obstructions.
- ❏ Rules for the track are posted.
- ❏ Projections on the track are padded or illuminated.
- ❏ Gym equipment is inspected before and during each use.
- ❏ The gym is adequately supervised.
- ❏ Galleries and viewing areas have been designed to protect small children by blocking their access to the playing area.
- ❏ The gym (floor, roof, walls, light fixtures, and so on) is inspected on an annual basis for safety and structural deficiencies.
- ❏ Fire alarms are in good working order.
- ❏ Fire extinguishers are up to date, with note of last inspection.
- ❏ Directions are posted for evacuating the gym in case of fire.

From American Sport Education Program, 2012, *Coaching youth basketball*, 5th ed. (Champaign, IL: Human Kinetics).

Informed Consent Form

I hereby give my permission for _____ to participate in _____ during the athletic season beginning on _____.
Further, I authorize the school or club to provide emergency treatment of any injury or illness my child may experience if qualified medical personnel consider treatment necessary and perform the treatment. This authorization is granted only if I cannot be reached after a reasonable effort to do so.

Parent or guardian: _____

Address: _____ Phone: (   )_____

Cell phone: (   )_____

Other person to contact in case of emergency: _____

Relationship to person: _____ Phone: (   )_____

Family physician: _____ Phone: (   )_____

Medical conditions (e.g., allergies, chronic illness): _____

_____

_____

_____

My child and I are aware that participating in _____ is a potentially hazardous activity. We assume all risks associated with participation in this sport, including but not limited to falls, contact with other participants, the effects of weather and traffic, and other reasonable conditions of risk associated with the sport. All such risks to my child are known and appreciated by my child and me.

We understand this informed consent form and agree to its conditions.

Child's signature: _____ Date: _____

Parent's or guardian's signature: _____ Date: _____

From American Sport Education Program, 2012, *Coaching youth basketball*, 5th ed. (Champaign, IL: Human Kinetics). Adapted, by permission, from M. Flegel, 2008, *Sport first aid*, 4th ed. (Champaign, IL: Human Kinetics), 15.

Injury Report Form

Date: _____ Time: _____ a.m.   p.m.

Location: _____

Player's name: _____ Age: _____ Date of birth: _____

Type of injury: _____

_____

Anatomical area involved: _____

_____

Cause of injury: _____

_____

Extent of injury: _____

_____

Person administering first aid (name): _____

First aid administered: _____

_____

Other treatment administered: _____

_____

Referral action: _____

_____

Signature of person administering first aid: _____

Date: _____

From American Sport Education Program, 2012, *Coaching youth basketball*, 5th ed. (Champaign, IL: Human Kinetics).

Emergency Information Card

Player's name: _____ Sport: _____ Age: _____

Address: _____

Phone: ( )_____

Provide information for parent or guardian and one additional contact in case of emergency:

Parent's or guardian's name: _____

Address: _____

Phone: ( )_____ Other phone: ( )_____

Additional contact's name: _____

Relationship to player: _____

Address: _____

Phone: ( )_____ Other phone: ( )_____

Insurance Information

Name of insurance company: _____

Policy name and number: _____

Medical Information

Physician's name: _____ Phone: ( )_____

Is your child allergic to any drugs?   Yes   No

If so, what? _____

Does your child have any other allergies (e.g., bee stings, dust)? _____

Does your child have any of the following?   Asthma   Diabetes Epilepsy

Is your child currently taking medication?   Yes   No

If so, what? _____

Does your child wear contact lenses?   Yes   No

Is there additional information we should
know about your child's health or
physical condition?   Yes   No

If yes, please explain: _____

Parent's or guardian's signature: _____ Date: _____

From American Sport Education Program, 2012, *Coaching youth basketball*, 5th ed. (Champaign, IL: Human Kinetics).

Emergency Response Card

Be prepared to give the following information to an EMS dispatcher.

Caller's name: _____

Telephone number from which the call is being made: (   )_____

Reason for call: _____

How many people are injured: _____

Condition of victim(s): _____

First aid being given: _____

Location: _____

Address: _____

City: _____

Directions (e.g., cross streets, landmarks, entrance access): _____

_____

_____

Note: Do not hang up first. Let the EMS dispatcher hang up first.

From American Sport Education Program, 2012, *Coaching youth basketball,* 5th ed. (Champaign, IL: Human Kinetics).

About the Authors

The fifth edition of *Coaching Youth Basketball* was written by the American Sport Education Program (ASEP) in conjunction with USA Basketball's Don Showalter.

Showalter has coached the USA Basketball Men's Developmental National Team for four years, leading them to gold medals at the 2009 and 2011 FIBA Americas U16 Championship and the 2010 FIBA U17 World Championship. He was named the USA Basketball Junior Developmental Coach of the Year in 2009 and 2010 and National Coach of the Year by the National High School Athletic Coaches Association in 2009 and coached in the prestigious McDonald's All-American Game in 1999. Showalter was the head boys' basketball coach and activities director at Mid-Prairie High School in Wellman, Iowa, from 1984 to 2012 before accepting the head coaching position at City High School in Iowa City. His winning percentage is .669 (557-275), and he has been named Iowa Basketball Coaches Association Coach of the Year nine times. Showalter has directed basketball camps all over the world, including Russia, Mexico, Switzerland, Italy, Belgium, England, and Scotland.

ASEP has been developing and delivering coaching education courses since 1981. As the nation's leading coaching education program, ASEP works with national, state, and local sport organizations to develop educational programs for coaches, officials, administrators, and parents. These programs incorporate ASEP's philosophy of "Athletes first, winning second."